HRM, Work a... in China

To what extent has China embraced human resource management in the Western sense? This exciting new book investigates this and many other important and controversial questions whilst examining human resource management, work and employment in China and the changing nature of these vital elements of society and business. Over the last few years there has been a growing interest in the way patterns of employment relations are changing in China; there have been radical reforms of workplace welfare and social security provisions.

Fang Lee Cooke addresses a number of thematic issues such as the growing inequality in employment, public sector reform, pay systems, vocational training and small private businesses. These themes are developed through a combination of rigorous empirical research and secondary data analysis which explores the distinct incentives and pressures facing different sectors and ownership forms in shaping their human resource strategies. The book offers an invaluable insight into the workings of the political, social, economic and business dimensions of Chinese society. The author also draws attention to the considerable similarity in the problems faced by both China and the developed economies in an increasingly globalised economic environment which will prove essential reading for all those studying or with an interest in human resource management, employment relations, international business or Asian studies.

Fang Lee Cooke is a Senior Lecturer in Employment Studies at the Manchester Business School, University of Manchester.

HRM, Work and Employment in China

Fang Lee Cooke

Routledge
Taylor & Francis Group

LONDON AND NEW YORK

First published 2005
by Routledge
2 Park Square, Milton Park, Abingdon, Oxon OX14 4RN

Simultaneously published in the USA and Canada
by Routledge
270 Madison Ave, New York, NY 10016

Routledge is an imprint of the Taylor & Francis Group

© 2005 Fang Lee Cooke

Typeset in Sabon by
Keystroke, Jacaranda Lodge, Wolverhampton
Printed and bound in Great Britain by
Cromwell Press, Trowbridge, Wiltshire

British Library Cataloguing in Publication Data
A catalogue record for this book is available from the British Library

Library of Congress Cataloging in Publication Data
Cooke, Fang Lee.
  HRM, work, and employment in China / Fang Lee Cooke.
    p. cm.
  Includes bibliographical references and index.
  1. Industrial relations–China. 2. Personnel management–China.
  3. Free enterprise–China. 4. State-owned enterprises–China.
  5. Employee rights–China. 6. Employees–Training of–China.
  7. Labor policy–China. I. Title.
  HD8736.5.C66 2005
  331.1'0951–dc22   2004012607

ISBN 0–415–32783–0 (hbk)
ISBN 0–415–32784–9 (pbk)

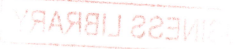

Contents

Tables

- Chapter 7 is based on an earlier version of Cooke, F. L. and Rubery, J. (2002) 'Minimum wage and social equality in China', project report on *Minimum Wage and Employment Equality in Developed and Developing Countries*, Geneva: the International Labour Organisation (ILO).
- Part of Chapter 8 comes from Cooke, F. L. (forthcoming, 2005) 'Employment relations in small commercial businesses in China', *Industrial Relations Journal*, 36, 1 (January).

Abbreviations

ACFTU	All-China Federation of Trade Unions
ACWF	All-China Women's Federation
COE	Collectively owned enterprise
ESO	Employee share ownership schemes
FDI	Foreign direct investment
HRM	Human resource management
ICT	Information and communication technologies
ILO	International Labour Organization
JV	Joint venture
MNC	Multinational corporation
SOE	State-owned enterprise
TVE	Township and village enterprise
WTO	The World Trade Organization

1 Introduction

Introduction

China has one of the largest labour forces in the world with a population of nearly 1.3 billion, over half of whom were in employment in 2002. About two-thirds of them are rural workers. China also has one of the highest labour participation rates in the world (over 80 per cent). As one of the largest exporting countries and the second largest beneficiary country of foreign direct investments (FDIs), China presents itself as one of the economically most important nations in the world. However, China's increasing inter-dependence with the world economy has been achieved through a period of political, social and economic change over the past twenty-five years. A major implication of these profound changes is how employment is (re-)organized and work experienced by its 0.7 billion workers (see Tables 1.1 and 1.2). Indeed, the employment landscape has changed significantly over the past two decades in at least three major dimensions.

First, lay-offs and early retirement had been a standard feature for state-owned enterprise (SOE) employees from the mid-1990s to the early 2000s when millions of workers were laid off, many of them consequently becoming bewildered and unsuccessful job seekers. This radical downsizing was accompanied by a series of far-reaching reforms in personnel/human resource policies and practices in the state sector, with the erosion of job security and welfare provision and tightened performance management as the major outcomes. If changes at enterprise level during the first wave of SOE reforms in the mid- and late 1980s were limited, then the level of organizational change and innovation of management techniques since the mid-1990s was far more evident (Ding and Warner 1999). These institutional discontinuities brought to an end the organized dependence of the state workers on their employer (Walder 1986; Lee 1999), which was crucial for sustaining paternalism, and called for a new mode of managing employment relationships.

A second major change has been the rapid growth of the private sector with the emergence of diverse ownership forms, for example, multinational corporations (MNCs), international joint ventures (JVs), domestic private

Table 1.1 Population and employment: 1985–2002 (end-of-year figure) (figures in 1,000 persons)

Item	1985	1990	1995	2000	2002
Population at the year-end	1,058,510	1143,330	1,211,210	1,267,430	1,284,530
Urban	250,940	301,950	351,740	459,060	502,120
Rural	807,570	841,380	859,470	808,370	782,410
Male	547,250	589,040	618,080	654,370	661,150
Female	511,260	554,290	593,130	613,063	623,380
Employment					
Employed persons[a]	498,730	647,490	680,650	720,850	737,400
Staff and workers[b]	123,580	140,590	149,080	112,590	105,580
Registered unemployed in urban areas	2,390	3,830	5,200	5,950	7,700
(Urban registered unemployment rate %)	(1.8%)	(2.5%)	(2.9%)	(3.1%)	(4.0%)

Source: adapted from *China Statistics Yearbook* 2003: 26–7, 123.

Notes

[a] Employed persons refer to the persons who are engaged in social working and receive remuneration payment or earn business income, including total staff and workers, re-employed retirees, employers of private enterprises, self-employed workers, employees in private enterprises and individual economies, employees in township enterprises, employed persons in rural areas, and other employed persons (including teachers in the schools run by the local people, people engaged in religious profession and servicemen).

[b] Staff and workers refer to the persons who work in, and receive payment from units of state ownership, collective ownership, joint ownership, shareholding ownership, foreign ownership, and ownership by entrepreneurs from Hong Kong, Macao and Taiwan, and other types of ownership and their affiliated units. They do not include (1) persons employed in township enterprises, (2) persons employed in private enterprises, (3) urban self-employed persons, (4) retirees, (5) re-employed retirees, (6) teachers in schools run by the local people, (7) foreigners and persons from Hong Kong, Macao and Taiwan who work in urban units, and (8) other persons not included by relevant regulations (original notes from *China Statistics Yearbook* (2003), the Ministry of Statistics of China: 181).

Table 1.2 Rural labour force by sector: 1978–2002 (end-of-year figure) (figures in 1,000 persons)

Year	Total	Farming, forestry, animal husbandry and fishery	Manufacturing	Construction	Transport storage, post and communication services	Wholesale, retail trade and catering services	Other non-agricultural trades
1978	306,380	274,880	17,340	2,300	800	520	5,210
1980	318,360	283,340	19,420	2,830	900	670	5,880
1985	370,650	303,510	27,410	11,300	4,340	4,630	13,190
1990	477,080	333,360	32,290	15,230	6,350	6,930	17,980
1991	480,260	341,860	32,680	15,340	6,550	7,230	19,100
1992	482,910	340,370	34,680	16,590	7,060	8,140	23,020
1993	485,460	332,580	36,590	18,870	8,000	9,490	36,710
1994	488,020	326,900	38,490	20,570	9,080	10,840	40,650
1995	490,250	323,350	39,710	22,040	9,830	11,700	43,800
1996	490,280	322,610	40,190	23,040	10,280	12,620	44,160
1997	490,390	324,340	40,320	23,730	10,580	13,820	46,840
1998	490,210	326,260	39,290	23,940	10,880	14,620	49,340
1999	489,820	329,120	39,530	25,320	11,160	15,850	47,990
2000	489,340	327,980	41,090	26,920	11,710	17,520	54,420
2001	490,850	324,510	42,960	27,970	12,050	18,650	56,150
2002	489,600	319,910	45,060	29,590	12,590	19,970	58,160

Source: adapted from *China Statistics Yearbook 2003*: 26.

firms, private small and self-employed businesses, township and village enterprises (TVEs), and the privatization of state-owned enterprises. Whereas access to 'good jobs' (in MNCs and JVs) is available to younger, male, skilled and educated workers in the private sector, the majority of workers may be segregated along lines of gender, employment status, residence status and market capacity.

Third, continuing urbanization has attracted an influx of migrant rural workers to urban areas who overcrowd certain segments of the job markets with only restricted opportunities accessible to them. The vast majority remain overworked, poorly paid and under/unprotected. Despite their pivotal contribution to a burgeoning economy in China, these workers have very few labour rights, and where the rights exist, they tend not to be actively policed. Many rural migrant workers have little cultural or technical knowledge, and institutionalized discrimination and the less-than-sympathetic attitude from the labour authorities further constrain their opportunities for employment and job choices.

It is apparent that China's opening up of its economy has had demonstrable effects on most sectors of its industrial economy, directly through the establishment of MNCs and JVs, and indirectly through the impact that competition and liberalization are having on SOEs and domestic private firms. While some workers are facing a greater level of employment insecurity and worsening terms and conditions, others are presented with wider occupational/career choices, job mobility and higher rewards for skill and performance level. Employers in general are encountering increasing pressure for quality, adaptability, and performance enhancement. This calls simultaneously for the need for labour protection and the introduction of new human resource management (HRM) techniques that provide better pay and greater career prospects, and intrinsic value to cope with these new demands. A key question is to what extent the state and employers are under pressure or have incentives to implement these policies which are essential to safeguard workers' basic labour rights and to improve productivity.

The increasing presence of MNCs in China may on the one hand act as a driving force for disseminating 'best practice' of HRM, upgrading technology, raising productivity and labour standards, and helping China to make the transition to a higher value-added economy. Indeed, this positive impact of MNCs has been evident in recent trends of adoption by domestic Chinese firms of HR practices that are associated more with 'Western practices', or at least, represents a marked divergence from the traditional Chinese personnel practices (see Chapter 9). On the other hand, MNCs may have little interest in these tasks other than using China as a low-cost mass production base that can be replaced when its comparative advantage declines. China's attraction to FDIs comes mainly from its favourable financial policy and the abundant supply of cheap and willing labour rather than a high-skilled base of its workforce. These investment attractions serve as a disincentive for a high commitment model of HR policy. Over the past two decades, about 60 per cent of the foreign investments in China have concentrated in the manufacturing industry relying on the intensive use of labour rather than technological sophistication. This investment pattern has, however, started to change and there is now an increasing level of investment in the high-tech sectors, such as telecommunications and electronics, where skilled and professional workers are the key assets in these industries.

While the state may face the dual burden of having to provide employment as well as employment protection for its workforce, local governments may come up with different solutions to labour problems or confused interpretations of the national regulatory framework. For governments and policy makers, there is a widely held assumption that employment under any conditions is the objective to be maximized. For many employers, any imposition of labour regulations may threaten their ability to survive, especially where there is limited scope for transferring the increased costs to prices. For many workers, any paid work, no matter how low the wage level may be or in what forms they are paid, is better than no work, given the lack of (adequate) social security provision for the majority of workers. The prospect of articulation of labour rights is further obscured by the weak, if it ever exists, voluntary collective bargaining system in China where trade union organization is legislatively under the command of the Communist Party.

Furthermore, organizations may have divergent notions as to what constitute appropriate employment/HRM practices for their immediate concerns. Where new HR initiatives have been adopted (e.g. performance management systems, employee share ownership schemes, and enterprise culture management initiatives), the degree of their success remains difficult to assess precisely.

The complexity of this employment environment and the proliferation of employment policies and practices have led to a growing interest in the way patterns of employment relations have changed in China in the past two decades or so. Studies reported in Western literature have drawn our attention to changes in employment relations in organizations of different forms of ownership, for example, state-owned enterprises, collectively owned enterprises (COEs), joint ventures and newly privatized firms. These studies (e.g. Morris *et al.* 2001; Cooke 2002; Taylor 2002) have in general highlighted the withdrawal of state intervention in employment relations at enterprise level and a trend towards greater diversity in and marketization of the employment relationships. These are taking place in parallel with the introduction of more statutory labour regulations, notably the Labour Law of China (1995), and the radical reforms of workplace welfare and social security provisions.

Another growing body of research literature is that of human resource management in China, often through micro empirical studies of state-owned enterprises, joint ventures, multinational corporations, and more recently but to a lesser extent, township and village enterprises. In particular, the HRM practices in MNCs and JVs have been studied quite extensively (e.g. Verburg

1996; Child *et al.* 1997; Goodall and Warner 1997; Bjorkman and Lu 1999b). A common finding in these studies is that there are significant differences between HRM practices in the home countries of the MNC and those in their operations in China. However, research findings show that foreign managers have gained increased control over HRM issues (Child 1994). In addition, HRM practices in domestic Chinese companies are reported to have changed considerably over the past two decades (Bjorkman and Lu 2001). A central focus in this body of literature has been the extent to which China has embraced HRM in the Western sense.

While these studies have made significant contributions to our understanding on issues related to human resource management, work and employment in contemporary China, there remain major issues which have not been sufficiently explored but are of growing importance if we are to have a more comprehensive understanding of China. For example, in what ways do patterns of employment policies and practices differ among different ownership forms? What are the major reform initiatives in the state sector including SOEs, governmental organizations and public sector organizations? Are recent HR policies of the state sector having any noticeable impact on workforce behaviour? Given the well-documented state control in the determination of wage structure and level in the state sector, do its grassroots employees have any role in shaping the distribution outcome? Relatedly, given the well-known Chinese egalitarian culture, to what extent are employees receptive to new pay initiatives aimed at differentiating and motivating their performance? What types of training interventions are in place at both macro and micro level to address the long-existing skill shortage problems of China? Given the long-term state pledge on gender equality and the high proportion of women in full-time employment in China, are Chinese women faring better than their counterparts in other countries in terms of their employment conditions and career prospects? More broadly, who are the major disadvantaged groups of workers in the labour market and in what ways are they being disadvantaged? What are the state interventions to eliminate inequalities in the system and how effective are these interventions? What are the employment terms and conditions and other HRM practices in the private small business sector where managerial skills of the (owner-) employers may be relatively low and where state intervention may be deliberately weak and the workers least protected? On a brighter note, what are the major challenges of HRM in China in general and what are the new HR practices favoured by organizations? What is the role of MNCs and JVs in disseminating Western HR practices in China? And are there any signs of convergence of HR practices within China and towards Western practices? This book aims to address some of these questions by exploring a number of thematic issues as follows.

Choice of themes and organization of the book

Employers' labour/HR strategies are intricately linked with the institutional context, including the labour and product market and the regulatory framework, under which they operate. The examination of HRM practices at both the organizational and societal level in a developing country like China where the institutional context is rapidly changing therefore needs to be situated in a broader context of how work is experienced and employment opportunities structured. As Rubery and Grimshaw (2003: 5) observe, 'In each society there are different ways of organising employment, reflecting the various institutional arrangements in place to generate skills, regulate the employment relationship and shape the wage structure'. Similarly, Boxall and Purcell (2003: 111–12) argue that the social and technical organization of work is 'a fundamental building block in HRM' because it has a most profound influence on people's experience of employment, including the level of skill and training required, job satisfaction derived, motivation to perform, and opportunities to participate in decision making.

The topics selected for discussion in this book reflect the most significant developments that have taken place in China in employment and work in the past two decades. In particular, they are selected for one of three reasons. First, where important changes have taken place, for example, the restructuring of employment and HR policies in the state sector. Second, where 'new' developments of HRM have taken place, for example, performance management system, employee share ownership schemes, and enterprise culture management. There are two dimensions to these 'new' HR aspects. One is that these issues may not really be 'new' to HR practices in China, but may have gained 'renewed' interest in recent years. The other is that they are relatively 'new' in the time span of the past five decades. Third, they are important issues that have received little attention in the existing literature, for example, private small businesses, groups of workers who are peripheral in the labour market, and gender issues. Some of these issues may have long existed while others are (temporary) outcomes of recent changes.

Consequently, this book is organized both by sector and theme. This is because, first, there are the sector-specific changes which affect the way human resources are managed (e.g. the state sector), and the growth of new sectors (e.g. private small businesses), the characteristics of which directly shape the employment practices in these sectors and influence how work is experienced by its workers. This gives rise to Chapter 3 and Chapter 8 in which sector-specific issues in HRM and employment relationships are discussed. Second, certain key aspects and problems of HRM are shared by many organizations both in the state and private sectors, such as skill shortages, training, pay and recent developments in HRM. This gives rise to Chapters 4, 5 and 9 in which these thematic issues are explored. Third, certain groups of workers (e.g. female workers, laid-off workers and rural migrant workers) face barriers in employment that are specific to them, often to their disadvantage (e.g. gender inequality and low pay). This gives rise to Chapters 6 and 7 in which the unpromising employment and career prospects for these workers are analysed.

There is also a temporal dimension to the sequence of the chapters in which the first half of the book deals with issues that have existed for a long time and focuses on the role of the state as the major employer and as a legislator. The second half of the book contemplates the more recent phenomena including issues of inequality in employment practices outside the state sector despite the existence of employment regulations. This is in the context of the downsizing of the state sector, reduced direct intervention from the state, and the increase of employment-related legislation. While the earlier chapters feature organizations which have a relatively long history (e.g. state-owned), later chapters focus more on organizations in relatively new forms of ownership as a result of China's political and economic reform since the late 1970s (e.g. small and private businesses, TVEs).

It must be pointed out here that this arrangement is by no means a clear-cut divide. While some of the themes form chapters of their own, others run through several chapters in the book. For example, public sector reforms, vocational and enterprise training systems, pay systems, and employment in the informal sector are discussed in individual chapters, whereas other themes, such as workers' representation, inequality in the workplace and labour market, and recruitment, feature, in various depth, in several chapters covering different sectors.

Considerable attention is paid to two main themes in the discussion. One is the role of employment regulations in the shaping of human resource management and employment practices. Regulations and administrative policies examined here include, for example, that of equal opportunity, the Labour Law, minimum wage and skill training. Employment regulations receive considerable attention in this book because the existence and effectiveness of employment regulations in a country is an important indication of a government's commitment to safeguard the minimum level of labour rights of its labour force. Regulations play an important role in an employment environment such as that of China where incentives may be low for employers to invest in their HRM in order to elicit effort and commitment from their workers, and therefore, without a certain level of regulation to guarantee the minimum standards of labour, at least in theory, employers may be heading for a 'race to the bottom'.

The other is the related theme of growing inequality in employment and HR policies in China. There are two strands to this theme. One is to do with gender inequality in employment and management. While full-time employment for women in China has been the norm for the past five decades, this apparent equality is quantitative rather than qualitative, with the majority of women clustered at the lower end of the job ladder. Women encounter increasingly blatant discrimination in recruitment, pay, promotion and retirement. Some of these discriminations are institutionalized in legislation whereas others are embedded in the culture. As Lee (1999) points out, despite the constitutional prescription for gender equality, national statistics and empirical evidence clearly reveal the prevalence of gender segregation and gender wage gaps. This conforms to the universal pattern in which women are segregated into occupations that are lower paid, largely labour-intensive and less prestigious. The degree of gender and wage inequality is a result of the institutional structures of China, as it is for other countries, that guide wage determination, education level, skill development, job allocation and career prospects at both societal and organizational level. The other strand examines employment inequality from a different angle, between (urban) workers in the formal sector and those in the informal sector (many of whom are rural migrant or laid-off workers). Whereas the former generally enjoy much better employment terms and conditions, the quality of work and employment protection for the latter are inferior by far. Yet this group is making up an increasingly large proportion of the workforce in China as a result of recent changes, an emerging employment pattern which also coincides with the international trend of informalization of employment and employment relations.

One deliberate omission from this book is a specific chapter on trade unions and workers' representation. This omission is mainly to do with the fact that much has been written on the subject (e.g. Hoffman 1981; Warner 1990b; White 1996; Levine 1997; Ng and Warner 1998; You 1998; Ding and Warner 1999; Sheehan 1999; Chan 2001; Cooke 2002). These studies have provided a comprehensive and similar picture of the state of affairs of trade unionism in China. Given the existing body of knowledge on the subject and the absence of major developments in the role of trade unions in China, it was decided that the finite space would be given to other topics that have been less fully explored. None the less, issues related to trade unions and workers' representation are discussed in various chapters where appropriate, often through the revelation of the lack of involvement and impact of the trade unions and the absence of alternative mechanisms of workers' representation. For example, Chapter 2 outlines briefly the role of the trade unions in China in general; Chapter 8 draws our attention to workers' apathy towards unionism and alternative official channels of resolving labour–management disputes; and the role of the trade unions in the future is discussed briefly in the concluding chapter (Chapter 10).

Another intentional omission is a chapter on HRM in MNCs and JVs for the similar reason that it is a relatively well-researched area, with many of the existing empirical studies on HRM in China drawn from these types of organizations. However, the characteristics of HR practices of these firms and the role of MNCs and JVs in influencing HR practices in China are discussed in various chapters as part of the wider picture of employment policies and practices in China.

In short, the book is organized with the view that, to understand patterns of adoption of HRM in China, it is necessary to contemplate its broader context of work and employment systems from a historical perspective, especially the legislative role of the state in a nation in which control tends to be centralized but enforcement of law is paradoxically weak. However, given the extent of change experienced in China and the complexity of the employment environment, it is difficult to embrace the breadth of the topics without losing a level of depth, a situation compounded by the gaps in available information. Based on the rationale outlined above, the chapters are organized as follows.

This introductory chapter provides a rationale for the book in terms of its importance, relevance and timeliness for a number of thematic issues chosen for discussion. It also lays out the structure of the book and provides a brief summary of the tasks of each chapter. Sources of statistics and empirical data used in this book are described, in addition to a brief explanation of the conceptual framework used for the book.

Chapter 2 outlines the broad characteristics of employment relations of different ownership forms, namely that of the state sector, MNCs and JVs, domestic private firms, and TVEs. Major differences in the employment/ HRM policies and practices between these firms are highlighted in view of the political environment under which different ownership forms emerged in China's economy. Characteristics of the labour market and the frame-work of employment regulations are also discussed. The chapter then draws our attention to issues related to the increasingly inadequate mechanisms of workers' representation and the rising incidence of labour disputes in the recent period of radical changes. This chapter provides the broad context under which more detailed discussions are carried out in subsequent chapters.

Chapter 3 explores a number of issues related to the reforms in the state sector. For example, what are the major sources of pressure for state sector reform in China? What approaches has the state adopted to introduce the changes into each of its sectors and what are the sources of conflict and resis-tance, if any, from the workforce? To what extent is China's state employer embracing the notion of HRM that is becoming increasingly popular in the country? What are the major HR problems encountered by the state employer? What HR initiatives are implemented to combat these problems and how effective are they? Examination of these issues is intended to shed light on the institutional and cultural characteristics of China's state sector, one that is still dominant in the economy of the country, employing a large proportion of the workforce. While much has been written on recent reforms of state-owned enterprises, little is revealed in Western literature about the changes that have taken/are taking place in the public sector and governmental organizations in China. This chapter adds knowledge to the latter by reviewing the pressure for and the process and outcome of the reforms in these two sub-sectors of the state sector in comparison with that of the SOEs.

Chapter 4 discusses issues related to the pay system and the development of new pay initiatives in China. The pay system in China demonstrates a number of unique characteristics which differ from that in other societies, such as the egalitarian culture, the relatively high proportion of bonuses in the total package of pay, and the significant role of workers in controlling the distribution of bonuses. Pay is perhaps the only aspect of HRM in China in which grassroots workers exert extensive control in its (egalitarian) distribution. A main feature of the pay system in the state sectors is the tension between the lack of input of employees in the formal wage set by the state on the one hand and their role in maintaining the low earning differentials among themselves on the other. While employees have little influence in the formal wage structure, they play a fundamental role in preserving the egalitarian and seniority culture in the distribution of bonuses and other material incentives, regardless of the relative efficiency of individuals. Attempts from the top to increase wage differentials between individuals according to performance may be mediated during implementation at the operational level. In the private sectors, seniority and egalitarianism still remain characteristic in employees' attitudes towards pay, albeit diluted by employers' constant attempts to introduce performance-based pay and pay confidentiality, especially in joint ventures and foreign firms. Recent reforms in the state sector and the growth of private domestic and foreign firms also lead to a greater variety of pay schemes, such as employee share ownership schemes and chief executive pay schemes. Many of these initiatives have not been explored in existing studies on China. In particular, the chapter addresses the following questions. In what ways do the political and ideological concerns which were traditionally so important to the governance of the state sector pay system have to give way to the more social and economic considerations underpinning recent reform efforts that tensions have arisen to challenge the status quo? To what extent do characteristics of pay in the state sector reflect themselves in the private sector? What are the characteristics of the pay system in the growing private sector in terms of wage level and determination process, for example? What are the recent innovations in pay schemes and how effective are they as HR initiatives? The investigation of these issues is essential in order to understand the changing characteristics of pay policies and practices in China in a period of vast change.

The effectiveness of a country's skills training system is essential to maintaining and improving its competitiveness in the global economy. Chapter 5 deals with both vocational and enterprise training in order to provide an overall picture of the skills training system of China. It is important to discuss both at the same time since they are the two major sources of skills provision and many of the issues are interrelated. China has often been criticized for the low quality of its labour supply and its skills shortages have been blamed as the cause of its low level of technological innovation and low productivity. However, there is a lack of a holistic understanding of what shapes the vocational training system and enterprise training practices. Although existing empirical studies do cover issues related to training, they have focused primarily on management training or employee training at enterprise level.

A systematic review of the vocational training system and practices of enterprise training as part of the country's human resource strategy is important to shed light on the extent of its skill problems and their likely causes. What, then, is the reality of skills training in China? Who are the major players? What role do the state and employers play? To what extent have the state and employers taken up skills training as a deliberate human resource development strategy at national and organizational level? What are the main characteristics of vocational and enterprise training in China and what have been the major problems facing training institutions and enterprises? How is the training provision distributed? Who are the likely groups of workers missing out in the training network? What are the prospects of training in China in light of its recent WTO (World Trade Organization) accession, an increasing level of foreign investment into the country, and, more importantly, its recent radical restructuring of the state sector and rapid expansion of the private sector including the informal sector? Finally, to what extent do the training and skills shortage problems of China resemble those of the rest of the world, now that skills shortage seems to be widely reported both in developed and developing economies? These are the issues that are explored in this chapter.

Chapter 6 discusses a number of issues related to gender inequality in the labour market, and in the HR policy and practice of organizations. Gender is an extremely important issue because employers' labour/HR strategies are far from being gender-neutral. Even if they are intended to be, the implications for different genders are likely to vary because of their differing personal conditions and social positions, which in turn determine their positions, and how they position themselves, in the organization and society. This is especially the case in China where problems faced by women in employment in recent years feature prominently in media reports but remedial actions appear to have limited impact. This chapter reviews the role of the state in promoting gender equality as part of its socialist agenda in the past five decades and the effectiveness of the equal opportunity regulations. It highlights barriers that Chinese women encounter in various stages of their employment, including recruitment, career progression, displacement and retirement. The chapter concludes that there may be a slippage in recent years in the level of gender equality that has been achieved during the earlier years of socialism as a result of the marketization of the economy and the weakening effect of state intervention despite the increase of legislation.

Chapter 7 continues along the same line of discussion of inequality in employment, focusing on those who are peripheral in the labour market and labour protection, including the ex-SOE laid-off workers and the rural migrant workers who are the low-paid groups. The chapter discusses issues related to the legislative framework and implementation of the minimum wage regulations that were introduced by the state in the mid-1990s with the aim of providing a minimum level of earning protection to these workers. However, the effect of the regulations proves to be limited so far.

In particular, controversy and confusion arise as to who should pay a minimum wage, who should be paid and at what level. The ineffectiveness of the implementation of the regulations may be attributed to a number of reasons, not least the indifferent attitude of the employer who has the burden to pay, the worker who should benefit, and the labour officials who have the responsibility to enforce the regulations.

Chapter 8 focuses on the employment policy and practice of a sector – the private small businesses – that has been largely ignored in the literature so far. Despite the growing social and economic importance of private small businesses in China, there remains a significant gap in our knowledge of employment relations in these firms, in sharp contrast to the proliferating literature on HRM in larger firms in recent years. Given the continuous growth of small businesses and self-employment (officially classified as the 'individual economy'[1]) and given their relatively (re-)new(ed) appearance as a form of ownership in China and their increasingly important role in the economy and employment since the early 1980s, it is necessary to investigate the nature of their employment relations. For example, what are the employment relations settings in these firms? How systematic are their HR procedures? What are the key HR and employment characteristics, for instance, in terms of recruitment, training, pay, working time and owner–worker relations? To what extent do external bodies such as the trade unions, labour authorities and other workers' associations have influence over the employment issues in the private small businesses? How knowledgeable are owner managers and workers about employment legislation and what is the level of adherence? In what ways are patterns of employment relations in this sector similar to and/or different from those which prevail in the public and larger private sectors in China? To what extent do they resemble the findings of the small sector in other countries? These are the major issues that are investigated in this chapter.

Chapter 9 brings HRM back under the spotlight by exploring recent trends of HR initiatives adopted by different firms (e.g. SOEs, larger private firms, MNCs/JVs and TVEs) in China. It addresses an important question: Is HRM taking root in China? The chapter draws our attention to the increasing diversity of HR practices in China as a result of the emerging varieties of ownership forms and the growth of new industries. It reveals signs that the rapid growth of private businesses and foreign firms is adding forces for change in the SOEs and public sector organizations, especially in areas such as recruitment, reward and performance management. The phenomenon of enterprise culture management is analysed as a 'new' HR initiative fashioned by SOEs, MNCs/JVs and domestic private businesses. In addition, the chapter explores the extent to which new ways of delivering the HR function in the Western countries, for example, the outsourcing of HR services and the growing use of e-HR, have been adopted by firms in China. The chapter further contemplates the role of MNCs and JVs in disseminating 'best practice' HRM in China and the level of convergence between the two. The chapter paves the way for the concluding chapter in which issues concerning HRM, work and employment are summarized in the context of the international trend of HRM and the globalized economy. This helps us to predict the future prospects of HR and employment practices in China.

The concluding chapter contemplates a number of challenges facing the state, the trade unions, the human resource function and researchers in the management of human resources and industrial relations in China. More specifically, it highlights the role and strategic plan of the state in employment creation and skills training as was set out in Premier Wen's Government Report speech to the 10th National People's Congress in March 2004. The chapter also discusses the challenges faced by the trade unions and points out their strategic tasks. This is followed by a summary of the major challenges to HRM in China and highlights the need to professionalize the HR function. The chapter finally points out a number of research implications for both Chinese and Western academics and the need for a new approach to comparative study that should transcend economic and geographic boundaries.

Sources of statistical data and empirical evidence

This book draws its statistical data and empirical evidence from a number of sources. First, it draws its secondary data from published official statistics and government policy documents, newspapers, articles from academic and practitioners' publications in both the Chinese and English languages. Literature in the Chinese language was collected in China mostly by the author and that in English was collected in the UK, again by the author. Research in social science in general and in employment and organizational studies in particular has been relatively limited and unsophisticated in China in comparison with that in the West, especially in the form of detailed and micro-level studies in order to build up the body of knowledge and analytical framework.

A leading source of statistical data is from the *China Statistics Yearbook*, the most comprehensive and authoritative source of quantitative data available on China. Statistics of different periods are used because this is a book that reviews the historical development of personnel and HR policy, work and employment in China. It is therefore important to use statistics of different periods to provide readers with a more complete picture of its development. It needs to be pointed out here that statistical information available in China on employment is regarded as rather rudimentary, in terms of both quantity and quality. Breakdown data are rarely available. National statistics often fail to detail gender differences, especially in employment-related data, making gender statistics study extremely difficult (Zheng 2001), although the situation is beginning to improve. The issue of gender discrimination in employment has been even less well studied, even though China has the largest female labour force in the world (Meng 1998). Similarly, limited statistics are available on the growing private and small business sectors to enable us to draw a detailed picture of employment patterns and to carry out cross-sectoral comparison. This volume therefore tries to piece together the available information on employment and management, but many gaps remain.

Second, many of the chapters are informed, and some primarily so (e.g. Chapters 3 and 8), by the ongoing empirical research that the author has been conducting since the mid-1990s on issues related to human resource management, gender equality and employment practices in China. These fieldwork studies include: reforms in the state-owned railway industry, privatization of the state-owned enterprises, joint ventures in the brewing industry, reforms in the civil service and public sector organizations, employment relations in the private small and self-employed businesses, employment conditions in private manufacturing firms, employment practices in community services, and HRM practices of wholly foreign-owned firms in China. Most of these studies were funded from a range of sources, such as the British Council, the Nuffield Foundation, the Department for International Development and the British Academy. Interviews and questionnaire surveys were the main methods of data collection, supplemented by company documents, where available, and a limited amount of observation during site visits. Access to these studies was mainly through the network of personal friends rather than official arrangements, a relationship that increases the level of readiness of the informants to disclose sensitive information related to the issues explored. These studies were conducted mainly in the Guangdong Province of southern China (one of the economically most developed provinces in China) where much of the fieldwork was conducted. Caution must therefore be taken in generalization. In any case, it is hazardous to generalize about China, one of the reasons being the country's considerable diversity (Child 1996).

Third, this book benefits from the author's personal experience of having lived and worked in China for many years, which provides a valuable pre-understanding of the political, cultural and economic dimensions of Chinese society necessary for the interpretation of the issues concerned here. However, the author has been careful in being as objective as possible in interpreting the data and expressing views on the issues under discussion.

The author is conscious of the fact that data presented in this volume may not be completely up to date because of the rapid development in China and the lead time in the production of the book. However, at least it serves as a reference for discussion and a milestone that captures a specific moment in time of China's social and economic development.

Conceptual framework

This book adopts the term 'human resource management' (HRM) in a broad sense. As Budhwar and Debrah (2001) point out, there are a number of reasons why HRM has to be defined in its broadest sense when exploring HRM in developing countries, including the very question of whether or not it exists and variations in models. Moreover, while the meaning of HRM was widely debated in the 1980s and early 1990s, 'it has become the most popular term in the English-speaking world referring to the activities of management in the employment relationship' (Boxall and Purcell 2003: 1). For example, Boxall and Purcell (2003: 2–5) define HRM as covering all workforce groups, involving line and specialist managers, incorporating a variety of management styles, involving managing work and people both collectively and individually, and embedded in industries and societies.

The term HRM was introduced to China in the early 1990s as a result of joint teaching programmes between Sino-Western universities and the importation of management techniques by MNCs and the foreign partners of JVs (Warner 1992). It should be noted here that, while the concept of HRM has grown in popularity in recent years, there is considerable divergence in the ways in which 'human resource management' is interpreted and understood in China. 'Human resource management' is often misleadingly used as a more fashionable synonym for 'personnel management' without attempting to differentiate the differences (Warner 1997b), a practice also noted in other countries such as the UK.

For the purpose of this book, the term 'personnel management/ administration' is generally used to describe the management of personnel in the predominantly state sector for the period prior to 1980 when radical economic reforms started, leading to the proliferation of business ownership forms outside the state sector. The term 'human resource management' is used for state-owned enterprises, collectively owned enterprises, joint ventures, multinational corporations and large private firms to reflect the relatively more formal and planned nature of their staffing policy and practice since 1980. The terms 'employment policy and practice' and 'labour strategy' are used for township and village enterprises, private small businesses and sweatshop manufacturing firms to reflect their informal, *ad hoc* and even exploitative nature in the management of labour. It must be pointed out here that these are loosely defined typologies rather than categorical classifications, since it is dangerous to polarize China's employment policy and practice as 'the best practice' of blue chip multinationals versus exploitation of sweatshop manufactories in the backyards of prospering economic cities. In addition, the term 'employment relations' is used in a broad sense to cover a wide range of issues which fall within the scope of analysis of both human resource management and industrial relations, especially for Chapter 8 on private small businesses. This is because it is felt that some of the employment practices reported here cannot be comfortably classified as HRM, even when interpreting the term in the broadest sense.

It has been noted, however, that through economic reform and the influx of foreign direct investment, the traditional personnel function in China has started to take a new form of HRM in recent years, and that the diffusion and transfer of HRM have been more extensive in MNCs (Goodall and Warner 1997; Braun and Warner 2002). In any case, if HRM is seen as a strategic approach to managing labour/human resources with more emphasis on planning and flexibility, in contrast with the traditional reactive and administrative approach to personnel management, then the overall trend in China appears to be moving towards a more planned, strategic and flexible approach to the management of human resources, albeit an approach mainly found in the formal sector. In that sense, we can reasonably justify the use of the term HRM to describe employment policy and practice in China, at least for some sectors and types of employing organizations.

Summary

In summary, the purpose of this book is to develop a better theoretical and empirical understanding of the differing incentives and pressures facing different sectors and ownership forms in shaping their human resource strategies. It addresses several thematic issues that have been under-explored in the existing Western literature on HRM, work and employment in China, but are having growing significance in China as a consequence of its recent reforms. At the macro level, the book explores how the economic and political institutions of China may have a direct and significant effect on the ownership and governance structure of firms and the resultant patterns of human resource policies and practices. At the organizational level, the book contemplates how organizational level strategies may be important in the adaptation and diffusion of certain employment and HR practices. At the individual level, the book reveals how employment and career opportunities are structured for and work is experienced by millions of workers in China, with some being more lucky than others.

This book does not claim to be the authoritative study on HRM, work and employment in China. Rather, it takes the opportunity to fill some of the gaps in the literature and to present readers with some of the latest research findings in a rapidly changing country. More importantly, it serves as a spur to stimulate further interest in and debate on China where opportunities for its social and economic development are as promising as the challenges it faces are uncompromising. Where possible, the book draws attention to the similarities of many of the issues and problems faced by developed economies in the management of human resources, whereas previous discussions have focused mainly on the differences between the two types of economies. It is felt that the contribution of a study of HRM, work and employment in China will be limited without relating the patterns displayed in the system to those demonstrated in the systems of other economies in an increasingly globalized economic environment. In other words, the study of China should not be carried out in isolation. Instead, it should be situated in the global context.

Note

1   This book follows the European Union (EU) definitions using employment figures as the sole criteria, i.e. those with up to nine employees are classified as micro enterprises and those with between ten and ninety-nine employees as small enterprises (Storey 1994: 13). In addition, it is the official convention in China that private businesses which employ fewer than eight workers are classified as self-employed businesses or individual economies, whereas anything above is classified as private businesses.

2 Employment relations in China and its institutional context

Introduction

The once state-controlled and state sector-dominant personnel administrative system of China has been through a period of profound change as a result of the political and economic reforms experienced in the past two and a half decades. This chapter first provides a historical overview of the personnel system in the past five decades or so since the founding of Socialist China in 1949. Much of it is related to the state sector, because the state has been the major employer in the past and because SOEs and public sector organizations are the areas where HRM has experienced the most radical changes in recent years under the economic and social welfare reforms. The chapter then outlines the institutional environment for the growth of the private sector since the late 1970s and the characteristics of the employment policy and practice in these private ownership forms. In particular, the chapter focuses on foreign investments, domestic private firms, and the township and village enterprises. The characteristics of the labour market, the framework of employment legislation, and the (welfare) role of the trade unions and the Workers' Representatives Congress are also discussed. This chapter serves as a backdrop for the more thematic discussions of HRM, work and employment in China in subsequent chapters.

The development of the personnel system in the state sector

For the first three decades of Socialist China until the end of the Cultural Revolution in 1976, the personnel management system was highly centralized by the state under the planned economy regime (see Chapter 3 for more detail). Personnel management during this period exhibited two major features in terms of its governance structure and the content of personnel policy. First, personnel policy and practice of organizations were strictly under the control of the state through regional/local labour departments. Centralization, formalization and standardization of personnel policies and practices were the primary tasks of the Ministry of Labour (for blue-collar workers) and the Ministry of Personnel (for white-collar and managerial staff) (see further discussion below). The state not only determined the number of people to be employed and sources of recruitment, but also unilaterally set the pay scales for different categories of workers. State intervention was also extended to the structure and responsibility of personnel function at the organizational level. Managers of all levels were only involved in the administrative function and policy implementation under rigid policy guidelines (Child 1994; Cooke 2003a). Second, for most people, entering employment was a 'once-in-a-lifetime' event with 'lifelong' job security. Wages were typically low but compensated by a broad range of workplace welfare provisions, including housing, pensions, health care, children's schooling, transportation to and from work, and employment for spouses and school-leaving children, as part of the responsibility of the 'nanny' employer (Warner 1996a; Cooke 2000). These characteristics were once dominant in the personnel management system of the country because, until the 1980s, the vast majority of Chinese employing organizations were state owned, with a minority collectively owned and even fewer privately owned. Three-quarters of urban employees worked in state-owned units (see Table 2.1).

The situation of state dominance began to be changed in the late 1970s, following the country's adoption of an 'open door' policy to attract foreign investments and domestic private funds in order to revitalize the nation's economy. In parallel to this economic policy, the state sector has witnessed radical changes in its personnel policy and practice, as part of the Economic Reforms and the Enterprise Reforms begun in the early 1980s. One of the major changes has been the rolling back of direct state control and the consequent increase of autonomy and responsibility at enterprise level in major aspects of their personnel management practices. This change was accompanied by a series of state-driven personnel initiatives which sent shock waves to individual employees as well as to the country's economy as a whole. The objective of these initiatives was to bring to an end the planned state economy characterized by 'high employment rate', 'high welfare', 'low wage' and 'low productivity' and to introduce the market economy 'with Chinese characteristics' in which competition and incentive were two major ingredients. As a result, rapid and fundamental changes in Chinese HRM policies had taken place during the 1980s and especially during the 1990s (Easterby-Smith *et al.* 1995).

In particular, the 'Three Systems' reform has been implemented in most (state-owned) organizations since the mid-1990s (see Chapter 3 for more detail). These include: fixed duration individual and collective labour contracts instead of jobs-for-life; new remuneration systems to reflect performance, post and skill levels; and new welfare schemes in which all employers and employees are required by law to make contribution to five separate funds: pension, industrial accident, maternity, unemployment and medical insurance (Warner 1996b). The new welfare system is intended to shift the huge welfare burden from being borne by the (state) employers alone towards

Table 2.1 Employment statistics by ownership in urban and rural areas in China (figures in million persons)[a]

Ownership	1978	1980	1985	1990	1995	1998	2000	2001	2002
Total	401.52	423.61	498.73	647.49	680.65	706.37	720.85	730.25	737.40
Number of urban employed persons	95.14	105.25	128.08	166.16	190.93	206.78	231.51	239.40	247.80
State-owned units	74.51	80.19	89.90	103.46	112.61	90.58	81.02	76.40	71.63
Collectively owned units	20.48	24.25	33.24	35.49	31.47	19.63	14.99	12.91	11.22
Co-operative units	—	—	—	—	—	1.36	1.55	1.53	1.61
Joint-ownership units	—	—	0.38	0.96	0.53	0.48	0.42	0.45	0.45
Limited liability corporations	—	—	—	—	—	4.84	6.87	8.41	10.83
Shareholding corporations ltd	—	—	—	—	3.17	4.10	4.57	4.83	5.38
Private enterprises	—	—	—	0.57	4.85	9.73	12.68	15.27	19.99
Units with funds from Hong Kong, Macao and Taiwan	—	—	—	0.04	2.72	2.94	3.10	3.26	3.67
Foreign-funded units	—	—	0.06	0.62	2.41	2.93	3.32	3.45	3.91
Self-employed individuals	0.15	0.81	4.50	6.14	15.60	22.59	21.36	21.31	22.69
Number of rural employed persons	306.38	318.36	370.65	472.93	488.54	492.79	489.34	490.85	489.60
Township and village enterprises	28.27	30.00	69.79	92.65	128.62	125.37	128.20	130.86	132.88
Private enterprises	—	—	—	1.13	4.71	7.37	11.39	11.87	14.11
Self-employed individuals	—	—	—	14.91	30.54	38.55	29.34	26.29	24.74

Source: adapted from China Statistical Yearbook 2003: 126–7.

Note
[a] Since 1990, data on the economically active population, total employed persons and the subtotal of employed persons in urban and rural areas have been adjusted in accordance with the data obtained from the 5th National Population Census. As a result, the sum of the data by region, by ownership or by sector is not equal to the total (original note from China Statistical Yearbook, 2003: 123).

a tripartite system that involves the employer, the individual employee and the social insurance company.

In SOEs and public sector organizations, a system called 'competing for the post' was also introduced in the mid-1990s in which employees would be assessed (through tests) once a year on their competence to work in a particular post. Those who came last would be laid off and further training would be given to increase their competence while they were waiting for a post. In addition, there has been an ongoing wage reform in the state sector since the late 1970s which aimed to establish a closer link between performance and reward, although its effectiveness remains controversial (see Chapter 4 for further discussion).

The State Economy Commission issued a document in 2001 (No. [2001] 230) which requires SOEs to deepen the above 'Three Systems' reform by viewing it as their top priority. The document reasserts that SOEs are required to establish a system in which managerial workers should compete for their posts with both upward and downward mobility. SOEs are also required to establish an independent employment system without interference from other bodies. Employment contracts are signed and employees need to compete for their post through competency tests. Finally, SOEs are required to establish a reward system which provides greater links between (individual) performance and reward as a motivational mechanism.

Many of the above changes in the state sector were initiated by the state and carried out at organizational level under the top-down approach with little consultation with the trade unions (see discussion below on the role of trade unions) or employees. These changes also took place alongside the most radical change in the SOEs in the past decade: downsizing. Started in the early 1990s as part of the programme of restructuring and revitalizing the outmoded SOEs, this initiative reached its peak in the late 1990s after Premier Zhu Rongji's announcement of his SOE reform plan in 1997. In the five-year period between 1998 and 2002, a total of over 27 million workers had been laid off from SOEs (*China Statistics Yearbook* 2003) through early retirement and performance review. Laid-off workers were expected to receive retraining for re-employment, a process in which the trade unions were able to play a more visible role. Similar reforms have been implemented in the civil service and public sector organizations since the late 1990s, but on a much less drastic scale (see Chapter 3).

In general, SOEs tend to have the following characteristics in their personnel policy and practice in comparison with that of other forms of ownership. They have established personnel policies and practices and clear lines of control in the management structure. They have a relatively high level of workplace welfare provisions, even though at a reducing level. They have espoused policy of trade union involvement and employee participation through the Workers' Representatives Congress in enterprise decision making and management. In addition, they have high levels of trade union recognition and membership, and a relatively lower level of labour disputes and, where it occurs, both sides tend to seek formal mechanisms to resolve the dispute (see discussion below).

The growth of non-state sectors and their characteristics of employment policy and practice

The deepening economic reform in the past two decades has led to the emergence and expansion of a variety of ownership forms (see Table 2.1; also see Child and Tse (2001) for a more detailed discussion of goals, means and limiting forces in institutional reform in China). Broadly speaking, and for the convenience of discussion in this book, these ownership forms may be classified as: state sector organizations; collectively owned enterprises; foreign-owned businesses, including MNCs, JVs and investments from Hong Kong, Macao and Taiwan; domestic privately owned firms and self-employed businesses; and township and village enterprises. These forms of ownership arise from different political and economic backgrounds and are engaged in different types of product and labour markets and therefore with employment policies and practices that are distinct to their form. While employment policy and practice of COEs share considerable similarities to those of the SOEs in part due to a level of state intervention in the past and relatedly in part due to their decades' modelling of the state sector, those in the other ownership forms are rather different.

Foreign investments

In the past two decades the Chinese economy has increasingly become highly export-oriented, which has made the country the second largest recipient of FDI worldwide (after the USA) for the past decade. This is due largely to two factors: investment incentives offered by the Chinese government, and the country's abundant availability of cheap labour. It has been argued that the strong emphasis on foreign investment and foreign trade has been one of the key factors, if not the key factor, in the unprecedented growth of the Chinese economy in recent years. Attracting FDI has been an important part of China's open door economic policy since 1978. For example, a total of 34,171 project agreements were signed in 2002, with a total amount of capital of nearly $83 billion. Of these, 24,930 agreements were in manufacturing with a total amount of capital of nearly $60 billion (*China Statistics Yearbook* 2003).

In the early stages of the 'open door policy', the Chinese government decided that in order to control the operations of foreign companies in China, foreign direct investments would be confined to joint ventures with local (state) partners. Numerous restrictions were also imposed on the joint ventures in their operations, including the management of human resources. For example, Child (1994) observed that the personnel area was where Chinese authorities have been most actively involved in international joint ventures.

In spite of the regulations that the joint ventures' board of directors could decide on employee compensation, local personnel and labour bureaux tried to control the salary levels paid to Chinese employees. In addition, there was strong pressure on JVs not to lay off workers.

However, the level of control and influence from the local authorities began to ease off from the early 1990s (see Chapter 9 for further discussion). Today, more than two decades after China issued its first joint venture law in 1979, foreign companies have considerably more latitude in their business operations in China. Since 1986, joint ventures have been granted the freedom, at least in principle, to decide on the recruitment and reward of their employees (Pomfret 1991). The Chinese government now permits 100 per cent foreign ownership in most industries and the number of new wholly owned foreign subsidiaries surpassed that of equity joint ventures for the first time in 1998 (Bjorkman and Lu 2001).

During the early and mid-1990s, a popular way of reforming and revitalizing SOEs in China was to convert them into joint ventures with foreign investors. It is a practice called 'grafting' (*jiajie*) encouraged by the government. There are two ways of forming these joint ventures. One is for the Chinese SOEs to convert their existing production buildings, equipment and land into shares in the joint venture, while the foreign partners invest capital, technology or equipment. The other is for the Chinese SOEs to restructure themselves into share-holding companies first, and then to transfer part of their shares to the foreign investors (Gu 1997). Other important reasons for Chinese partners entering a joint venture agreement include the desire to acquire knowledge, the latest technology and management skills, and the desire to generate export income (Brunner *et al.* 1992).

MNCs and JVs are therefore major employers in China whose employment policy and practice has a strong bearing in reshaping the pool of human resources and the experience of work for a significant proportion of workers. While MNCs and JVs operate at different ends of the market and may deploy potentially polarizing human resource strategies, (e.g. blue chip MNCs and JVs employing mainly urban workers with relatively higher skills and qualification levels vs. sweatshop manufactories employing predominantly rural migrant workers), they appear to share a number of characteristics. Taking the extreme cases out of the equation, the differences between these firms in terms of their employment policy and practice may be in the degree of implementation rather than in kind.

Generally speaking, they tend to be flexible in their observation of the employment regulations contingent to their perceived risk (of non-observation) and financial burden of the enterprises (see Chapter 6 and 7). There is a higher level of job insecurity from the workers, especially the older ones, with fixed-term employment contracts being the norm. There is generally a lower level of social security provision than in the state sector but higher than the domestic private and self-employed businesses. However, wage levels are generally highest in this sector (see Chapter 4), attracting many job candidates who desire to work in the sector. This is in part because MNCs and JVs are required by regulations to pay wages at a level no lower than the average wage of the same industry in the local area. There is also a relatively high level and variety of health and safety and skills training. For instance, the car factory Volkswagen in Shanghai has an average of 5 per cent of employees receiving off-the-job training every day. Many blue chip MNCs and JVs also pride themselves on employee training and development.

There is a disproportionally higher level of labour disputes that are also more collectively involved compared with the state sector (see Table 2.7). This is perhaps due to the fact that blue chip MNCs and JVs are a small proportion in this sector and that sweatshop manufacturers have been a major source of labour disputes in contemporary industrial relations in China (see e.g. Chan 2001). Compared with the state sector, there is a much lower level of union recognition with varying roles of the trade unions. A better management–labour relationship tends to exist where a trade union is recognized with a competent union chairman in place who has established a good relationship with management. They take a cautious approach to collective negotiation for fear of the wider implications for other establishments of the MNC outside China. None the less, collective agreements have generally been considered beneficial to the improvement of the investment environment. However, there is a relatively low level of employee participation and union involvement in decision making (Zhang 2003).

Domestic private firms

The rapid growth of domestic private businesses in China has been one of the most notable phenomena in its economic development since the 1980s. Once existing as a marginal and marginalized economic force in the country (because its capitalist ideology was seen as undermining socialist values), the sector was gradually given more freedom to grow, and full legal rights were granted in 2000 (see Parris 1999; Zhang and Ming 1999; Child and Tse 2001; and Chapter 8 for detailed discussion). In the past twenty-five years, this sector has been growing steadily in terms of the number of entities, size of the workforce and industrial output. Its scope of business has been expanding into a diverse portfolio, although commercial services and labour-intensive light manufacturing industries remain its main territory. While the growth of this sector is country-wide, the East and South coastal areas have been its key base of growth. While small businesses remain central, the size of firms appears to be growing. Their organizational structure is becoming increasingly formalized, with limited and share-holding entities becoming the main stake of private businesses. The growth (both in size and number) of private firms and their growing formalization is, to a certain extent, a result of the increasing incidences of privatization of SOEs and COEs since the late 1990s. According to the Fifth Survey of Private Enterprises carried out at the end of 2001 (*China Private Economy Yearbook* 2003), 8 per cent of the

3,258 private businesses surveyed reported that they had already acquired bankrupt SOEs, while another 14 per cent expressed that they had plans to do so. In addition, nearly 3 per cent had subcontracted poor performing SOEs and another 7 per cent had plans to do so.

Compared with SOEs and larger firms in other ownership forms, private businesses tend to have a stronger adaptability to market trends because of their relatively simple product structure and technology. They mainly operate in the gaps and niches of products where larger enterprises have not yet set foot. They are highly profit driven and therefore more adventurous and opportunistic, but with a relatively lower level of investment risk. In recent years, they have been playing an increasingly important role in the export of industrial products (Chen 2003).

As such, private enterprises have been a major source of job growth in the past twenty years (see Table 2.2). Between 1990 and 1999, the state sector shed nearly 18 million jobs. Another 18 million were shed from the collectively owned enterprises. In the same period, 28 million jobs were created by the domestic private and self-employed businesses and 5.5 million by foreign enterprises (Chen 2003). Over 62 million people worked in self-employed businesses as owners or workers in its peak year 1999. In the year 2000 alone, the private and self-employed sector accommodated 2.5 million laid-off workers, making up 70 per cent of the total number of laid-off workers re-employed (Wang, Y. J. 2003). By the end of 2002, 17 per cent of urban workers worked in private or self-employed businesses and 8 per cent of rural workers worked in the same sector (see Table 2.1). Nearly 47 per cent (38.1 million) of these workers worked in the commercial sector (wholesale and retail trade and catering services) and over 26 per cent (21.4 million) worked in the manufacturing sector (*China Statistics Yearbook* 2003).

There were over 2.4 million registered private businesses and over 27.7 million registered self-employed businesses by the end of 2002 (*China Statistics Yearbook* 2003). Most of these private businesses are small scale (with an average of fourteen employees in each business), and the self-employed businesses are even smaller by definition. Most of them have a short company history of under ten years (see Chapter 8, for example).

There are a number of characteristics in the employment policy and practice of these firms. Generally speaking there are few layers of management, often with combined operational and ownership rights. This to some extent facilitates direct control of the business and the workforce by the (owner-) manager. These businesses tend to have more flexible use of human resources than do SOEs in response to, and taking advantage of, the market environment, often through long working hours with workers peripheral in the labour market. They virtually have no union recognition, with weak bargaining power from the labour ranks and a high level of management/owner prerogatives. Labour turnover in this sector tends to be higher than that in other sectors. Social and workplace welfare provisions are limited, even though some of the provisions are required by the state. There is largely a

Table 2.2 Employment growth in the private and other forms of ownership: 1990–1999

Year	National growth	State-owned growth (%)	Collectively owned growth (%)	Foreign-owned growth (%)	Self-employed growth (%)	Private owned	Private-owned growth (%)
1990	155,100	2.35	1.34	40.43	8.45	1,700,000	3.66
1991	13,900	3.07	2.23	150.00	9.64	1,840,000	8.24
1992	11,700	2.11	−0.19	33.94	6.93	2,320,000	26.09
1993	12,500	0.28	−6.30	30.32	19.12	3,730,000	60.78
1994	12,400	2.69	−3.18	40.97	28.44	6,480,000	73.73
1995	11,100	0.42	−4.20	26.35	22.19	9,560,000	47.53
1996	13,300	−0.15	−4.16	5.26	8.73	11,710,000	22.49
1997	10,900	−1.78	−4.41	7.59	8.45	13,500,000	15.29
1998	5,100	−17.98	−31.91	1.03	12.37	17,100,000	26.67
1999	9,000	−5.37	−12.79	4.26	2.08	20,220,000	18.25
Average growth	11,100	−2.06	−7.78	28.07	12.84		31.67

Sources: adapted from *China Statistics Yearbook* 2000; *Forty Years of China Industry and Commerce Administration Management* 2000.

lack of long-term strategic planning and an absence of HR policies and procedures. Recruitment tends to be informal, often based on nepotism rather than on market competition (see Chapter 8).

The growth of TVEs

Built from the 'remnants of the disintegrating people's communes' (Garnaut 2001: 3), township and village enterprises have been praised as one of the wonders of the reforms by Chinese and Western commentators alike. Similar to the private and self-employed businesses, TVEs grew dramatically and played a significant role in creating jobs (mainly for the rural labour force) throughout the 1980s and 1990s. A major economic strategy by the Chinese government in the mid-1980s to combat the stagnating farming income was to stimulate non-agricultural production. This has led to the rapid growth of TVEs, from just over 1.5 million by the end of 1978 to a peak of nearly 25 million by the end of 1994 (see Table 2.3). Over the past two decades, TVEs have become the most vibrant part of the economy, absorbing surplus rural labour, processing agricultural products, and diversifying production into a range of consumer goods and products for both the home and export markets. The growth rate was explosive, with rural industrial output increasing by 21 per cent per annum from 1978 through to the early 1990s (Saich 2001). In 1978, taxes paid by TVEs were about 2 billion yuan; in 2002, this increased to nearly 279 billion yuan. In 1978, the operating revenue of TVEs was over 43 billion yuan; in 2002, it increased to nearly 12,976 billion yuan (*China Statistics Yearbook* 2003).

The presence of a readily available labour force (see Table 2.2) was crucial to the expansion of the TVEs, and the introduction of the household responsibility system in the rural economy (i.e. from collective contracting to household contracting of land for agricultural activities) made this available (Meng 2000). TVEs have, for the past ten years, been employing over 100 million people each year (see Table 2.3), surpassing the number of employees in SOEs. Although the total number of TVEs has slightly reduced to a steady level of around 20 to 21 million since the mid-1990s, the total number of people employed has been rising, from just over 28 million in 1978 to nearly 133 million in 2002 (see Table 2.3). This indicates that the size of TVEs is on the increase. Sources of their competitive advantages come mainly from favourable tax policies (free for the first three years) and the abundant availability of a highly mobile and flexible labour force.

Most TVEs are collectively owned by their local citizens or privately owned but may often be controlled by the local township and village governments in order to gain access to resources (e.g. bank loan and bureaucratic approval) that are only available to the formal sectors through controlled channels (Chang and Wang 1994). In addition, township and village officials have vested interests in being involved in TVEs, such as sharing the residual benefits. Compared with SOEs, TVEs may be more innovative, proactive and risk taking when they encounter the same adversarial business environment (Luo *et al.* 1998).

Given the diversity of the TVEs, in terms of, for example, geographical location, size of enterprise, ownership pattern and governance structure, and the limited data available on the sector, it is very difficult to provide an overview of the features of employment policy and practice in this sector. However, crude judgement may be made to suggest that while model TVEs do exist with systematic human resource policies in place, the majority of TVEs tend to operate with informal HR procedures (see Ding *et al.* (2004) for more detailed discussion of the variations in HRM of TVEs of different ownership). Senior managers are usually appointed by local governments. Recruitment is based largely on word of mouth from existing employees and from the local labour market. Nepotism is widely practised and the general education and skill levels of the workforce are relatively low, with a disproportionally small number of technical and professional staff or managerial talent. Training provision tends to focus on immediate production needs with little prospect of career development. There is a lack of rigorous performance management system other than basic performance-related pay, a practice similar to that of many urban domestic private firms.

Employment conditions in TVEs tend to be less favourable than those in the formal sector in general, if measured by employment security, wage level and labour protection, but will almost undoubtedly be better than farming. Employment regulations are often not implemented with the tacit approval of authorities in order to avoid costs that may hinder TVEs' existence and growth. For instance, there has been controversy as to whether minimum wage regulations should be applied to TVEs (see Chapter 7 for more discussion). Few TVEs contribute to social insurance for their employees. Only about 7 per cent of employees in TVEs are union members and the collective representation of TVEs employees may be largely voluntary and simultaneous when labour–management conflicts arise. There is little evidence of collective contract or collective bargaining (Ding *et al.* 2001). However, there appears to be a trend for HRM practices to be increasingly formalized as TVEs grow in size and maturity (Chow and Fu 2000). For example, managerial and technical staff may be recruited from a broader labour market to fill the skill gaps (Ding *et al.* 2001).

The labour market

The employment policy and practice of the above categories of employing organizations have a close two-way relationship with the labour market in China, which exhibits a number of (related) features. First, there are growing employment opportunities in the non-state sectors in parallel with the rising number of unemployed, in part as a result of the continuous downsizing in SOEs and COEs and the increasing mismatch of skills available and sought between the supply and demand side. China's official urban unemployment

Table 2.3 The growth of TVEs and employment in TVEs: 1978–2002 (end-of-year figures)

Year	Total TVEs[a]	Total Employees[b]	Farming, forestry, animal husbandry and fishery TVEs	Farming, forestry, animal husbandry and fishery Employees	Industry TVEs	Industry Employees	Construction TVEs	Construction Employees
1978	1,524.2	28,265.6	494.6	6,084.2	794.0	17,343.6	46.7	2,356.2
1979	1,480.4	29,093.4	443.9	5,330.0	767.1	18,143.8	49.7	2,984.5
1980	1,424.6	29,996.7	378.3	4,560.7	757.8	19,423.0	50.8	3,346.7
1981	1,337.5	29,695.6	319.0	3,799.4	725.4	19,808.0	48.3	3,488.3
1982	1,361.7	31,129.1	292.8	3,440.0	749.2	20,728.1	53.8	4,212.9
1983	1,346.4	32,346.4	269.8	3,092.2	744.0	21,681.4	57.0	4,827.2
1984	6,065.2	52,081.1	248.4	2,839.3	4,812.2	36,560.7	80.4	6,834.9
1985	12,224.5	69,790.3	224.2	2,523.8	4,930.3	41,367.0	82.6	7,899.5
1986	15,153.0	79,371.4	239.7	2,408.0	6,355.0	47,619.6	892.5	2,703.7
1987	17,502.4	88,051.8	231.2	2,441.8	7,082.8	52,666.9	902.5	3,739.8
1988	18,881.6	95,454.5	232.8	2,499.9	7,735.2	57,033.9	955.8	14,848.1
1989	18,686.3	93,667.8	226.8	2,393.0	7,364.7	56,241.0	925.5	14,037.3
1990	18,504.0	92,647.5	224.0	2,360.6	7,220.0	55,716.9	904.0	13,468.4
1991	19,088.8	96,091.1	230.9	2,430.8	2,425.7	58,135.5	888.1	13,843.3
1992	20,916.2	106,245.9	249.2	2,618.2	7,938.2	63,364.0	984.9	15,524.2
1993	24,529.0	123,453.0	279.0	2,854.0	9,184.0	72,596.0	1,217.0	18,269.0
1994	24,944.7	120,174.7	246.4	2,604.6	6,985.8	69,615.1	829.9	16,220.4
1995	22,026.7	128,620.6	277.7	3,135.2	7,181.6	75,647.2	1,067.5	19,325.2
1996	23,363.3	135,082.9	289.4	3,360.0	7,564.3	78,601.4	1,045.8	19,488.4
1997	9,075.0	91,582.8	214.6	2,769.6	3,782.2	61,494.4	416.2	12,734.0
1998	20,040.0	125,365.5	189.0	2,739.1	6,620.0	73,342.3	821.0	16,337.5
1999	20,709.0	127,040.9	165.0	2,473.8	6,735.0	73,953.2	825.0	16,134.5
2000	20,846.6	128,195.7	151.2	2,220.4	6,740.1	74,667.3	795.2	15,810.9
2001	21,155.4	130,855.8	127.4	2,000.3	6,721.7	76,151.1	762.6	15,644.1
2002	21,326.9	132,877.1	321.7	2,053.7	6,276.8	76,676.1	697.5	14,603.6

Source: adapted from *China Statistics Yearbook* 2003: 471–3.

Notes
1. In 1997 the statistical coverage of township and village enterprises was adjusted (original note), (therefore non-comparable with the rest of the statistics).
2. The number of TVEs includes three types of ownership: collectively owned, privately owned, and self-employed businesses.
[a] Number of TVEs, figures in thousands.
[b] Number of people employed in TVEs, figures in thousands.

rate stood at 4 per cent at the end of 2002, up from 3.6 per cent at the end of 2001 (*China Statistics Yearbook* 2003). The government admitted that the real rate would be closer to 7 per cent if laid-off workers of SOEs were included. Among the unemployed, laid-off workers (42.7 per cent in 2002) and university graduates (21 per cent in 2002) make up the largest proportion (*China Statistics Yearbook* 2003). Favourable policies, such as tax relief, are offered by the government to encourage laid-off workers and university graduates to take up self-employment in order to ease the pressure of unemployment. University graduates are also encouraged to develop their career in the north-west region of the country where the new focus of economic development is and where skills are most needed. Second, for those who are

Transport and storage		Wholesale and retail trade		Hotel and catering services		Social services		Other non-agricultural trades	
TVEs	Employees	TVEs	Employees	TVEs	Employees	TVEs	Employees	TVEs	Employees
65.1	1,038.3	123.8	1,443.3	—	—	—	—	—	—
82.1	1,169.0	137.6	1,466.1	—	—	—	—	—	—
89.4	1,135.6	148.3	1,530.7	—	—	—	—	—	—
88.9	1,073.8	155.9	1,526.1	—	—	—	—	—	—
95.8	1,129.4	170.1	1,618.7	—	—	—	—	—	—
91.6	1,097.1	184.0	1,648.5	—	—	—	—	—	—
129.6	1,293.0	794.6	4,553.2	—	—	—	—	—	—
106.1	1,141.8	6,881.3	16,858.2	—	—	—	—	—	—
2,619.8	5,412.6	5,046.0	11,227.5	—	—	—	—	—	—
3,252.4	6,231.4	6,033.5	12,971.9	—	—	—	—	—	—
3,725.5	6,841.6	6,232.3	14,234.0	—	—	—	—	—	—
1,798.8	6,993.7	6,370.5	14,002.8	—	—	—	—	—	—
3,814.0	7,112.2	6,342.0	13,989.4	—	—	—	—	—	—
4,003.4	7,323.1	6,540.7	14,358.4	—	—	—	—	—	—
4,369.5	7,997.4	7,377.7	16,743.4	—	—	—	—	—	—
4,864.0	9,314.0	6,563.0	14,078.0	—	—	—	—	—	—
3,691.1	7,255.9	7,596.3	16,145.3	2,929.3	4,181.7	—	—	2,665.8	4,151.6
4,951.7	9,520.3	6,977.7	16,774.2	944.5	2,252.2	—	—	626.0	1,966.3
5,464.9	10,623.2	7,617.1	24,478.7	—	—	—	—	—	—
1,430.6	3,820.3	2,110.8	6,229.9	867.5	3,477.4	—	—	253.0	1,057.2
4,148.0	8,863.4	5,455.0	14,189.0	2,211.0	7,676.3	—	—	595.0	2,217.9
4,127.0	8,857.2	5,831.0	15,140.2	2,414.0	8,349.0	—	—	611.0	2,132.9
4,125.2	8,984.9	5,913.0	15,569.3	2,491.9	8,640.4	—	—	630.1	2,302.5
4,128.6	9,026.9	6,141.7	16,437.4	2,627.0	9,245.4	—	—	646.4	2,350.7
3,801.3	8,616.2	6,271.2	16,912.7	2,110.2	8,307.8	1,062.9	3,019.4	785.3	2,687.6

in employment, they are likely to experience reduced job security, shortening duration of employment contract, and more frequent job changes. Third, wage gaps are widening in the context of a universal real wage increase (see Table 2.4 and Chapter 4). There is a rising level, albeit a moderate one, of employment-related social insurance in the private sector *vis-à-vis* decreases in the state sector, with an overall increase of insurance for the whole workforce. Fourth, the quality of the labour force, in terms of skill and educational levels, is rising steadily with growing productivity and labour costs (see Chapter 9 for further discussion on recruitment and labour market trends). Meanwhile, there are increasingly severe skills shortages that are believed to be inhibiting the adoption of advanced technology and the

Table 2.4 Wages: 1985–2002 (end-of-year figures)

Wages	1985	1990	1995	2000	2002
Total wages of staff and workers (100 million yuan)[a]	1,383	2,951	8,100	10,656	13,161
Average wage of staff and workers (yuan)	1,148	2,140	5,500	9,371	12,422
Pensions for retired staff and workers (100 million yuan)	145	396	1,306	2,733	3,659

Source: adapted from *China Statistics Yearbook* 2003: 32–3.

Note

[a] Total wages of staff and workers refer to the total remuneration payment to staff and workers in various units during a certain period of time. The calculation of total wages is based on the total remuneration payment to the staff and workers. Therefore, all the wages and salaries and other payments to staff and workers are included in the total wages regardless of their sources, category and forms (in kind or in cash). (Total wages of staff and workers in this yearbook include only total wages of fully employed staff and workers, excluding the living allowances distributed to those who have left their working units while keeping their labour contract/ employment relation unchanged.) (Original notes from *China Statistics Yearbook* 2003: 182).

development of high-tech industries (see Chapter 5). Fifth, there appears to be a decreasing level of job qualities, with fewer career opportunities in the state sector, lengthening average working hours and the rapid expansion of informal sector employment such as community services and hourly paid work (Cooke 2003c).

Perhaps the biggest opportunity and challenge in the urban labour market is the rural migrant workers who flood into town to make a living for themselves and their families in the country (see Chapter 7). They work on construction sites, in foreign-owned manufacturing factories, joint venture workshops, private enterprises, township and village enterprises, or community services where substandard employment terms and conditions may be the norm. As discussed above, the adoption of China's open door policy since 1978 and its subsequent shift from the state command economy towards the market economy has led to the growth of a variety of business ownership. Many of these businesses were set up along the eastern coastal areas due to their advantageous geographic locations. These businesses have attracted an overwhelming number of rural labourers from the poor inland areas, who flocked to fill up the largely low-skilled, low-wage and long-hour job vacancies. According to national statistics, there were some 50 million rural migrant workers working in the city by 1995, representing a quarter of those working in the urban area (Chen *et al.* 2001). This figure fell slightly and was maintained at a level of 45 million throughout the late 1990s due to the government's attempt to protect the laid-off workers in the labour market by restricting the influx of rural labourers. It is estimated that there will be a new entrance of at least 6 million rural migrant workers into the urban labour market each year in the next few years (The Project Team of

Social Situation Analysis 2002), many of whom may be working in TVEs and small private businesses where the level of state intervention has been deliberately weak.

Employment regulations

Two separate ministries, namely the Ministry of Labour and the Ministry of Personnel, are responsible for the management of labour and personnel in China. The former covers manual employees and those whose jobs are closely related to physical activities while the latter covers managers, technicians, political staff, and office and clerical employees. They are responsible for labour and personnel policies through their detailed regulations covering issues related to working conditions, recruitment procedures and standards, selection and promotion, salary and bonus levels, and training.

In light of the diversification of ownership forms, the rapid growth of the private sector, the emergent labour market, and the rising number of unemployed and laid-off workers, the state has issued a series of employment-related legislation in order to regulate the labour market and to offer employment protections to workers. As a result, the majority of the employment regulations in China were issued in the past twenty years. Major labour regulations include: the Labour Law of China (1995) which provides the overarching framework of employment regulations; the Trade Union Law (1950, 2001) which sets out the scope of responsibilities of the trade unions; and the Provisions Concerning the Administration of the Labour Market (2000) which sets out the basic principle for the governance of the labour market. Other regulations include: a series of gender-related legislation in order to improve gender equality in employment (see Chapter 6); the minimum wage regulation issued in 1993, which aims to provide a wage floor to the low-paid groups of workers (see Chapter 7); and the training regulations (see Chapter 5). In addition, each sector may be issued with sector-specific regulations, such as the civil service, foreign firms and joint ventures.

In spite of the perceived ineffectiveness of the employment regulations in China (Warner 1996b; Cooke 2001; Cooke and Rubery 2002), these regulations do, at least in principle, provide a legal framework under which HR practices, such as recruitment, training, working time and pay should be carried out. For instance, all employers are now required by the Labour Law of China (1995) to sign an employment contract with their workers, by adapting a standardized employment contract provided by the local labour authority to each specific post. While the initial intention of introducing the fixed-term employment contract in SOEs in 1986 was to increase motivation by removing job security, the purpose of signing employment contracts in the private firms is primarily to protect individual workers against irresponsible employers who may try to evade their responsibilities as employers. Many of these workers come from rural areas and have little knowledge of their employment rights. According to the Labour Law (1995), the employment contract should include: length of the contract, work content, health and safety protection and working conditions, remuneration, discipline, conditions for termination of contract, and liability for violating the employment contract. Employers are required to specify in the contract any other clauses that are not included in the standardized contract. Where changes are to be made in the employment contract, they need to be recorded in the contract and signed by both parties. The contract also specifies the employment rights for workers against unfair dismissal and whistle blowing of malpractice of employers. The length of the employment contracts with shopfloor workers may vary from one to three years, depending on the source of the workforce (e.g. urban vs. rural migrant workers) and types of firms (e.g. state-owned vs. FDI manufacturers whose production volume may fluctuate radically depending on orders).

In terms of working time arrangements, the Labour Law of China (1995) specifies the number of hours (no more than forty-four hours, now reduced to forty) workers should work in a normal working week and the number of hours of overtime they should be expected to work (no more than thirty-six hours per month). It needs to be pointed out here that the vast majority of workers work full-time in China, as part-time working is still a relatively new concept with insufficient interest from both the employers and the workers. While these working time regulations are followed by most state sector organizations and many larger private enterprises (Zhang *et al.* 2002), they are often not adhered to by private small business employers, FDI factories or TVEs. In general, workers in the private sector work much longer hours than the norm, a situation compounded by the low level of rest days and holidays that are given to the workers (see Chapter 8 for examples). Equally, there is much implementational latitude in the enforcement of the minimum wage regulations, for example, whether or not the regulations should apply to TVEs. The labour officials' monitoring role of labour rights enforcement is often compromised by conflicting demand that is placed on them to attract external funding for employment and economic growth. Moreover, as Knight *et al.* (1999) observe, decentralization in the state sector also gives rise to principal–agent problems where financial interests of the two diverge.

In a recent nation-wide development aimed to protect the rights of migrant workers, a new regulation was issued in January 2003 that allows rural migrants the legal right to work in cities and prohibits employment discrimination on the basis of residency. The new regulation also enables the municipal police authority to provide urban residency documents to migrants who find employment in the city. This is a marked change from the existing rules, which confine rural migrant workers to temporary jobs without access to social welfare in an attempt to prevent the influx of migrant labour into the city. This new regulation is likely to increase competition in the labour market.

The role of the trade unions and Workers' Representatives Congress

Only one trade union – the All-China Federation of Trade Unions (ACFTU) – is recognized by the Chinese government, with its formal national union structure dating back to the early 1920s in support of the Communist Party revolution. The current structure of the Chinese trade union organization has not changed drastically since 1949 (Warner 1990b), although there has been an expansion of union membership as urbanization has drawn more workers into industry (Ng and Warner 1998). Drawing their membership from all sorts of occupations and sectors including manual and non-manual workers in factory, hospital, school and university, the trade unions do not have any distinctive 'trade' characteristics, as they all belong to the same 'father' – the ACFTU. Two major pieces of law provide the legal framework for the role of the unions: the Trade Union Law (1950), which was replaced by the recently amended Trade Union Law (2001) in response to the rapid growth of the private sector, and the Labour Law (1995).

Under the Socialist system in which labour and capital are perceived to share the same interests, trade unions' activities are focused on the provision of welfare and entertainment for employees under the leadership of the Communist Party, although union officials would be consulted for disciplinary and dismissal matters. They carry out this function effectively by acting as a 'conveyor belt' between the Communist Party and the workers (Hoffman 1981). (See You (1998) for a more detailed review of the earlier political debate within the Party in the 1950s on the role of ACFTU; and Sheehan (1999) for a historical overview of the role of the trade unions in brokering the party–worker relationship.) Although union membership level is generally high in SOEs (see Table 2.5 and 2.6), people join trade unions by default (to be seen as supportive to the Party and to enjoy the associated welfare benefits) rather than by desire. In some ways, it is a form of social exclusion not to be a union member in the state sector. For example, in the past, temporary workers (many of them from rural areas) who carried out laborious and tedious work undesired by urban workers were usually non-union members and did not share the same level of workplace benefits as permanent workers.

With the growth of new ownership forms, the welfare role of the state has largely disappeared. The seemingly harmonious management–labour relationship has been replaced with one which is characterized by conflicting interests, rising disputes and increasing inequality in contractual arrangements between management and labour. However, the role of the trade unions, or more specifically the union officials' perception of their duties, remains little changed. They still continue to carry out their traditional functions such as organizing social events, taking care of workers' welfare, helping management to implement operational decisions, and co-ordinating relations between management and workers (Verma and Yan 1995). In

Table 2.5 Union membership density in organizations where unions were established

Year	Number of staff and workers	Membership	Membership density (%)
1952	13,932,000	10,023,000	71.9
1979	68,972,000	51,473,000	74.6
1980	74,482,000	61,165,000	82.1
1985	96,430,000	85,258,000	88.4
1990	111,569,000	101,356,000	90.8
1995	113,214,000	103,996,000	91.9
2000	114,721,000	103,615,000	90.3
2001	129,970,000	121,523,000	93.5
2002	144,615,000	133,978,000	92.6

Source: adapted from *China Statistics Yearbook* 2003: 823.

Table 2.6 Number of grassroots trade unions and union members in 2002

	Number of unions	Number of members
Total	1,712,528	133,977,709
Enterprise of domestic funded		
State-owned	118,687	39,230,472
Urban collectively owned	56,810	6,595,280
Co-operative	18,644	2,523,384
Joint-owned	1,880	222,187
Limited liability corporations	28,287	6,345,196
Shareholding corporations ltd	14,707	6,000,635
Privately owned	989,481	23,394,323
Others	2,096	5,810,863
Funded by entrepreneurs from Hong Kong, Macao and Taiwan	11,044	1,650,487
Foreign funded	11,633	2,197,030
Township and village enterprises	119,443	9,836,832
Public sector organizations	209,752	20,895,883
Party agencies and governmental organizations	111,388	7,733,383
Others	18,676	1,541,754

Source: adapted from *China Statistics Yearbook* 2003: 585–8.

addition, skills training and assisting laid-off workers to regain employment have been two major functions of the trade unions.

In theory, trade unions have been given a newly regulated monitoring role. According to the Labour Law (Chapter 1, No. 7), 'Trade Unions shall represent and protect the legal rights and interests of workers independently and autonomously and develop their activities according to the law'. In practice, this proposition is rarely fulfilled. Past and contemporary empirical evidence hardly supports the notion of trade union autonomy in China, whether it is for trade unions in large SOEs or in private or foreign-owned enterprises (Warner 1995; Ng and Warner 1998; Chan 2000; Warner 2001; Cooke 2002; Ding *et al.* 2002). Although union organizations have a relatively strong presence in some traditional state-owned industries, such as the railway industry (Cooke 2000), union officials in China have generally been considered unfamiliar with the Western style of collective bargaining, 'with their serious lack of the necessary back-up bargaining resources, skills and capacities' (Warner and Ng 1999: 307). Trade union officials in China are often in their post not because they are the best candidates for the job, but because they have appeared to be, for various reasons, 'unsuccessful' in their previous managerial posts (Cooke 2002). It has been reported that some trade union officials took pride in considering themselves to be representatives of the enterprises. Some even confronted workers on behalf of the management during the handling of labour–management disputes, forgetting that they should be representing the workers' interests instead (e.g. Lu 1999; Sheehan 1999).

In the private sectors, union membership levels are far lower than in the state sector and union activities are less popular (e.g. Levine 1997; Ding and Warner 1999), largely due to the state and employers' bipartisanship and employers' unilateral power. It is estimated that only about 30 per cent of private organizations have established unions. Many firms do not recognize trade unions, asserting that the union's (welfare) functions are still carried out by the firm despite the absence of union organization (e.g. Cooke 2004c). While labour officials often confuse the role of trade unions with that of a welfare function, demand from workers to establish a trade union may be low in part because they are unfamiliar with the concept of workplace representation but more so because of their perceived ineffectiveness of such an organization (Cooke 2002). For firms that have union recognition, union independence and effectiveness remains highly questionable (e.g. Ding *et al.* 2002). Union chairs are often party secretaries, enterprise managers, or other senior managerial staff (Chan 1998). Membership level is usually high at over 90 per cent once a union is recognized. Workers are urged to join the union as part of the workplace routine procedure. The ineffectiveness of the trade unions is reflected in the finding of the Fifth Survey of Private Enterprises (*China Private Economy Yearbook* 2003), which reveals that union recognition appears to have little impact on wage levels, although the coverage of social insurance is marginally higher, with less than 20 per cent coverage in unionized enterprises, but, it remains a long way away from what is required by the state.

The formal 'representative function' of the unions, according to the Labour Law (1995), is supplemented by the trade union-guided Workers' Representatives Congress which is an organization formed by workers' representatives (Zhu 1995) and a format of workers' representation in the workplace. Initially introduced in the late 1940s, the Workers' Representatives Congress has been given an enhanced role since the 1980s as a result of the marketization programmes. It has the legal right to:

Deliberate such major issues as the policy of operations, annual and long-term plans and programmes, contract and leasing responsibility systems of management; it may approve or reject plans on wage reforms and bonus distribution as well as on important rules and regulations; it may decide on major issues concerning workers' conditions and welfare; it may appraise and supervise the leading administrative cadres at various levels and put forward suggestions for awards and punishments and their appointment and approval; and it democratically elects the director.

(Liu 1989: 5–6)

Again, in reality, the role of the Workers' Representatives Congress remains less than effective (Benson and Zhu 2000). The Workers' Representatives Congress is required by law to hold an annual meeting in which workers may raise issues of concern. This, however, does not often happen. Even when it is held, it is mostly a symbolic gesture and an opportunity for a party for everybody involved.

In short, there is no real 'partnership' between management and trade unions, or 'employee voice' in the management–labour relations in China. While unions may appear to be sympathetic to the plight of employees, their lack of autonomy from the state prevents any concerted action designed to influence the government (Frenkel and Peetz 1998). However, the dominance of state influence in the state-owned sectors and the weakness of trade unions in employment relations in China as a whole do not mean unilateral determination of employment practices by (state) employers. During the state planned economy period, conflict between management and workers as a result of the dominance of the Party within enterprises has been 'a far more common feature of industrial life in China than is generally recognized' (Sheehan 1999: 2). By the early 1990s, there was a growing incidence of 'wildcat' strikes without any union presence or organization, especially in foreign (including and especially in Hong Kong, Macao and Taiwan) funded enterprises (see e.g. Chan 2001). These industrial actions by unorganized workers (or unrecognized unions) reflect both the ability of enterprises to prevent unionization and the failures of existing official unions (Frenkel and Peetz 1998). In 1994, the number of officially recorded labour dispute cases brought before arbitration panels was 19,098; by the end of 2000, this number had risen to 135,206 cases, an increase of seven times in seven years (Wang, H. L. 2002). The number of cases from foreign funded and private enterprises was also high in comparison with the total number of people employed in these enterprises (see Table 2.7). Major issues of disputes involve wage, labour contract, social insurance and welfare, and work injury.

The rising level of industrial conflicts has led to the recognition of the need for collective negotiation as a mechanism to resolve disputes. Since the mid-1990s, enterprises have been encouraged by the state to establish a collective negotiation system, an area in which trade unions are expected to play an important part. The role of the trade unions in the new context of employment relations in China will be discussed further in the Conclusion (Chapter 10).

Conclusions

The changing composition structure of business ownership in China since the 1980s with the shrinking share of state ownership and the rapid growth of private and foreign-related firms undoubtedly has major implications for the patterns of employment relations at a macro level, as evidenced in the discussion in this chapter. While radical changes in the state sector have fundamentally altered relationships between the state employer and its employees, the influx of rural migrant workers as a peripheral workforce in the urban areas adds further pressures and challenges to the state, the trade unions, the employers and the urban workers in various ways. An inevitable outcome is that urban employees are increasingly concerned with their declining employment and career opportunities and are increasingly dissatisfied with management (Frenkel and Peetz 1998). As globalization places more competitive pressure on firms, work is being intensified with increasing incidences of violation of labour rights, against a backdrop of introductions of labour protection regulations. The role mapped out for the trade unions under the Chinese Communist government is clearly inadequate in dealing with the increasing tensions between labour and management, especially in the private sector.

However, there are major differences in employment/HRM policies and practices between firms of different ownership, as was observed by other authors (e.g. Child 1994; Verma and Yan 1995; Warner 2001). For instance, Zhu and Dowling's study (2002) found that ownership did have an impact on staffing practices, with collectively and privately owned enterprises having fewer formal HR practices. Ding and Warner (1999) further noted that JVs had a more systematic HRM than did SOEs. These differences in the approaches to HRM are likely to result in different HR outcomes. For example, Chiu (2002) revealed that state and non-state workers differed in their organizational commitment. Chiu's finding is supported by Wang's study (2004) of SOEs and foreign invested enterprises. There may be scope for, and a level of, convergence in HR practices among firms of different ownership forms in the future. This may be especially the case as the positive impact of MNCs and JVs' HRM practices becomes more widespread (see Chapter 9 for further discussion) and the effect of employment regulations more apparent (Warner 2001). Nevertheless, it is highly likely that major differences will persist, with polarizing employment terms and conditions that reflect, at least partially, the firms' business and labour strategy. Likewise, certain culturally embedded practices may still prevail, such as the perceived importance of distributional equity and the persistent gender discriminations. Some of these issues will be discussed in more detail in the following chapters, beginning with the reforms in the state sector.

Table 2.7 The disposal of labour disputes (2002)

	Total	Increase from previous year[a] (%)	SOEs	COEs
No. of cases left over from last period	12472	43	3031	1854
Cases accepted	184116	20	45215	27253
No. of cases appealed by employer	11863	50	2921	1718
No. of cases appealed by worker				
No. of collective labour disputes	172253	17	42294	25535
No. of persons involved	11024	12	3387	1911
No. of persons involved in collective disputes	608396	30	206182	91656
Cause of the disputes	374956	31	140566	59643
Labour remuneration	59144	31	10610	7453
Social insurance and welfare	32622	5	9402	5972
Work injury	23936	32	3619	3263
Occupational training	1070	−15	300	126
Change of labour contract	3765	−12	1280	643
Release from labour contract	30940	7	8795	4274
Termination of labour contract	12908	25	5153	2383
Laid-off	2169	no data	1306	465
Others	17562	15	4750	2674
No. of cases settled	178744	19	43610	27269
By manner of settlement				
By mediation	50925	19	12870	7830
By arbitration lawsuit	77340	7	21062	12179
Others	50479	44	9678	7260
By result of settlement				
Won by employers	27017	−14	7982	4548
Won by workers	84432	18	21167	14437
Won partly by both parties	67295	43	14461	8284
No. of cases not settled	17844	36	4636	1838
No. of cases arbitrated by other means	77342	21	16656	13843

Source: adapted from *China Statistics Yearbook* 2003: 824–5.

Note
[a] calculated from the total of previous year.

Hong Kong, Macao, Taiwan and foreign-funded enterprises	Shareholding joint-ownership enterprises	Limited liability corporations	Private enterprises	Individual economy	State organs and institutions	Others
1716	1404	1676	1715	474	409	193
22930	19809	19264	30618	6564	4593	7870
1460	1368	1911	2095	234	93	63
21470	18441	17353	28523	6330	4500	7807
1196	1095	979	1818	261	225	152
78604	46748	57208	88913	18588	8741	11756
50135	24376	31333	51608	9587	4183	3525
8304	7216	6358	12169	3008	1050	2976
3257	3123	2763	5502	860	1045	698
2876	2108	3033	6226	1465	266	1080
275	125	68	95	10	51	20
290	512	302	357	66	91	224
4193	3524	3890	3368	766	1081	1419
1301	1030	1291	1066	146	346	183
13	134	105	43	19	47	37
2412	2307	1454	1792	224	616	13333
22008	18741	19013	29828	6489	4546	7240
5963	4955	4485	9720	2238	1160	1704
10677	8571	7421	10780	2503	2026	2121
5368	5215	7107	9328	1748	1360	3415
3267	2809	2499	3390	561	892	1069
10463	9081	7224	14208	3376	2018	2458
8278	6851	9290	12230	2552	1636	3713
2638	2472	1927	2505	549	456	823
16503	4285	10182	11221	2751	1013	888

3   Reforms of the personnel system in the state sector

Introduction

Reforming the state sector has been an issue of top priority for the Chinese government in the past decade. Overstaffing, low efficiency and a high level of bureaucracy have been major problems shackling the performance of the state sector which is increasingly under competitive pressure from the private sector and facing the need for modernization if China wishes to launch itself as a major player in the international arena. Major changes have been made in employment policies and practices in the state sector, which, until the latest employment reform started in 1997, had a massive workforce and an enormous payroll (see Table 3.1). The state sector consists of mainly SOEs, public sector organizations and governmental organizations. Among them, SOEs and the public sector employ the majority of the state sector workforce. While the former has been shrinking since the mid-1990s, the latter has experienced a slight growth in the number of employed, because it was the SOEs that were the main targets for downsizing and not the public sector. For example, by the end of 1996, over 18 million workers were employed in the public sector with a total wage bill of nearly 126 billion yuan (*China Statistics Yearbook* 2003). By the end of 2002, the public sector had a workforce of over 20 million with a total wage bill of nearly 300 billion yuan (*China Statistics Yearbook* 2003).

For decades, China has been using the same set of personnel management policies, which was established during the early years of Socialist China, to cover a wide range of occupational staff working in the state sector, from managers and professionals in SOEs to actors and medical doctors in the public sector (who were all classified as 'state cadres'). The highly centralized and undifferentiated approach to personnel management was much flawed in that seniority was the key promotion criterion and poor performers were tolerated. In addition, differing occupations which required widely varying skills all shared a similar pay structure. A central feature of the reforms has been the development of sector-specific HR policies based on their own characteristics, although the underlying principles appear to be similar.

This chapter focuses mainly on the recent reforms since the mid-1990s, namely that of the mass-scale downsizing of the SOEs, the reform of HR policies in the civil service, and the more recent attention to public sector reform, with the higher education sector as the pilot reform cases. Particular attention will be given to HR aspects such as recruitment, performance assessment and promotion, pay and retention, which have been the major issues of reform. Some of these issues will also be discussed more broadly in other chapters, for example, pay (Chapter 4), training (Chapter 5) and recruitment (Chapter 9). The main body of this chapter is divided into three sections, each dealing with reforms in one sector – the first one on SOEs, the second on the civil service and the third on the public sector. These sections describe the pressures for reform in each of the sectors, the processes in which the reforms are carried out, as well as the implications for the workforce.

Reforms in the SOEs

Much has been written on China's economic reform, particularly on SOE management (e.g. Walder 1986; Granick 1990; Child 1994; Lin 1998; Forrester and Porter 1999; Hassard *et al.* 1999; Meng 2000). There have been several scholarly books which provide a historic-political overview of SOEs in China and their reforms in the 1980s and 1990s (e.g. Warner 1992, 1999b; Child 1994; You 1998). These works piece together a detailed picture of the earlier reforms on the SOE management system, including the introduction of the Director Responsibility System and the management education and training programme. The main purpose of the earlier reforms in the 1980s and early 1990s was to better integrate government adminis-tration and enterprise management while also developing a sense of enterprise on the part of managers and workers within the companies. Research on the recent reform of downsizing and privatization of SOEs (e.g. Cooke 2000, 2002; Morris *et al.* 2001; Taylor 2002) also highlights the political force of SOE reforms and their lasting impact on political, economic and social change in the country. It is the latest round of reform that has the most significant HR and employment implications for state employees. This section will therefore focus on the more recent reform – notably the mass down-sizing beginning in the mid-1990s, and its related changes in HRM and impact on the laid-off workers. It is the intention here to provide only a brief account of these issues since they have been extensively discussed in various publications mentioned above.

Traditionally, SOEs in China, which employ the majority of the workforce, have been the patron of the workers' welfare. There was a high level of organized dependence of workers on their state employers (Walder 1986) in which the enterprise is a personification of the state's paternalistic ideology with comprehensive welfare provision extended to the family network of the employees. Enterprises were typically overstaffed and productivity was low. The open door policy since 1979 and the opening up of private sectors made it necessary for the state to reform the SOEs to make them more efficient and competitive, mainly by shedding a large number of workers,

Table 3.1 Number and total wages of staff and workers in state-owned units by sector

Sector	1980		1985		1990	
	No.ᵃ	Wageᵇ	No.	Wage	No.	Wage
Total	80,190	77.24	89,900	138.30	103,460	295.11
Farming, forestry, animal husbandry and fishery	7,400	4.89	7,260	6.87	7,370	12.03
Mining and quarrying	6,210	5.84	7,060	10.34	7,860	23.43
Manufacturing	26,010	28.97	29,750	50.40	33,950	108.93
Production and supply of electricity, gas and water	1,120	1.19	1,340	1.71	1,830	4.94
Construction	4,750	5.97	5,450	12.00	5,380	21.15
Geological prospecting and water conservancy	1,870	6.37	1,960	2.77	1,940	4.88
Transport, storage, post and telecom services	4,980	5.88	5,850	10.30	6,600	21.46
Wholesale and retail trade and catering services	10,050	8.30	8,000	14.97	9,470	30.82
Finance and insurance	630	0.59	930	1.38	1,450	3.97
Real estate	330	0.28	320	0.41	400	0.97
Social services	1,300	1.45	1,810	2.93	2,360	7.27
Health care, sports and social welfare	2,170	1.99	2,720	3.77	3,230	8.51
Education, culture and art, radio, film and TV	7,570	5.56	9,250	10.93	11,120	23.86
Scientific research and polytechnic services	1,040	0.87	1,290	1.63	1,480	3.60
Government agencies, Party agencies and social organizations	4,760	3.79	6,910	7.87	9,030	19.29
Others	—	—	—	—	—	—

Source: adapted from *China Statistics Yearbook* 2003: 134–5, 152–3.

Notes
ᵃ Figures in thousands.
ᵇ Figures in billion yuan.

linking performance to reward and job security, and privatization. A two-track reform policy was adopted by the central government: corporatization of large SOEs and privatization of small and medium-sized (SMEs) ones. The purpose was twofold: to reduce the government's burden of bailing out the smaller firms in trouble; and to raise finance in order to relocate workers in the state sector. In 1997, the new Premier Zhu Rongji proposed that those state enterprises which had been making a loss for years would be given 'just three years to sort themselves out, even though it means sacking millions of workers' who were typically low-skilled with few marketable qualifications (*The Economist*, 13 June 1998: 73). If the dramatic economic reform of China since 1979 has been somewhat piecemeal, then this round of reform was by far the most radical and far-reaching.

1995		1997		1998		2000		2002	
No.	*Wage*	*No.*	*Wage*	*No.*	*Wage*	*No.*	*Wage*	*No.*	*Wage*
109,550	810.00	107,660	940.53	88,090	929.65	78,780	1,065.62	69,240	1316.11
6,340	23.01	5,880	26.28	5,250	24.99	4,750	26.01	4,100	27.81
8,340	51.62	7,720	57.43	5,960	51.39	4,480	49.60	3,470	59.32
33,260	276.01	30,110	299.34	18,830	272.43	14,150	288.26	9,790	321.90
2,370	19.70	2,570	26.88	2,420	29.34	2,330	36.12	2,200	46.74
6,050	60.98	5,770	67.33	4,440	63.50	3,720	66.96	3,020	79.03
1,320	7.98	1,250	9.17	1,130	9.22	1,070	10.75	940	11.75
6,770	56.56	6,810	70.28	5,840	69.35	5,490	72.04	4,980	99.01
10,610	75.81	10,370	848.50	6,940	74.66	5,310	71.89	3,650	70.39
2,030	19.79	2,100	28.80	2,080	31.96	2,000	39.97	1,840	55.04
610	5.49	640	7.51	630	8.97	600	11.65	570	16.48
3,150	26.43	3,450	35.74	3,220	37.43	3,140	47.28	3,110	64.66
3,790	25.38	4,020	34.81	4,100	39.53	4,190	51.70	4,270	70.62
12,650	69.08	13,620	93.11	14,080	107.05	14,470	141.03	14,520	200.22
1,670	12.14	1,670	16.19	1,550	17.26	1,470	22.45	1,330	28.95
10,190	55.95	10,740	74.40	10,790	83.54	10,860	109.04	10,530	147.40
420	4.04	950	8.41	840	9.03	760	10.87	910	16.78

HR policy of the downsizing SOEs

For the existing workforce, three strands of human resource policy were implemented in an attempt to increase labour productivity.

1 The use of an employment contract system to replace jobs for life

The employment contract system was introduced for both management and ordinary workers to replace the old system in which managers were appointed by their superiors and workers were employed for life. The rationale of the contract system is to allow greater freedom both for the firm and the individuals in entering/terminating their employment relationship. It also reduces the job security of individuals so that they would be more motivated to work and to update their skills. Piloted in the early 1980s in China (Ng and Warner 1998), this contract system 'was systematized under the 1992 "three systems" (*san gaige*) reforms' and the Labour Law of China (1995) (Warner 1999a: 10). By now, the vast majority of employees are employed under the contract system. In many SOEs, tasks and responsibilities of each post are now defined in terms of quality and quantity of work, assessment criteria, pay and other employment conditions. While senior managers' reward and, to some extent, tenure are linked to the performance of the enterprise, a system called 'competing for the post' is practised on ordinary employees (see Chapter 2). This system effectively injects an element of job insecurity which serves as an incentive for employees to become more competitive by upskilling themselves.

2 Linking remuneration to the post

There have been several attempts at pay reform in the state sector in general and SOEs in particular in the past two decades (see Chapter 4). In the mid-1990s, the distribution system in SOEs was readjusted in order to reflect more appropriately the differences in the skills requirement and performance between different types of jobs. Pay is now to be linked to the financial return of the business unit and the performance of the individuals. Under this new initiative of pay, the total wage bill within each business unit of an organization is fixed. Wage increase for workers within each unit depends on the reduction of labour with maintained productivity. Equally, increased number of workers (in order to meet production targets) will not warrant an increased wage bill at business level, as was found to be the case in the Guangzhou Railway Corporation (Cooke 2000). This acts as an incentive for workers in each unit to increase their productivity and become more committed to and more involved with their business. This new reward system which includes both individual and collective bonus elements is also noted by Warner (1995). In addition, wage differentials (known as 'position wage') are increased significantly between skilled, dangerous, specialist jobs and non-skilled jobs, and between active workers and laid-off workers (Huang 1998). Again, this acts as an incentive to attract people to upskill themselves for the more demanding jobs. This new performance-based remuneration system reflects one of the 'three systems' reforms implemented more widely at a national level (Warner 1996a). For example, in his research conducted in six Beijing state-owned manufacturing enterprises, Child (1995) found that more components were introduced into their payment systems 'in an attempt to link monetary reward more closely to variations in (1) responsibility, (2) technical expertise, (3) enterprise performance and (4) individual performance' (Child 1995: 5).

3 Developing human resources through employee training

Although enterprise training in China tends to be undervalued and under-invested (see Chapter 5), some large SOEs have been making more efforts to enhance the skills and educational levels of their workforce as part of the reform programme. For example, the Guangzhou Railway Corporation has an extensive training programme which follows a medium- and long-term plan covering different groups of the workforce and at different levels. Its target of employee qualifications is ambitious with over 20 per cent of the total workforce technically skilled workers; 80 per cent of the administrative staff college qualified; and 80 per cent of the office-based knowledge workers possessing university degree qualifications (Cooke 2000).

One major HR initiative in SOEs and more generally the state sector is the relatively high level of investment in management training. Many SOEs encourage and fund their key employees who desire to undertake further training courses (e.g. a second degree in management or certificate courses). Management training and qualifications also become a prerequisite for promotion. In many organizations, young professional workers (below 35 years of age) who are considered by management to have the potential for career advancement will be hand-picked and sent away for further education and training. Well-performing SOEs also tend to provide a favourable employment package with career prospects to attract special talents/skills from the external labour market, and to retain and motivate those who are already in the company, as a means of competing against the private sector.

For the office/shopfloor workers, continuous training is provided (often in compliance with the state's training regulations) in order to enhance their work-related skills and adaptability. Each worker is expected to receive one month's (skills) training each year. As mentioned above, an annual competence assessment is given to each on-the-job worker. Those who fail or come last in the test will be laid off until they are retrained and pass the re-test. Training provision for workers is aimed to standardize their performance, raise their quality of service and market awareness, and develop their potential. It is also strategically linked, at least in theory, to other HRM practices such as appraisal for promotion or upgrading of skills level which is in turn related to remuneration. It needs to be pointed out here that neither the training nor the competence test that follows is considered to be stringently implemented in many organizations (see Chapter 5).

Redeployment projects for laid-off workers

According to the official statistics, a total of over 65 million workers (including those who have regained employment elsewhere) were laid off between 1993 and 2000 (Chen *et al.* 2001: 122). A nation-wide redeployment plan is in place as part of the downsizing programme which aims to help those made redundant regain employment (Cooke 2000; Lee and Warner 2002). This plan includes skills training, internal redeployment in existing businesses and by developing new ones, and providing employment information on the external labour market in co-ordination with local employment agencies. Training and employment centres have been set up to facilitate redeployment projects. All these services are provided free of charge or at minimum cost.

All employees who have been laid off or transferred to another post are to be given skills training according to the skills required for the new job and the background of the worker. Although no guarantee is given for a new job, attempts are to be made by their employers to find vacancies within the enterprise to accommodate them, often by squeezing temporary workers out of their posts. However, these workers may have to compete for their new post. Training services are also provided to enhance the employability of those who are willing to seek employment outside. Larger SOEs tend to have subsidiary businesses which, while undergoing a fundamental shake-up themselves to improve performance, have been used as the 'refugee centres' for those cleared off from the mainstream businesses. Since the early 2000s, even these shelters were full or abolished due to loss-making, and laid-off workers simply have to find alternative employment in the labour market or become unemployed.

The continuous job shedding in SOEs and COEs, the large influx of rural migrant workers and the annual addition of a large new labour force mean that it is now becoming more and more difficult for laid-off workers to regain employment. Re-employment rates have been declining since the turn of the new century with equally declining job quality. This issue will be discussed more fully in Chapter 6 (on gender implications) and in Chapter 7 in which their positions in the labour market are compared with those of rural migrant workers.

SOEs privatization

Privatizing small and medium-sized SOEs has a far-reaching impact in both economic and political terms: 'nationally they make up 99.8 per cent of industrial concerns, employ 75 per cent of the workforce, produce 60 per cent of the GNP, and submit 40 per cent of taxes' (You 1998: 169). The privatization of SOEs also fundamentally alters the nature of employment relations once characterized by central planning, low pay, low productivity, slow pace of work and relatively harmonized labour–management relations in which employees had no real voice in the business but could expect to be relatively well-looked after by their state employer. The mass change of ownership from the former SOEs has resulted in the national system of employment relations losing much of its distinct characteristics on the one hand, while creating a context for the reshaping of new employment relations at enterprise level on the other. As Kochan (1996) observes, the critical HR challenges facing firms in China are liberalizing the labour markets and decentralizing management authority without disintegrating into civil and political unrest.

In general, the privatization of SOEs has brought differing effects to their workers in terms of their employment conditions and their wider experience of work. While the experience of some of them may have been enhanced, many may encounter worsening experience. Broad generalization is difficult to make, but empirical evidence does provide an insight into indicative trends of the widening variations of HR practices in the privatized firms.

For example, privatized enterprises involving joint venture with foreign firms tend to have a more formalized HR system with clearly defined rules and regulations covering all aspects of the operation. These firms enjoy more autonomy to recruit from the labour market, and may introduce new reward and promotion/demotion procedures based on competence and performance instead of seniority and equity. Employees in these enterprises tend to have more training opportunities as a result of technological investment and implementation of quality initiatives. These activities may take place together with the practices of teamworking, functional flexibility and work intensification. However, there is a generic problem of how far HR policies from the Western headquarters may be transferred to the Chinese establishments where institutional and cultural arrangements differ considerably (see Chapter 9 for further discussion). It has been widely noted that these HR policies are not necessarily well received by the Chinese employees who particularly resent the idea of pay secrecy (Child 1996; Bjorkman and Lu 1999a, 1999b; Cooke 2002).

On the other hand, privatization may further weaken the chance of survival of troubled SMEs, if the new management team only aims for short-term personal gain at the expense of the firm's long-term survival. As Cooke's study (2002) reveals, training opportunities may not exist for employees, reflecting the absence of training in many small and private firms in China over which the state has little influence and to which it lends little support. The drive for quality assurance accreditation may be merely a pursuit for corporate image rather than anything in substance.

While pay, promotion opportunities and skills levels may have increased for workers in some privatized firms, these benefits tend to come with the conditional requirements of different workplace attitude and behaviour such as obligation for responsibility and orientation of quality, competence and performance. They are also accompanied by work intensification, increased job insecurity and a weakening, if not disappearing, grassroots voice due to the trade union's ineffective representation of the workforce's interests in the new form of employment relations (Benson and Zhu 2000; Cooke 2002). As Warner (1997a: 31) points out, the improved living standards (because of a higher real income) for most Chinese workers may have been exchanged for reduced employment security and welfare coverage, 'particularly with the on-going dilution of the "iron rice bowl"'.

Similarly, Taylor's study (2002) of privatization of SOEs points to increased discipline, tighter budget control and heightened threat of job insecurity. These are, Taylor argues, really what privatization amounts to, at least in theory. However, Taylor's study (2002: 268) suggests that 'privatization has very definite but limited impacts on the reconstitution of industrial relations in privatized firms' in part due to the gradualist approach that the Chinese government has taken in the transition towards a market economy.

What, then, have been the changes in the personnel system in the civil service?

Reforms in the civil service

Civil service in China

The term 'civil servant' only came to be used in China in the 1980s to describe its administrative officers in governmental organizations, known as 'state cadres'. Civil servants are those employed by the state (at central, regional and local level) who, on behalf of the state, manage the social public good exercise administrative power and carry out public functions. Employees of legislative bodies are included in government personnel. 'Employees of state enterprises are not civil servants, and less obviously, neither are employees of state institutions (including educational, research, sports, health and cultural institutions)' (Chew 1990b: 773).

Unlike some countries whose civil service system has suffered in recent decades from political uncertainty as a result of changes of government regimes and whose civil servants may be poorly paid, China's civil service exists in a relatively stable political environment. Working in a governmental organization as a civil servant is considered to be prestigious and desirable in China which yields authoritative power and consequently material rewards. Much of these rewards, often classified as 'grey incomes' and un-approved by the state, are difficult to capture, therefore making it difficult, if not impossible, to compare the real earnings of civil servants with those of professionals in other sectors. To date, civil service jobs remain some of the most popular ones among university graduates.

Seven reforms of the civil service in five decades

In the past five decades, the Chinese governments have carried out seven major reforms on its civil service, three in the 1950s and early 1960s, two in the 1980s and two in the 1990s. These reforms aimed to reduce the financial burden of the government, and in more recent years, to facilitate its economic reform towards a market economy by removing the government's control over SOEs, and by simplifying the decision-making process and reducing inter-departmental conflicts. While the first five reforms were mainly to do with reducing the number of governmental departments and downsizing the workforce (see Cooke (2003b) for further discussion), the last two reforms in the 1990s were considered to be more radical and had stronger elements of HRM. This subsection therefore focuses on these two latest reforms.

The sixth reform of the civil service in China began at the end of 1992 in the wake of the formal implementation of the 'Civil Servant System' which was to begin in 1993. The agenda of the three-year reform programme was that only a proportion of the existing staff in governmental organizations would be transferred to the Civil Servant System and given the 'civil servant' title (Tong *et al.* 1999). The reduction in the number of staff was to be achieved through the reduction in the number of organizations and through an assessment process to identify the good performers from the old state cadre system and put them on to the new civil service system. The primary objective of this performance review process was to identify and remove those who were deemed unqualified to create a lean but efficient civil service workforce (Song 1999).

The latest reform was initiated at the end of 1997 and formally launched in March 1998 by the then newly elected Premier Zhu Rongji. Fifteen government ministries were to be axed or merged by the end of the year and three million civil servants were to be made redundant in three years (Zhang, Z. W. 2000). The demand for a slimmer and better civil service was heightened when millions of SOE workers were laid off and when thousands of Chinese citizens were complaining bitterly about the bureaucracy and corruption of government officials (*The Economist*, 14 March 1998: 83). The 1998 reform was considered to be one of the largest, most radical and ambitious plans for restructuring governmental organizations since the founding of Socialist China in 1949 (Song 1999). As with previous reforms, the biggest problem was how to deal with those staff made redundant. Only this time the problem was more prominent for two reasons. First, a larger number of people were displaced; and second, many of them were removed from high-ranking positions.

In previous reforms, displaced staff were simply moved from one organization to another, while the 1998 reform programme required that all staff made redundant be removed completely from any organization of the ministry (*Jin San Jiao* 1998). The new reform programme allowed ministries to retain their laid-off staff for a maximum of three years during which ministries were responsible for offering retraining programmes to these staff in order to create re-employment opportunities for them. The retraining was almost compulsory for the displaced staff. Displaced staff were encouraged to find new jobs outside the civil service sector within the three-year period in which the government looked after their wages and welfare. Those who had professional skills were encouraged to work in SOEs where management or other specialist skills were in great demand. Those who were willing to take up jobs in local governments in remote and poor areas would be offered extra incentive and subsidies. Financial assistance would also be provided to those who wished to join the market economy and set up their own business, a package similar to that offered to employees made redundant in SOEs (Cooke 2000).

Pressure for the reforms

The pressures for these reforms came from political, economic and institutional directions and have become more compelling in recent years. First, the civil service in China was considered to be bureaucratic with a declining credibility of the administrative offices and officers. Second, China's economy has experienced structural change in the industrial sectors in the past twenty years (Guo 1996). Sectoral and enterprise ownership change (from state-owned to private-owned or joint venture) meant a shrinking territory for the dominance of the state as an employer. The state also recognized that there was a need to change its role to match the need of the new economic environment. This included transforming the government functions from economic planning to macro-level adjustment, reducing functional control over business organizations, while strengthening the role of the government in social administration, law enforcement and public service (Zhang, Z. B. 2000). The ideology of the government was to move from controlling society to providing services to society. This brings us to a third and most important set of pressures for reforming governmental organizations. For decades, the government's regulating role has been confused with and compromised by that of the entrepreneurship in which many local governments were also the owners of many businesses (Guo 1996; Zhang, Z. W. 2000). Many of these businesses were poorly operated with mounting debts. In addition, governmental organizations have over the years grown to be functionally overlapping with the inherent disadvantages of infighting, unclear responsibility, low efficiency and overstaffing (Chow 1991). Eliminating inter-departmental conflicts, increasing efficiency and transparency were thus vital if the economy was to move forward.

In many ways, the pressures of reform reflect recent worldwide trends of devolution of responsibilities, cost reduction, enhancement of accountability and responsiveness, and adoption of 'best practices' across sectors and countries in public administrations (Straussman and Zhang 2001). It is also against this background that the 'Civil Servant System' was introduced in 1993 as a more strategic approach to reforming and managing the human resources of the civil service.

The 'Civil Servant System' and human resource implications

The year 1993 saw the introduction and implementation of the 'Provisional Regulations for State Civil Servants' (hereafter 'Regulations') in China. The adoption of the Civil Servant System was considered to be the most comprehensive reform package ever initiated with an aim to create a well-qualified and professional civil service workforce (Tong *et al.* 1999). It indicates the first step taken by the state towards the establishment of a new personnel system with Chinese characteristics in the management of its civil service. The Regulations lay down the most detailed employment and

HR procedures under which a civil servant may be recruited, assessed, promoted and rewarded, disciplined or dismissed and so on. In particular, the
Regulations place great emphasis on the recruitment, performance appraisal
and assessment, promotion, reward and disciplinary procedures in the hope
of improving transparency and efficiency of the personnel administration.
A new salary structure is in place, and a performance recognition system has
been developed as well as a Code of Conduct for civil servants, as a move
towards greater accountability and higher quality of public service.

Civil servants in China may be broadly categorized into two types. The
first type are the administrative civil servants who make up the greater part
of the civil service workforce. They usually enter the service from the bottom
through recruitment examinations and other assessments. The second type
are civil servants in leadership (managerial) positions who are normally
promoted from the ranks and 'exercise the functions of political control
during their term of office' (Cabestan 1992: 422).

Recruitment

For years, recruitment in governmental organizations has been based on two
sources: graduate recruits and nepotism. University graduates are recruited
each year into governmental organizations where they start from the bottom
rank as a cadre and work their way up gradually. Since the introduction of
the Regulations, individual organizations have the autonomy to decide who
to recruit into the civil service, although the number of staff in this category
is largely controlled by the central personnel authority. Civil servants are
recruited directly into individual organizations, where they may remain
throughout their careers. Because of the high social status traditionally
afforded to government service as a profession, large numbers of applicants
compete for relatively few places. In recent years, the government has been
raising the requirements of entry-level qualifications for civil servants, believing that the recruitment and initial placement of civil servants are crucial
determinants of the enduring quality of the civil service. Most applicants
must now have at least university degrees. Meanwhile, the government
has opened its recruitment doors to people from all walks of life in order
to attract talent into the civil service workforce. Job applicants have to go
through a competitive recruitment process which is ensured by intensive
entrance examinations, in addition to other selection mechanisms, such as
interviews and assessment centres. Examination has been the major mechanism in the Chinese history for recruiting mandarins. This reflects the Chinese
belief that examination provides an impartial selection method in which
the most talented are identified and selected. The (re-)new(ed) emphasis
on examination as a recruitment assessment mechanism is, however, also
an attempt to block the influx of nepotism which has been a long-standing
recruitment practice in the past. The recruitment procedures specified in
the Provisional Regulations for State Civil Servants are a bid for a fair and

efficient system of recruitment and promotion that is open, transparent and competitive.

Training and assessment

Training has been a key HR feature in China's civil service system in the past two decades. In general, training provision is divided into three categories: pre-post, on-the-post and post-promotion training. According to the Regulations, all newly recruited civil servants must go through pre-post training before they start work. Once they are in the post, regular training courses are provided. Training contents range from dissemination of government documents to new IT skills, management skills or new procedures relating to the profession. The government recognizes that updating the skills and knowledge of the civil servant force is a compelling task in modernizing the service, since most of the civil servants are originally state cadres who lack modern management knowledge and new professional/technical skills. According to a survey carried out in several administrative bureaux in Beijing, about 50 per cent of the civil servants in these organizations were not equipped with the required level of knowledge or skills in subjects such as law, finance, accounting, taxation, foreign languages and computing (Zhu, L. M. 2000). Even the younger civil servants who hold higher educational qualifications still require further training in civil service administration.

Another type of civil servant receiving training are those who have just been promoted or are already in leadership positions. Although large-scale management training has been a key feature in China's economic reform since the early 1980s, in which a large number of state cadres have been sent to universities for management training (Warner 1992; Child 1994), the latest training initiative for newly promoted leaders is compulsory. As from 2001, all newly promoted senior managers below 45 years of age at township level must pass their qualifying exams in political theory. Those who fail the exams will not be allowed to take up the posts.

Performance assessment and promotion

The Regulations further specify that civil servants are required to have a formal annual assessment which includes written exams and performance record inspection. The assessment results are graded and referred to for promotion and reward. Like most civil service systems in the world, China has an internal career development scheme, which governs promotion on the basis of ability, training received, seniority and so forth. There are a total of ten broad grades in the civil servant echelon from a junior officer to the premier. The higher the rank, the higher the educational qualification required from the job holder. Promotion to the next grade requires a minimum service period in the current rank, and the higher the rank, the longer the minimum service (usually five years) required in the previous rank. Public opinion is another new criterion which promotion seekers need to satisfy. In the past few years, more and more local governments have adopted the election model for appointing their managerial posts. They are widening the source base of candidates and targeting for higher managerial posts in larger numbers. By the end of April 2000, over 48,000 organizations in twenty-nine provinces had implemented the system of 'getting the post by competition' (*jingzheng shanggang*). Among those organizations, over 900 were of provincial level, over 7,000 municipal level, over 22,000 township level and over 18,000 community level. More than 1,000 posts in governmental ministries and commissions were open for competition, in addition to 350,000 posts at provincial, municipal and township levels (about half of which were at township level) (Zhu, H. 2000). However, public election for managerial posts applies mainly to junior and middle-ranking positions rather than to the senior positions, although there are signs of increasing use of elections to appoint high-ranking officials.

Introducing these types of competition and performance appraisal for promotion challenges the tradition of lifetime entitlements and seniority-based advancement in the civil service in China and may indeed spur civil service performance. It gives organizations legitimate reasons for retraining and/or removing poor performers.

Retention and dismissal

Although the Provisional Regulations for State Civil Servants were introduced in 1993, it was the 1998 reform that pushed its implementation to new heights. In particular, labour mobility both within and outside the service has played an increasingly important role in the latest civil service reform which saw the beginning of the end of lifelong mandarins. As a policy, those who fail their annual exam assessments are offered one of three options: demotion, retraining and waiting for a post (*deng gang*), or resignation. As the level of reform deepens and the implementation of the Regulations becomes more widespread, thousands of civil servants may be seeking a career change in the wake of a radical management overhaul. According to statistics from the Ministry of Personnel, over 10,000 senior managers (director or '*chu*' level) of municipal level and above who were deemed unfit for the posts have been demoted since 1995; over 15,000 civil servants have been dismissed, and some 28,600 resigned between 1996 and 2002. Meanwhile, by 1999, over 2,600 farmers and 10,600 workers had been recruited, through examinations, as civil servants by regional governmental organizations (Zhu, L. M. 2000).

Some local governments are also beginning to make a serious effort to improve the quality of public services. For instance, the Guangzhou City Government issued its first preliminary regulation in 2003 which specifies the standards of behaviour of civil servants in their provision of public service

(*Yangcheng Evening News*, 9 July 2003). The regulation states that if a complaint is made on three occasions against a civil servant by the general public for valid reasons, then this civil servant will be removed from the post or demoted. If another three valid complaints are lodged after the demotion, dismissal will then take place.

Pay

In many developing countries, civil servants have been poorly paid and difficult to retain, and pay has therefore been a major feature in their reform (De Haan and Van Hees 1996; Nunberg 1997; Schiavo-Campo *et al.* 1997; McCourt 2001). In China, however, retention of civil servants has generally not been a problem and pay has not been a major part of its civil service reforms. Civil service pay has witnessed only three reforms in the past five decades: 1955, 1985 and 1993 (Yang and Gao 2001). These reforms were part of nation-wide wage reform in the state sector (see Chapter 4). The aims were twofold: upward adjustment of wages to match rising living costs, and introduction of an incentive mechanism to motivate individual performance. These reforms were generally considered by scholars of China to be insufficient and of little real impact (e.g. Chew 1990a, 1990b; Warner 1996a; Yu, K. C. 1998; Cooke 2000). None the less, these pay reforms have not had any negative impact on civil servants' pay. In fact, they were given a substantial pay rise in 2001. This was part of a wider decision of the government which aimed to increase the income of the whole population to combat the impact of the slowdown of the world's economy on China. In a proposal launched in April 2001, it was decided that from October 2001, all civil servants were to be given a pay rise of 15 per cent on average. The basic wage gap between the lowest and the highest grade was widened from between 50 and 480 yuan to a new range of between 100 and 850 yuan. At the same time, a thirteen-month salary system was implemented to replace the twelve-month system. In light of the worsening corruption among government officials and the rising discontent of the public, there has been an ongoing debate in recent years on the plausibility of increasing the income of governmental administrative staff to foster an honest civil service workforce.

Effectiveness of the new human resource policies

If the focus of the earlier reforms was primarily to do with downsizing in order to control the bloated army of administrative cadres, then the latest reform is a major leap towards building a lean and smart force of civil servants. More recent civil service reforms have also been closely linked with the public sector and SOEs reforms in China in that many of their new HR policies shared many similarities. It is a strong indication that the state employer was moving towards an era of strategic HRM. However, the HR policies manifested in the 'Provisional Regulations for State Civil Servants' are not without problems in their implementation.

For example, the civil service training system in China is in its early stages of development as a result of the establishment of the 'Civil Servant System' which aims to professionalize the service. New training methods and contents need to be developed urgently to replace the outmoded ones which were based on monotonous method and old ideology. This poses a demanding challenge for the training institutes and trainers to innovate their training service. At present, most of the teachers in administrative institutes are professional teachers with little practical experience of the civil service function. One way of addressing the issue is to bring in senior civil servants on a part-time basis to pass on their firsthand experience. This occupational and organizational boundary crossing on a formal basis remains as yet an unfamiliar exercise for many individuals and organizations, although part-time working as a second job to sell professional expertise (often on an informal basis) has been a common practice in the past two decades. In addition, recent downsizing of the civil service has led to a reduction in the average age of the workforce, with 60 per cent below the age of 40 and the majority of middle-ranking officials below their mid-forties. This is not necessarily an advantage to both the individuals and the organization, because valuable skills and knowledge accumulated by the experienced civil servants may have been lost.

The performance appraisal policy is supposed to serve as an incentive as well as a pressure for individuals to develop themselves. In theory, the implementation of annual exam assessments for civil servants offers a real opportunity and a formal mechanism for governmental organizations to shed under-performing personnel and improve the quality of their staff. In reality, many governmental organizations tend to diverge from the rules in order to protect the reputation of the individuals who perform poorly. The opportunity of exercising this discretion is to a great extent facilitated by the perceived ideological unsoundness and the implementational difficulty which have long been associated with performance appraisal, a management technique that has been much criticized in the Western literature of HRM (e.g. Grint 1993; Bowman 1994; Coates 1994; Randell 1994; Tziner 1999). This technique has encountered the similar 'what to measure' and 'how to measure' problems in China (Chow 1994; Tong *et al.* 1999). Additional problems in performance management in China are related to its strong egalitarian culture and network style of social relationship. Awards for outstanding performance rarely go to the real winners. Instead, people within the organization may take turns to win the award prize in order to maintain harmonization (Shirk 1981; Yu, K. C. 1998). The implementation of disciplinary and dismissal procedures has been lenient in part due to the Chinese emphasis on harmony rather than justice and in part because of the network (*guanxi*) relationship in which disciplining one person may upset another in an important position.

In terms of promotion policy there has been a shift in emphasis in China, like many countries, from seniority to merit as the main criterion for granting salary increments and promotion. In practice, however, the appraisal of every civil service employee's merits on a regular, objective, fair and consistent basis is extremely difficult and calls for enormous resources, so much so that seniority continues to play a very important role in promotion, particularly in the lower grades.

Conflicts also arise between the new recruitment policy (of selecting the best people) and the promotion policy in which a fixed quota is imposed by the state for each rank. A minimum number of years of service is required for each promotion in order to control the proportion of civil servants in the senior ranks and that in the lower ranks. Although the in-post tenure requirement may be slightly relaxed for those who demonstrate an excellent performance record and loyalty to the Party, the quota system means that promotion is not guaranteed even if one meets all the requirements if there is no vacancy available. An alternative is for the person to be transferred to another department which has a suitable vacancy. This creates yet another set of problems for the organizations and the individual concerned in a country where public service employees are generally not very mobile, either voluntarily or involuntarily.

In short, successive reforms have seen a level of progress in tackling the problems of overstaffing and under-performance in the civil service. Many elements of its HR reform strategy share considerable similarities with those adopted in the SOEs. The early twenty-first century is seeing increasing determination from more and more regional and local governments to build a more qualified and motivated workforce through open and competitive recruitment selection and performance assessment involving public opinion. For example, by the end of 2002, over 69 per cent of the five million civil servants were university graduates, an increase of 37 per cent from 1993 (*Yangcheng Evening News*, 14 August 2003). However, there is still a long way to go before we can say that China possesses a first-class civil service force with progressive HR strategy and high-quality service.

Reforms in the public sector

Public sector organizations in China are known as *shiye danwei* in Chinese. It usually refers to those public sector organizations providing public goods and services to citizens, which are non-profit making, maintained by the state fiscal expenditure and under the control of government departments (Cheng 2000). Public sector organizations in China mainly include science, education, culture, health and sports institutions, with the exclusion of public corporations (see Table 3.2).

Compared with the SOEs and the civil service, public sector reform has been lagging behind, although the government is now turning its attention to it. A net result of the situation is that the sector has continued to grow and is becoming an increasingly heavy burden on the state. Most public sector organizations are dependent on state funding, but they are given the

Table 3.2 Number of employees and average wage in the public sector in China in 1996 and 2002

Sector	End of 1996		End of 2002	
	Number employed[a]	*Average annual wage*[b]	*Number employed*[a]	*Average annual wage*[b]
Health care	3,671	6,975	3,998	15,281
Sports	76	7,719	74	17,999
Social welfare	154	6,420	195	14,265
Higher education	1,094	7,591	1,155	21,270
Secondary schools	4,046	6,071	4,796	12,910
Primary schools	5,250	5,566	5,720	11,478
Culture and art	576	7,117	590	16,925
Radio, film and TV	440	6,184	437	14,452
Scientific research and polytechnic service	1,658	7,984	1,332	19,006

Sources: adapted from *China Statistics Yearbook* 1997, 2003.

Notes
[a] Figures in thousands.
[b] Figures in yuan.

autonomy to carry out business activities by using the state's property and to share the profit internally without paying much tax.

Although there are several subsectors in the public sector, this section will focus mainly on the reform of higher educational institutions. This is in part because this sub-sector is the pioneer in current public sector reform, with a high level of political sensitiveness, and in part because it is a large sub-sector which has been expanding in the past two decades, especially since 2001 following the state's decision to expand the sector. In 1985, there were a total of 1,016 universities with 344,000 full-time teachers (there were virtually no part-time workers in China in those days) and 1.7 million students in enrolment. In 2000, there were 1,041 universities with 463,000 teachers and 5.56 million students. By the end of 2002, there were 1,396 universities with 618,000 teachers and over nine million students (*China Statistics Yearbook* 2002, 2003).

The reform of the personnel system in the higher education sector in China may be divided into three periods since 1978 (Ma and Liu 1999; Dong, Y. X. 2001). The first period was between 1978 and 1987 when all the academics who had been wrongly prosecuted or sidelined during the Cultural Revolution were reinstated and promoted accordingly. The positional assessment and designation (*zhicheng pingding*) procedure was adopted once again to assess and decide the grades of academics. The appointment system (*ping ren*) was first adopted which offered academics positions according to their academic capacity. The personnel department at organizational level was given more autonomy to manage their function. The second period was from 1987 to 1992 when the reform was deepened with further devolution of power. Universities were given a total wage bill with which they could organize its distribution. The appointment system was adopted more widely and a system was developed to encourage and promote young, talented academics with a range of motivational mechanisms. The third period began in 1992. A number of laws have been introduced since then, including 'The Education Law' (1995), 'The Teachers' Law' (1994) and 'The Higher Education Law' (1999). All academic staff were put on an appointment system. Further reforms were carried out on the selection and recruitment of new academics to build a core team. In 1999, the Educational Ministry stressed in its key priorities for the year the need for the higher educational institutions to deepen their internal management reform. However, these reforms have not really made fundamental changes to the HR system of universities.

The early stage of the personnel system reform in higher education in the 1980s focused on internal restructuring in which the 'iron wage' and 'iron chair' (position) tradition was shaken but not the 'iron rice bowl' (Cheng 2000). As a result, recruitment and releasing remained a major problem, due in part to the absence of an independent social insurance system to take over the people made redundant, a problem shared by the SOEs and civil service. Universities generally encountered problems in retaining key personnel in teaching and research, especially for the leading edge and popular subjects, mainly because of low pay and poor housing provision. Although many universities have tried to introduce favourable conditions to attract talented academics, these practices have not really solved the retention problem. In addition, it has been difficult, if not impossible, to get rid of those who were considered incompetent for their post, which left no space for the university to recruit good candidates. Universities also tended to have a distorted ratio between teaching and administrative staff, with the latter grossly overstaffed.

Into the twenty-first century, the personnel system of the higher education sector still carries many of the characteristics of the planned economy. Historically, the higher education and governmental organizations shared a similar personnel system designed and controlled by the state employer. In other words, academics were managed the same as cadres. For many, a university still resembles a miniature society akin to that of large SOEs prior to their reform in recent years. It is essentially a closed and self-sustained system with a large number of overlapping and overstaffed administrative departments and supporting functions. This is in part a result of the need to accommodate some of the family members of the academics whom the university is keen to attract and retain.

In theory, the new personnel/HR system of higher education is guided by similar principles to that of the SOEs and civil service. Key elements in the new HR system include greater link between performance and job security, pay and promotion. In particular, the new system of the higher education sector aims to enforce:

- the system of employment contract and appointment to the post;
- the policy of open selection and employment;
- the policy of positional wage, performance-related pay and promotion/demotion.

However, this system has not been implemented effectively. In addition to the recruitment and releasing problems, the appraisal of academic performance has been a difficult task and its current system leaves much to be desired (Wang *et al.* 2002). Most assessment criteria focus on research instead of teaching and on the quantity of teaching rather than its quality (Shi 1999). The dual-sourced pay package implemented in 2000 which is made up of salary paid by the state and allowances by the university drawn from its own source of income also attracts much resentment from the lower ranking academics because of the perceived unfair wide differentials to their disadvantage. In principle, the differential of basic salaries between the lowest and the highest rank of academics is about 3.3. However, the differential of allowances is as high as 16.7 times, making the average differential of earnings about 8 times. This figure would be much higher if other sources of income from advisory and consultancy work were taken into account, for example, that which senior academics are able to generate due to their social network and prestige (Wang, C. H. 2003).

Nevertheless, one aspect of the HRM in which the higher education sector has made continuous efforts is its high investment in the training and development of academic staff. Over the past two and a half decades, a large number of academic staff have been sent abroad or to other universities for further training. This is in spite of the fact that this effort has virtually served as a brain drain for China, since the majority of those who were sent abroad in the earlier years failed to return to China.

The year 2003 marked the time when the focus of state sector reform turned to the public sector, notably the higher education sector. The plan for public sector reform (*Yangcheng Evening News*, 23 February 2003) is that all staff will be transferred to the contract employment system by the end of 2005. It is planned that it will take five years to normalize and standardize the new system. This reform plan will affect 1.3 million organizations and 30 million employees. It is the third major personnel reform in the state sector following the SOEs and civil service reforms. Key universities (e.g. Beijing and Tsinghua universities) and media organizations (e.g. the China Central TV Bureau) will be the forerunners of the reform. For universities, the key personnel issues in the new wave of reform are job design, appointment to post, performance appraisal, distribution and accommodating displaced staff. However, leaders of higher rankings are not to be put on contractual system yet. Those who have twenty-five years (or more) of tenure are offered a permanent employment contract. The biggest problem in the reform is again how to deal with those who are made redundant from their original posts. This worry has, to a certain extent, prevented any radical action in the reform process. For example, by early 2003, over 60,000 employees had been offered a contract by their employers, with only 250 made redundant (*Yangcheng Evening News*, 23 February 2003). It is likely that universities will adopt the same policy as those in SOEs and civil service organizations in accommodating those who fail to be reappointed to their original posts, i.e. by discharging the temporary workers to make way for the unappointed ones who are deemed suitable for the temporary posts. Administrative departments will be merged and downsized like governmental organizations.

Diverse employment strategies with permanent, fixed-term and temporary contracts are being used at the same time. Many large organizations are now adopting a flexible employment strategy in order to reduce the number of permanent staff. For example, the China Central TV Bureau (CCTV), the state's mouthpiece and one of the most high-profile public sector organizations in the country, operates on a three-tier workforce system of what they call the core layer, the close layer and the loose layer. The core layer and the majority of the close layer consist of some 2,400 employees as the quota allocated by the state. The third layer makes up some 60 per cent of the total workforce, most of whom are contracted to work on specific programmes on a temporary basis (*Yangcheng Evening News*, 21 November 2002).

One of the reform pioneer universities is Beijing University. It is one of the two most prestigious universities in China whose every move has strong political significance. It revealed its draft plan in early 2003 for public comments and suggestions on the university's proposed reform of its academic staff's employment and promotion systems. The eminent reform was to be the most radical of its kind for nearly a century and has attracted heated debate among scholars. According to the plan, the ultimate objective of the university is that 'every lifetime professor in the university is a first-class scholar'. The basic features of the reform plan are as follows:

1   academic staff will be employed with inter-grade mobility;
2   a last-number elimination system will be instituted to abolish poor academic departments or subject groups;
3   a competition mechanism with the external labour market will be introduced for employment and promotion;
4   in principle, no graduates of the university will be recruited directly to the teaching and research posts;
5   a judging panel of professors will be set up for academic staff appointment and promotion.

The objective of the reform is, similar to that of other state sectors, to introduce a sense of insecurity in the employment and promotion system in order to encourage competition, enhance performance and promote staff mobility. It is believed that, in many faculties, 80 per cent of the academic achievements and reputation are created by the 20 per cent of excellent academics. The biggest problem is that a large proportion of the posts are high-ranking academic posts and none of these highly paid post occupants wishes to leave.

This reform plan has met with strong criticism mainly from the junior/middle-ranking academics, as they are the people most likely to be adversely affected by the reform. In principle, if the reform plan goes ahead, these academics are entitled to renew their employment contract twice. If they fail to secure a promotion during this period, their contract will not be renewed. Once they are promoted to a full professorship, they are then entitled to a permanent employment contract. This proposed system is somewhat similar to the American one of 'up-or-out', although the American universities also have permanent posts for junior/middle-ranking academics. There are over 8,000 academic staff in Beijing University, only 10 per cent of whom are in the junior/middle-ranking group who are arguably the youngest, most energetic and best educated with the most up-to-date knowledge (*Yangcheng Evening News*, 4 July 2003). However, this is also the group which has the weakest voice in influencing the decision making of the university.

As the rhythm of drumming for reform accelerates, more and more universities are now under pressure to carry out reform of their personnel system in order to improve their quality and efficiency. It needs to be pointed out here that not all universities will adopt the same reform plan as that of Beijing University. Instead, they are expected to formulate their own plan based on their specific situation, drawing on lessons and good practices from other universities.

Conclusions

This chapter has described the major reforms of the personnel systems in the SOEs, civil service and public sector organizations. While the key principles of the reforms in these sectors share a number of similarities, such as downsizing, performance-related reward and promotion, and contract employment, specific challenges encountered by each sector in its human resource management vary. For example, while the civil service and governmental organizations remain employers of choice for many well-qualified job seekers, SOEs have encountered a severe brain drain to JVs, MNCs and domestic blue chip enterprises. Similarly, the Chinese universities have generally suffered serious brain drain problems since the 1980s and faced difficulties in recruiting talent, although these situations are improving.

The reforms in the state sector also have varying degrees of implications for workers, with some better cushioned against the shock of economic displacement than others. What is unclear is the extent to which these reforms have impacted on the (psychological) experience of work of those who have survived the job cuts and the extent to which they have been able to adapt to the new system.

4 Pay systems and recent remuneration schemes

Introduction

Pay is not only an important part of the human resource strategy, but also an important topic for research in work and employment, and a frequent source of tension in labour–management relations. Pay determination involves a host of stakeholders and is influenced by a range of factors such as legislation, government policies, unions and professional associations' policies, sectoral performance, and labour market conditions. Pay reform in China is a subject that has received considerable attention from scholars on China over the past two decades, although most of these studies have focused mainly on pay systems in the SOEs (e.g. Howe 1973; Walder 1987; Chew 1990a, 1990b; Tung 1991; Jackson 1992; Korzec 1992; Takahara 1992; Child 1994, 1995; Nyaw 1995; Warner 1996a, 1997a; Yu, K. C. 1998). This is understandable since most of the changes in the pay systems, as part of a wider reform, have occurred in enterprises which have been increasingly released from the once tight state control on their affairs. Despite the quantitative and qualitative significance of government organizations and the public sector as part of the state sector in China, insufficient information is known about their pay policy and practice, and any changes that may have taken place in the wake of the market economy. In addition, the diverse features manifested in the pay practices in the expanding private sector have received little attention, as have recent developments in pay schemes in general.

This chapter provides an overview of the pay system in China. It begins with a major section that focuses on the state sector. This is necessarily the case due to the overwhelming dominance of the sector in the whole economy for the past five decades until recent years. In particular, major reforms in the state sector pay system are reviewed and their effectiveness assessed. The section also discusses the process of pay determination and explores social norms that govern the distribution of pay. In the discussion, more attention will be paid to government organizations and the public sector rather than SOEs because the former have been insufficiently studied whereas the latter have received much more attention elsewhere, as was pointed out at the beginning of this chapter. The second section then outlines the main features of pay practices in the private sector. It highlights patterns of rising wage gaps among different groups of workers as a result of the varying levels of economic performance of different sectors, and the bargaining power of different groups of workers. The third section discusses new forms of remuneration schemes, paying particular attention to employee share ownership schemes. More generally, the chapter highlights several sets of tensions manifested in the pay systems in China which have arisen as a result of socially embedded values, and recent political, social and economic reforms. These tensions still need to be addressed by the state and employers if the pay systems are to achieve greater sectoral efficiency and social equality.

Pay system of the state sector

The pay system of the state sector in China has experienced three major reforms in the past five decades: 1953 to 1956, 1985, and 1993, with several minor adjustments in between (see Korzec (1992), Takahara (1992) and Child (1994) for more detailed discussion on the subject). Each of the three pay reforms was an adjustment to the social and economic development of the era. The aims were twofold: upward adjustment of wage to match rising living costs, and the introduction of an incentive mechanism to motivate individual performance. For decades, state sector employees who performed wildly different tasks with varying skills requirements shared a similar pay structure, the main differences being manual workers and state cadres. In the 1993 pay reform, new pay structures were introduced for each of the four categories of workforce. The separation of the pay structure was aimed to reflect more closely the nature of their work and the sector they were in.

The first reform

The first reform took place between 1953 and 1956 in two waves. The purpose of the first wave in 1953 was to bring to an end the dual system of pay made up of material supply and monetary wage and to move to a salary-based pay system (Tien 2000). This pay reform also introduced, for the first time, the grading system to classify each employee's level of pay based on the principle of 'distribution on the basis of labour'. The second wave, carried out in 1956, saw the introduction of a nation-wide Soviet-style wage grade system in order to, it was believed by the policy makers, increase productivity (Takahara 1992).

From 1956 until 1978, the wage structure was essentially frozen. The wage level was kept deliberately low in order to keep prices down. The objective of the 'rational low wage system' was to create more urban employment so that 'everyone has a meal to eat'. It was also aimed to discourage rural workers from migrating into cities. Wage incentives were basically restricted, and wage adjustments took place more as a passive means of political appeasement than as a positive means of economic stimulation (Takahara 1992). In short, there was little change in the system of wage determination and levels of pay for state sector employees in the two decades. With the state allocating the wages and the enterprise management acting as the distributor, workers had little influence on the state wage policies (You 1998). The absence of wage rises and the rising prices led to a long-term decline in real wages that was believed to have undermined workers' morale. This was considered to be a contributing factor to the poor performance of labour productivity in the 1970s (Korzec 1992).

The second reform

The second major pay system reform was implemented in 1985. The thrust of this reform was to introduce what was known as the 'structural wage system' with positional wage as its main component. This system was based on the four major factors emphasized by the International Labour Organization in 1950: knowledge required; responsibility assumed; work intensity involved; and working conditions (Hu and He 1992). Under the structural wage system, a wage package consists of four parts: basic wage, positional wage, longevity pay and bonus. Basic wage was the same for everybody irrespective of their hierarchical position whereas positional wage was based upon one's managerial or technical position and responsibility. Longevity pay was a relatively moderate amount of subsidy which accrued each year to a maximum of forty years. A special favourable rate was introduced to occupations that were considered to be low paid given their responsibility and for which recruitment and retention might be a problem (e.g. teachers, nurses and sports trainers). The fourth component – the bonus – was designed to reward those with outstanding performance.

The objectives of a structural wage system were both economic and political. Its introduction abolished the previous wage grading system, which was criticized for having too many sets of wage standards; causing discrepancies between positions and wages; creating a great deal of irrationality in the wage differentials; and causing conflicts between various personnel. This new system saw the reintroduction of bonus incentives and has, operationally, made it 'easier to quantify the worker's performance and easier to link such performance to pay' (Zhao and Nichols 1996: 14). In theory, the structural wage policy represented a marked shift from the earlier egalitarian wage principle by placing far greater emphasis on one's position which should reflect competence and responsibility, i.e. 'to each according to one's work'. It was intended to enhance workforce morale by improving the linkage between workers' responsibility and wages, defining more persuasive wage differentials among them, and guaranteeing their basic livelihood. It was also, for China, an attempt to move away from the Soviet-style grading system and to build in greater rewards for flexibility.

This major reform was complemented by a number of minor adjustments between 1986 and 1992. For example, public sector employees were given the largest ever wage increase on the grounds that their wages had been unreasonably lower than those of employees in enterprises who received bonuses. The aims were to increase the wage gap between technical/ professional workers and administrative workers; to address the low wage problem of academics and other intellects such as doctors and engineers; and to raise the wages of schoolteachers and nurses by approximately 10 per cent of the sum of basic and position wages.

In SOEs, a system called the 'floating salary' was also widely adopted after the mid-1980s. This system was intended to replace the bonus system (at least in part) that was by then increasingly recognized to have failed to link pay directly to performance. The first form of floating salary introduced a variable element into the salary, which fluctuated according to the production volume of workers and according to the degree of responsibility, workload and/or enterprise profit levels for managerial and non-production workers. The second form of floating system was one that linked the total enterprise wage bill to the fulfilment of a predetermined enterprise performance indicator (Child 1996). In general, SOEs 'were introducing more components into their payment systems in an attempt to bind monetary reward more closely to variations in (1) responsibility, (2) technical expertise, (3) enterprise performance and (4) individual performance' (Child 1996: 187).

The second pay reform covered a period of eight years with limited success in the implementation of the structural wage system in part because it tried to cover too broad a range of occupations. The state had great difficulty in establishing a uniform national scheme of positions and position wages. In addition, position has not always been a reliable indicator of competence and performance, since promotion in China's state sector has often been based on seniority rather than on early signs of competence. This reform has also led to a relative wage reduction for public sector employees compared with that of enterprises, since the wage spread necessarily grew wider in part because SOEs were better able to increase the proportion of bonus wage (see further discussion below).

The third reform

The third pay reform was introduced in 1993 in which the state separated the pay system for the public sector from that for the governmental organizations (civil service) (Kang 1996). It also set up for the first time pay systems that were considered to be appropriate for each type of public service (Cheng 2000). This pay reform led to the establishment of five pay systems and two parts in order to reflect the diverse range of jobs in the sectors. To be more specific, the five pay systems referred to the individual system for each sector. Wage package within each pay system was divided into two parts: fixed-wage and flexi-wage, in theory a 70 per cent and 30 per cent ratio. This was the first step towards a differentiated management system of the public sector. This non-egalitarian system, it was believed, would motivate employees of each organization as their earnings were to be closely related to their performance both at individual and organizational level. Some organizations have implemented the 'internal structural wage' system based on this principle. This reform also increased wages for those jobs which were dirty, strenuous and high risk, and which were in remote areas in order to recruit and retain people (see also Chapter 3 for discussion of pay reform as part of the state sector reforms since the 1990s).

The above pay reforms are, however, generally considered by scholars to be insufficient, with little real impact in motivating the workforce, in rewarding the good performers or in enhancing the comparability of public sector pay to that of other sectors (Chew 1990b; Warner 1996a; Yu, K. C. 1998). Chew (1990b) asserts that the position salary introduced in the mid-1980s is a case of old wine in new bottles rather than a true innovation. However, what is most criticized about the state sector pay reforms is the state's lack of success in achieving its major objective; that is, to overturn the culture of egalitarianism (Child 1995; Zhang, Z. J. 2000) and to reinforce the principle of 'to each according to one's work' first advocated in the early 1950s. This attempt is often compromised by formal policy, for example, seniority pay (in the structural wage system), to cushion the negative impact on the older group of less qualified and/or physically able, and by informal practices of employees who control bonus distribution by taking turns to be the top bonus winner to ensure equity.

When implementing the performance-related pay elements of the pay reform, there is an undeclared but officially endorsed deviation from the principle of 'to each according to one's work'. For example, despite attempts to adopt merit criteria in the higher education sector, the most important determinant of academic promotion remains seniority (Johnson 1990). Academics typically move up one grade every year and are promoted to a higher rank every five years. In easing the tension between older and younger workers generated by merit-related pay, special favours are often given to older workers, and their relative lack of professional competence tends to be overlooked in the assigning of technical grades.

The introduction of a bonus as one of the four components in the new wage package in the mid-1980s gave organizational leaders a role in partially determining how reward was to be allocated among their employees. While the intention of the bonus was to enhance productivity by setting up a wage system with wider wage differentials, which was considered by policy makers a better reflection of the principle, 'to each according to one's work', this new right has not been embraced with enthusiasm by managers (Korzec 1992; Takahara 1992). Organizational leaders are well aware that employees preferred stability and relative equality of real earnings, and are therefore reluctant to implement policies which their workforce resent. Instead, organizational leaders prefer unsophisticated methods of reward distribution in order to keep everybody happy (Yu, K. C. 1998). Therefore the 'flexible' component of wage becomes another 'inflexible' part.

In general, the state sector wage reforms have created a new structure of interests with the withdrawal of the state from its direct involvement in micro remunerative matters. This transition has greatly affected the tripartite relationship between the state, enterprise management and workers (You 1998), and has become a major source of worsening management–labour relationships due to the widening wage gaps (Lee 1998). Industrial wages are now much less influenced by the state but have more to do with management competence and market factors. While the state expects to increase its revenue from profit-related tax from the enterprise, the enterprise is under strong pressure from its employees to keep more profits for itself so as to increase wages. This has led to an increased tension in which the state tries to control the floating part of an enterprise's wage bill, while the enterprise tries to reduce the fixed proportion within the overall income distribution (You 1998).

This apparent lack of effectiveness of the pay reforms has to be seen in the context of how pay is determined in terms of its governing ideology and key players in the determination process in the state sector, and what tensions exist in the system, although some of these characteristics are shared by the system in the private sector.

Pay determination in the state sector

In Western societies, and to an increasing extent in China, pay is considered to be of strategic importance for employee attraction, retention, motivation and performance which will in turn enhance organizational performance, even though the existence of such a link and the effectiveness of pay as a management strategy long remains debatable. Pay in the state sector in China has been treated, however, to a much lesser extent as a motivational strategy for pursuing organizational efficiency and effectiveness, until recent years, than it was as a necessity to cover the living costs of the employees themselves and their families.

This dominant ideology of wage distribution reflects the homogeneous nature of wealth distribution in China, despite its vast population, and explains its narrower wage differentials than one may find in more hetero-geneous societies. In particular, wage policy in the public sector in China has been, and still is, heavily influenced by two factors: political ideology and cultural belief. Both emphasize the need for egalitarianism in which material rewards are officially subjugated to ideology, and unpaid contribution is often praised and encouraged by the state employer. These ideologies trans-late themselves into the following norms which govern pay determination in China's public sector (and much of other sectors') pay system (Yu, K. C. 1998; Cooke 2004a).

1   *The contribution norm.* Seniority wage is a prime example of this norm in reward distribution.

2 *The effort norm.* Chinese employers tend to attach considerable weight to their employees' work attitude and the effort they have made in their work, often to the disregard of outcomes. This norm is typically applied in the selection for promotion and bonus allocation.

3 *The morality norm.* This is a distinct feature in China and one which has been given particular importance in the public sector. Morality includes one's political loyalty to the Communist Party, integrity of personality, diligence at work and quest for knowledge to improve one's intellectual horizons. So much so that morality not only plays a key role in the promotion decision but is also significant in the distribution of other kinds of rewards, such as pay, prestige, housing, and even opportunities for (overseas) business/training trips.

4 *The egalitarian norm.* Egalitarianism has long been recognized as a unique Chinese societal culture and continues to be a taken-for-granted assumption of fairness and equity in rewards. This is reflected, to some extent, in the narrow wage differentials between grades and between occupations in the state sector. But it is in the distribution of bonuses that the egalitarian norm plays the most significant role (see further discussion below).

Since the 1980s, SOEs have been given full autonomy in deciding how and when to reward workers under the guidance of the state wage regulations. A variety of wage practices emerged, the main objective of which is to link the rewards of workers to the levels of their individual performance and that of the firms, with workshops and production teams playing a key role. As a result, 'state micro wage policy no longer directly affects workers, whose lot is more intimately linked to the market performance of their employer' (You 1998: 23). Meanwhile, there is an increasing proportion of SOEs that have established the collective negotiation wage policy, usually through the involvement of trade unions and Workers' Representative Congress since the mid-1990s. This is essentially a requirement by the state to safeguard the financial interest of the workers, but its effectiveness remains modest due to the limited power of the trade unions, as was discussed in Chapter 2.

In the public sector and in governmental organizations, wage level is centrally determined by the state unilaterally, and managers of all levels are only involved in the administrative function and policy implementation. There is effectively no wage bargaining mechanism for the non-SOE state sector employees. Whereas trade unions in the public sectors of many developed and developing countries represent a major force in voicing concerns and mobilizing resistance, this function of the trade unions is largely absent from the state sector in China (Cooke 2000, 2002). Resistance to pay reform in the public sector in China remains unorganized and covert, where academics and professionals tend to conceal their discontent or express it in more subtle ways than enterprise workers.

The principle of 'to each according to one's work' is at odds with the public sector and civil service ethos of 'serving the people heart and soul' promoted by the state. Public sector and civil service employees are expected to serve the people and be rewarded by their job satisfaction instead of material/financial gains. However, the ideological rhetoric of 'serving the public' which disregards material reward is increasingly in conflict with the new-found materialism and the pressure for employees to be seen to have the same financial power as workers in other sectors. Temporary policy interventions are sometimes introduced at local level (usually municipal level) to ease recruitment and retention problems in certain occupations such as teaching. Local authorities of wealthier areas also take advantage of their higher purchasing power to attract talent from poorer areas, leading to a brain drain from those areas where this resource is even more crucial to their regional development.

Writers on pay (e.g. Kessler 1995, 2000; Rubery 1995, 1997; Poole and Jenkins 1998; Hastings 2000; White 2000) have highlighted the dynamic tension between the needs of the internal market for equity and fairness and the differential price at which labour may be purchased in the external labour market. In the case of public sector and governmental organizations in China, factors influencing the determination of its wage level are more closely associated with the internal labour market and organizational factors rather than being regulated by external factors such as the labour market. More weight is given to the job held and the time worked (seniority), and, more importantly, personal qualities (e.g. morality and loyalty) of the individual employee play a more decisive role in underpinning their pay level. The lack of leverage of external factors in pay determination has also allowed the state to maintain a low wage level and a broad-band grading structure for the public sector and governmental organizations in China, supplemented by relatively extensive, albeit shrinking, workplace welfare such as canteens, bonuses, allowances and material incentives. The principle is to guarantee a basic living standard for the majority of people.

For the employees, although radical economic and social reforms in recent years and the expansion of the non-state-owned sectors have, to some extent, changed the previously deep-seated psychological determinants of reward behaviour, two potent sets of rules based on 'equality' and 'equity' are still prevalent. In other words, equal right to reward is emphasized and differential reward is legitimate as long as it is based on an equitable way of differentiating performance (Sparrow 2000). Distributive justice (i.e. the degree to which a person perceives the tangible outcome of a decision to be fair) (Folger and Cropanzano 1998) plays a particularly significant role in Chinese workers' attitudes towards pay distribution which influences not only the effectiveness of pay reforms in the state sector but also the degree of success in the introduction of new pay schemes in the private sector (see further discussion below).

Characteristics of the pay system of the state sector

The relative rigidity in pay determination and the societal norms in pay distribution create a unique set of characteristics and tensions in the pay system of the state sector in China. First, conflict exists between the ideologies of 'to each according to one's need' and 'to each according to one's work' simultaneously promoted by the socialist state which unilaterally determines the form and level of pay as the employer. This conflict is sharpened in the public sector, as is the dilemma encountered by many governments under increasing fiscal constraints. On the one hand, they need to uphold the public service ethos and to contain public spending; on the other hand, they need to introduce incentives to motivate performance. A key feature of pay in the public sector is the lack of commitment of the state to comparability of pay levels with those prevailing outside the public sector, even though external comparability is often a central factor in pay practices. This lack of commitment has led to a decrease in formal real wage for the Chinese public sector employees in comparison with those in other sectors. Ironically, the inability to contain its swelling wage bill has been a perennial problem for the Chinese government.

Second, the wage structure of the state sector in China is, on the one hand, too controlled, too egalitarian and insufficiently tied to organizational efficiency and individual labour effort (Korzec 1992). On the other hand, the transparent structure of standard wages does not necessarily mean that it is easy to describe the income structure of state sector employees. The basic wage is but one of the components of the earning structure which plays a diminishing part in the total package of a Chinese worker's total earnings. Among the other components are subsidies of all kinds and sometimes illegal incomes (Child 1996). Subsidies and bonuses make up a large proportion of the total wage income of employees. It is not unusual for employees in state-owned organizations to receive more than thirty different items of subsidies in one given year. For example, it was believed that the annual growth rate of the average wage between 1985 and 1992 was 12.9 per cent while that of non-wage income was 25.2 per cent (Hu and Liu 1994). However, no adequate quantitative information is available about the distributive effect of subsidies within the state economy and no precise figures are known which reflect the real total work-related income. This lack of data also makes it problematic to compare the wages and earning levels of workers across different sectors in part because firms in the private sector may rely less heavily on subsidies to boost the wage level of their employees.

The tension is particularly acute between the tight and rigid control of the state in setting the basic wage structure and level and the uncontrollable opportunistic behaviour of individuals and organizations in seeking avenues to generate extra income. Since the mid-1980s, the government has given individual organizations a high level of autonomy to develop a portfolio of operational activities to generate income to subsidize the insufficient budget given by the state. Much of the income formed an important source of additional earnings (often in the form of bonuses, commodities and package holidays) for the employees of the organizations. The state's encouragement of business diversification and the lack of policy specification on the extent to which these commercial activities are allowed invited opportunistic behaviour by many organizations. They are often criticized by the media for using the public asset for commercial activities without paying for it, often for short-term gains. These activities also have a negative impact on the level of public service provision, since much of the resources are diverted. What is worse, many organizations even find excuses to charge the public for services they are entitled to free of charge. These practices are beyond state control, even though the state has made repeated efforts, for example, by introducing top limits for bonuses and a bonus tax, to curb the distribution of these benefits in an attempt to restrain inflation.

A third set of tensions in the pay system is the lack of input of employees in the formal wage set by the state and their role in maintaining the low earning differentials among themselves. Egalitarianism in order to maintain stability and harmonization remains another key characteristic of the pay system in the state sector in China. While employees have little discretion to oppose the formal wage structure set by the state and their SOEs, they play a fundamental role in preserving the egalitarian and seniority culture in the distribution of bonuses and other material incentives, regardless of the relative efficiency of individuals. Attempts from the top to increase wage differentials between individuals according to performance may be mediated during implementation at the operational level. It has been observed that the most noteworthy characteristic of the Chinese perspective on distributive fairness is one of egalitarianism. Chinese people are said to be very sensitive and to have low tolerance towards income gaps between people. They believe this to be potentially disruptive in collective social systems that regard group harmony and social adhesion as the top priority (Yu, K. C. 1998).

It has been widely noted that bonuses tended to be distributed equally to all workers and managers in a given job grade (Nelson and Reeder 1985; Laaksonen 1988; Korzec 1992; Takahara 1992; Warner 1997a; Freud 1998; Yu, K. C. 1998). In dividing grades for bonus distribution, managers often classify them into only two or three grades with small but symbolic differentials. Typically, at least 80 per cent of the staff are in the middle grade. Only a few people are given the first grade and even fewer are allocated to the bottom grade, usually reserved for people who have a long-term sickness record or who have made serious mistakes at work. Even when bonuses are eventually allocated, those rewarded for their competence and performance are hesitant to take the financial reward on their own without sharing it for fear that it would build a wall between themselves and fellow workers. It is not unusual for people to take turns in sharing the top grade of bonuses. Individuals who receive the top grade of bonuses more than once will have to step down or be pulled down by their colleagues from nomination as candidates for the top bonus in the next round. This egalitarian value remains a strong force of resistance to wage reforms in China's SOEs that aim to shift from an egalitarian to a performance-based system. SOEs have encountered many difficulties in implementing wage reform. 'Among these difficulties were implementing a performance-based wage system, linking increases in wages and bonuses with increases in productivity, the continued use of wages as a social stabilizer, the lack of job mobility and lingering ideals of egalitarianism' (Freud 1998: 114).

In order to avoid intra-unit disorder and to maintain their popularity, organizational leaders succumb to pressure for high and egalitarian bonus payments from their subordinates, who demand both compensation for price increases and equal or better treatment compared to other units through bonus distribution (Henley and Nyaw 1987; Takahara 1992; Easterby-Smith *et al.* 1995; Lee 1998). In fact, bonus has played a fundamental role, albeit often an unofficial one, in the state sector pay, as it has for other sectors over the past two decades. It is not only an important source of income to supplement the low wage level set by the state, but also a source of pressure for managers, a source of tension and earning differentials among groups of workers, and a source of inflation threat to the unstable economy.

Fourth, the ineffective interference from the state to contain unofficial income has led to the widening of earning differentials within the same sector due to the unequal opportunities available for individuals and organizations to attract income additional to the basic wage. This is despite the fact that pay in the public sector and governmental organizations in China has taken on a homogeneous pattern with little formal variation to reflect performance levels and nature of tasks. This problem is particularly pertinent in the education and health sectors (see Cooke (2004a) for more discussion). Geographical location adds to a further, if not the largest, source of intra-sector differentials in income. This is in part because spatial income inequality has long been a feature in China, a phenomenon which has become even more prominent since the mid-1980s, making it one of the most unequal of Asian developing countries (Khan and Riskin 1998). But far more importantly, this widening income gap is unofficial, if not illegal, and is to do with the level of wealth of those who seek public service.

Fifth, there is also a tendency towards widening wage income differentials across different sectors in the state sector, with the public sector employees generally in a more disadvantageous position than employees in other sectors (see Table 4.1). For example, the decades' suppression of public sector wage growth by the state has caused a widening wage gap between the public sector and profitable SOEs (e.g. utilities, telecommunications, banking) and private industries such as foreign-owned businesses and joint ventures in the more developed geographical areas (see Table 4.3). Although it is specified in the 'Teachers' Law' that the teachers' wage should be slightly higher than that of the civil servants, this has not been the case in reality.

In the past, the wage gap between public sector professionals, particularly academics, and manual workers (in SOEs and the private sector) was an

Table 4.1 Average annual wage of employees in the state sector by selected industry (figures in yuan)

Industry	1985	1990	1995	1998	2001	2002
Manufacturing	1,190	2,289	5,352	6,981	9,590	10,876
Electricity, gas and water production and supply	1,272	2,648	7,734	12,458	14,132	15,799
Transport, storage, post and telecom	1,383	2,697	7,572	12,613	14,318	16,030
Wholesale, retail and catering	1,087	2,028	4,568	7,414	8,220	9,444
Banking and insurance	1,234	2,200	7,595	13,729	16,605	19,648
Real estate	1,170	2,247	6,884	11,626	13,111	14,465
Health care, sports and social welfare	1,164	2,263	6,009	11,234	13,340	15,281
Education, culture and art, radio, film and TV	1,184	2,134	5,457	9,599	11,591	13,473
Scientific research and polytechnic service	1,268	2,411	6,835	13,221	16,218	19,006
Governmental organizations, Party agencies and social organizations	1,133	2,115	5,528	10,048	12,152	13,987

Source: adapted from *China Statistics Yearbook* 2003: 158–9.

ideological problem rather than a sectoral one. For decades, the academic's wage was in inverse proportion to that of manual workers. This situation was mocked by the maxim: 'Working with a razor blade is better off than with a surgical blade'. The state has made several attempts to address the issue, mainly through wage increases at national level and better housing conditions at organizational level. However, the overall wage gap between the academics and the manual workers remains too narrow.

Sixth, the current limited role of external factors in the pay determination in the public sector and governmental organizations should not be interpreted as a static state of affairs. As the market economy gradually takes root in China, there are signs that the labour market is playing an increasing role in the recruitment and reward of public sector and civil service employees, most notably teachers at all levels. Local institutions have been given the autonomy to make temporary adjustments to their employment package in order to ease their recruitment and retention problems. In 1998, the State Council issued the 'Provisional Regulations for Public Sector Organizations Registration and Management' to take effect from 1999. The aim was to grant public sector organizations their right as a legal entity so as to protect their legal rights as well as to regulate their market behaviour. Pressure is mounting for the state to redesign the public sector wage system in order to have a more effective central framework of incentives and reward which is flexible enough to accommodate local situations and at the same time perceived to be fair. For example, in 2001, many higher educational institutions doubled the salaries of their academic employees, and schoolteachers were also given a significant pay rise, in many cases doubling their salary. In addition, more and more universities are offering individual employment packages (including a handsome golden handshake, large sums for research funding and facilities, and employment for family members) to attract high-quality academics in order to maintain and boost the institution's reputation.

The above main section of this chapter has outlined the history and characteristics of the pay system in the state sector in China. Many of the characteristics are shared in the private sector; for example, the role of individuals in bonus distribution and employees' resentment of wage differentials as barriers to wage reform. It is to the pay practices in the private sector that we will now turn.

Wage determination and pay practices in the private sector

The diverse profile of the private sector and the scarcity of detailed studies and national statistics on its pay practices make it difficult for us to establish the precise patterns of the pay system in this sector. However, broad characteristics are discernible based on the available information.

First, in terms of wage determination, similar to the state sector, wage levels are largely decided by the employers with little scope for bargaining or workers' involvement. In theory, the state requires employers to set up a collective negotiation system with their employees (assisted by the trade union) to negotiate terms and conditions collectively. In practice, only a small proportion of the larger firms have done so and the extent of its effectiveness remains unknown. Whereas employees in the state sector can exert pressure on their managers for higher bonus income, workers in the private sector may be much less able to do so because of the threat of job loss. Equally, while a wage floor is required by regulations for foreign firms in China, domestic firms are relatively free to decide their wage levels. According to the regulations, foreign firms in China need to set their wage level at no lower than the local average wage for workers in the same industry. In addition, wage increases should take place in accordance with the financial performance of the firm. Where collective negotiation is recognized, collective bargaining of wages should form an important part of the collective negotiation. Regulation requirements and relatively better performance of foreign firms may be some of the reasons why wage levels are generally higher in these firms than in other types of ownership. At the other end of the spectrum, however, are the small private businesses and individual economy (self-employed businesses) in which pay is determined unilaterally by employers who are largely paying the market rate in any case and in which the enforcement of labour standards is at its weakest (see Chapter 8 for discussion). What is common, though, among firms in the private sector in designing the wage system is the strong emphasis on responsibility and performance at individual and/or group level. For example, Child (1994) observed that by the 1990s, job responsibility had replaced seniority as the most significant predictor of employee earnings. This trend is supported by Bjorkman and Lu's study (1999b) and Benson *et al.*'s study (2000) in which they found that all companies had some element of individual performance built into the wage system.

Second, similar to but worse than the state sector, there are increasing intra-sector gaps in the wage levels across different types of ownership in the private sector (see Table 4.3). Employees working in the lowest paying ownership units (co-operative units) earn just over 50 per cent of that earned by their counterparts working for the highest paying type of ownership (foreign-funded units). It must be pointed out here that these official statistics of wage levels have not taken into account the varying levels of employers' contribution towards social insurance for their employees. In general, a higher proportion of state sector employers and larger private sector employers make contributions to social insurance for their employees than smaller private ones. This is especially the case for TVEs, sweatshops premised on cheap labour supply of (rural) migrant workers, and small businesses operating in the peripheral markets (see Chapters 7 and 8 for more detailed discussion), many of which are not included in the national statistics. Neither have the official statistics taken into account any material incentives and subsidies which employees working for better paying employers are more likely to enjoy. Nor have these statistics taken into consideration the longer hours which employees in the worse paying firms may have to work to earn their wages. Should the broader terms and conditions of the different groups of workers be taken into the equation, the real wage income gaps would be likely to be far higher than the statistics currently suggest. The introduction of the minimum wage regulations is precisely a recognition by the state of the diversity and market function of pay and the consequent need to protect the disadvantaged workers in the private and informal sector. More generally, the polarization of high and low wages may reflect the differences in the broader patterns of human resource/labour management in these firms. Whereas the HR system in MNCs, JVs and high-performing (large) private firms may be more comprehensive, strategic and people-oriented, private and smaller businesses may adopt a shorter term and more *ad hoc* approach to the management of human resources that is highly sensitive to immediate operating costs.

Third, according to the national statistics, there are significant inter-sector pay gaps, with employees in the category of 'units of other types of ownership' (private sector) being the mostly highly paid in comparison with their counterparts in the other two categories of ownership – 'state-owned units' and 'urban collectively owned units' (see Table 4.2). While the wage gaps between the state-owned units and the units of other types of ownership are generally closing, the wage gaps between the urban collectively owned units and the other two categories remain significantly high, even within the same types of industry (see Table 4.4). This pattern of macro statistics is supported by micro studies. For example, Ding and Warner's study (1999) found that while the structure of pay in both SOEs and JVs had narrowed, the actual wage differentials between the two remained significant. Similarly, Knight *et al.*'s survey study (1999) revealed that equally productive people had different access to the better jobs and that the equally productive were paid differently in similar jobs. The unique institutional urban–rural divide in China may be seen as the main cause for the differences in supply prices (see Chapter 7). While urban workers are protected by institutional wage determination and by the government commitment to provide them with employment (although such a commitment has been significantly reduced in recent years), the wages of migrant workers are largely market-determined, compounded by the fact that their reservation wages are weakened by the lack of village opportunities, of information, and of social security (Knight *et al.* 1999).

Recent trends of pay

As we can see from the discussion in this chapter so far, there appears to be a convergent trend in the reward strategy in both the state and private sectors in China. That is, performance seems to be a key factor in the determination of the level of pay, although it is debatable how effective this has been. Firms

Table 4.2 Average annual wage of staff and workers and related indices

| | Average money wage (yuan) | | | | Indices (preceding year = 100) | | | | | | | |
| | | | | | Average money wage | | | | Average real wage | | | |
Year	Total	State-owned units	Urban collectively owned units	Units of other types of ownership[a]	Total	State-owned units	Urban collectively owned units	Units of other types of ownership	Total	State-owned units	Urban collectively owned units	Units of other types of ownership
1978	615	644	506	—	106.8	107.0	105.9	—	106.0	106.2	105.1	—
1980	762	803	623	—	114.1	113.9	114.9	—	106.1	106.0	106.9	—
1985	1,148	1,213	967	1,436	117.9	117.3	119.2	137.0	105.3	104.8	106.6	122.5
1990	2,140	2,284	1,681	2,987	110.6	111.1	108.0	110.3	109.2	109.7	106.6	108.9
1991	2,340	2,477	1,866	3,468	109.3	108.5	111.0	116.1	104.0	103.2	105.6	110.5
1992	2,711	2,878	2,109	3,966	115.9	116.2	113.0	114.4	106.7	107.0	104.1	105.3
1993	3,371	3,532	2,592	4,966	124.3	122.7	122.9	125.2	107.1	105.7	105.9	107.9
1994	4,538	4,797	3,245	6,303	134.6	135.8	125.2	126.9	107.7	108.7	100.2	101.5
1995	5,500	5,625	3,931	7,463	121.2	117.3	121.1	118.4	103.8	100.4	103.7	101.4
1996	6,210	6,280	4,302	8,261	112.9	111.6	109.4	110.7	103.8	102.6	100.6	101.7
1997	6,470	6,747	4,512	8,789	104.2	107.4	104.9	106.4	101.1	104.2	101.7	103.2
1998	7,479	7,668	5,331	8,972	106.6	106.1	102.5	97.7	107.2	106.7	103.1	98.3
1999	8,346	8,543	5,774	9,829	111.6	111.4	108.3	109.6	113.1	112.9	109.7	111.0
2000	9,371	9,552	6,262	10,984	112.3	111.8	108.5	111.8	111.4	110.9	107.6	110.9
2001	10,870	11,178	6,867	12,140	116.0	117.0	109.7	110.5	115.2	116.2	108.9	109.7
2002	12,422	12,869	7,667	13,212	114.3	115.1	111.6	108.8	115.5	116.3	112.7	109.9

Source: adapted from China Statistics Yearbook 2003: 151.

Note
a See Table 4.3 for breakdown of types of ownership in this category.

Table 4.3 Average annual wage of staff and workers in units of other types of ownership by registration status (figures in yuan)

Year	Total	Co-operative units	Joint-ownership units	Limited liability corporations	Shareholding corporations ltd	Others	Units with funds from Hong Kong, Macao and Taiwan	Foreign-funded units
1993	4,966	—	3,741	—	5,171	3,279	5,147	5,315
1994	6,303	—	4,982	—	6,383	4,954	6,376	6,533
1995	7,463	—	6,056	—	7,277	6,494	7,484	8,058
1996	8,261	—	6,856	—	7,623	7,131	8,334	9,383
1997	8,789	—	7,310	—	7,693	7,063	9,329	10,361
1998	8,972	6,054	8,431	7,750	8,833	6,133	10,027	11,767
1999	9,829	6,709	9,501	8,632	9,720	8,425	10,991	12,951
2000	10,984	7,473	10,663	9,766	11,131	10,223	11,914	14,372
2001	12,140	8,398	11,887	10,993	12,385	11,621	12,544	16,101
2002	13,212	9,484	12,451	11,997	13,850	10,242	13,756	17,892

Source: adapted from *China Statistics Yearbook*, 2003: 164.

Table 4.4 Average annual wage of employees in different sectors by industry in 2002 (figures in yuan)

Industry	Total	State-owned units	Urban collectively owned units	Units of other types of owner-ship
Manufacturing	11,001	10,876	6,749	12,027
Electricity, gas and water production and supply	16,440	15,799	13,051	19,271
Construction	10,279	11,231	7,745	11,358
Transport, storage, post and telecom	16,044	16,030	6,940	20,864
Wholesale, retail and catering	9,398	9,444	5,983	12,202
Banking and insurance	19,135	19,648	12,540	27,788
Real estate trade	15,501	14,465	11,504	17,630
Health care, sports and social welfare	14,795	15,281	10,738	14,548
Education, culture and art, radio, film and TV	13,290	13,473	8,036	17,008
Scientific research and polytechnic service	19,113	19,006	12,976	21,017

Source: adapted from *China Statistics Yearbook* 2003: 156–7.

in both sectors are now adopting similar wage structures that consist of basic wage, bonus and a range of allowances or subsidies, although details may vary from firm to firm. Meanwhile, more varieties of pay schemes have emerged, formulated by individual companies at their own initiatives, and for SOEs, encouraged by the state.

For example, in 2001, the Ministry of Labour and Social Security issued new instructions to SOEs to introduce new initiatives in their reward packages. According to the instructions, the new reward system should focus even more on workers' performance. Variable pay schemes, such as commission schemes and shares of stock, are also encouraged. Enterprises may reward key members of staff with stock options. Scientists are to be given the opportunity to trade their R&D achievements for shares in the enterprise, although this practice has existed for some years. For directors and executives, salaries will be determined after performance review meetings held with the board of directors and shareholders. The level of reward will be determined by their responsibilities and contribution to the business (*China Staff*, February 2001).

Pay rises and individualized pay packages are also used as the main methods for the recruitment and retention of key employees (such as managers and professional staff) by both the state and private sector employers. This has led to much larger pay gaps between key employees and average employees. For example, a recent survey conducted by the Guangzhou Labour and

Management Association on 180 foreign enterprises in Guangzhou reported that offering pay rises tended to be the main method used by these firms to retain their key employees. The survey revealed that an average annual salary increase of 6.1 per cent had been paid to senior staff in Guangzhou-based foreign firms in the 2002 to 2003 fiscal year, a slightly higher increase than that of the previous year. The survey also showed that general managers in Guangzhou earned an average annual salary of 476,000 yuan with top managers earning up to 1.16 million yuan. Sales managers (312,609 yuan) earned more than financial controllers (238,737 yuan) who in turn earned more than human resource managers (212,582 yuan) (*China Staff*, March 2003: 42). It should be pointed out here that many of these managers may be expatriates who are generally more highly paid than local Chinese managers. In addition, more and more foreign firms and joint ventures are employing Chinese staff instead of expatriates because the former are considerably cheaper to hire; however, their wage levels are increasing rapidly and have more than doubled in five years (*China Staff*, March 2003).

A large-scale survey on pay carried out in the four most economically advanced cities (Beijing, Shanghai, Guangzhou and Shenzhen) in 2003 found that, for more than half of the managers surveyed, cash payment made up over 80 per cent of their total annual wage income in the year 2002. About 70 per cent of the managers had bonuses which made up less than 20 per cent of their total annual wage income. About 60 per cent of the managers surveyed were satisfied with their wage and nearly 40 per cent of managers had higher expectation of their wage. However, over 10 per cent of the managers were unhappy with their wage income, an increase of 4 per cent from 2001 (Wang, Q. J. 2003).

At the grassroots level, there are signs that workers are beginning to believe that more pay for higher skills and contribution is fair and respond positively, albeit moderately, to performance-related pay initiatives, as is found in Sun's (2000) study of two SOE subsidiary plants.

In addition, employers deploy a dual labour strategy in employing their human resources. For example, a survey carried out in 2000 on 1,162 private high-tech enterprises revealed that employers used a dual labour strategy in which cheap labour and well-rewarded professionals and technical staff were deployed at the same time. While the former tended to have a low and undifferentiated wage package, the latter were offered a much wider variety of pay schemes. Among the enterprises surveyed, 52 per cent of them used one-off bonuses, nearly 8 per cent used share options, and over 12 per cent used profit sharing as financial mechanisms to retain and motivate their technical staff. For managerial staff, over 31 per cent of enterprises used annual profit-related salaries, over 41 per cent used operational responsibility bonuses and nearly 8 per cent used base wage plus bonus shares as incentives (Lu and Wang 2003).

Among urban enterprises, employee share-ownership schemes (ESOs) are becoming more widely adopted as a new pay initiative with the objective of motivating employees through financial participation. The rest of this section discusses ESOs in more detail.

Employee share ownership schemes

The earliest forms of ESOs emerged in the early 1980s when small and medium-sized enterprises asked their employees to invest their savings in the company to relieve the company's financial difficulties. ESOs in their formal appearance were first adopted in the early 1990s in small and medium-sized SOEs and a small number of large SOEs as experiments. This was followed by some TVEs and enterprises in other forms of ownership. Since 2000, ESOs have become an important agenda in the deepening reform of SOEs. By the early 2000s, thousands of SOE enterprises had implemented some forms of ESOs. For example, by the end of 1999, nearly 9 per cent of the SOEs in Shanghai had established ESO committees, with some 300,000 employees (6.56 per cent of all employees) as ESO members. In the first half of 2000, over forty ESO committees were registered from which enterprises have raised over a billion yuan of funds (Chi 2001). Local governments have also issued governing regulations on ESO implementation.

Benson *et al.*'s study (2000), one of the few micro-level studies existing on ESOs, found that in one company, employees were given priority in purchasing the limited shares of the company available to the public, whereas in another company shares were offered to employees in collective ownership. They found that profit-sharing schemes in the broad sense existed in half of the companies they studied. However, they found it difficult to assess the level of employee stock ownership in view of the vagueness of the ownership structure of Chinese companies.

ESO is promoted by policy makers, academics and managers in China as an enterprise management innovation. There are two general purposes for the adoption of ESOs. One is to use ESO as a form of employee welfare. The other objective is to motivate employees at work through financial participation. However, it is thought that the motivational effect of ESOs on workers has not been evident in enterprises that have implemented ESOs, although the effect has been more apparent on retaining (technical and managerial) key personnel. According to a survey on 1,235 enterprise managers in 2000, over 82 per cent of managers felt that insufficient incentives and restrictions were the main factors that affected their motivation at work (Chi 2001).

It has been noted, however, that there are several major problems that enterprises may encounter in the implementation of ESOs (Chen and Lin 2002). First, the long-term strategy of low wages and high welfare has prevented employees from accumulating savings to invest in ESOs. Second, the transferability of shares is currently restricted by most regulations. This makes employees reluctant to 'put all their eggs in one basket' without being able to get them out. Third, there is a strong element of egalitarianism in profit sharing, which defeats the purpose of motivation (Guan and Xu 1999).

Fourth, and perhaps more importantly, the motive of individual organizations (particularly their managers) in implementing ESOs remains to be questioned. It is recognized that the primary motive for managers to promote ESOs, often aided by local officials, is so that they can use the opportunity to profit themselves, their families and associates, seeing it as 'one last chance to get rich' (Saich 2001: 208). In addition, local leaders see the policy of promoting shareholding as a great opportunity to shed their responsibility for the state sector, to raise some much-needed capital and to profit at the expense of the state. This is particularly common at the township level. National statistics showed that by the end of 1997, one-third of the 500,000 township enterprises had been sold off or turned into shareholding co-operatives (*South China Morning Post*, 21 June 1998). It was estimated that 'spontaneous privatization' with the stripping of state assets has cost the state $6 billion a year over the past fifteen years (Hughes 1998: 75). An equally severe problem has been that of local authorities forcing workers to buy shares in enterprises so that they qualify as shareholding co-operatives, although it is unclear how pervasive this practice has been (Saich 2001). However, the purchase of these shares may neither turn the failing enterprise around nor give employees a real voice in the enterprise's decision making. Moreover, most shares may be held by managers who obtain the shares not necessarily through purchase but as a reward.

In spite of these problems and the apparent ineffectiveness of financial participation as a motivational mechanism noted in Western literature, ESOs are often promoted by the government and media as the new cure for China's long-standing motivational problem. In reality, it is often used to relieve the financial constraints of SOEs by transferring the risk to their employees. There is a lack of understanding from all concerned about the role of the schemes and how they should be managed. Companies also tend to underestimate the complexity of the management of the schemes and are less than well prepared for the problems that occur. More studies need to be carried out to explore how to design and implement ESOs at a strategic level, bearing in mind the diversities of enterprise ownership and workforce characteristics, if ESOs are to be more widely adopted as a successful HR initiative in the country.

Conclusions

This chapter has provided an overview of the pay system in the state sector in China in terms of its reforms, determination process, governing ideology and wage level position in comparison with that of other sectors. It has revealed a very different approach to pay determination than those in the Western countries in which more parties may be involved in the negotiation and determination of wage levels. Although the state sector pay system in

China has experienced several reforms in the past five decades, they are perhaps more accurately called adjustments, since the contrast between the old and the new is not necessarily clear-cut (Warner 1996a). While various pay schemes were introduced in an attempt to increase employees' motivation and productivity, these measures have generally not been considered sufficiently effective. This is in part, as Meng (2000) suggests, due to the lack of labour mobility (at least in the state sector) in China and in part because the motivational effect of pay has been controversial.

At a deeper level, the wage system has exposed tensions between the socially embedded values and the functional requirements for modernization (Child 1995). In many ways, tensions demonstrated in the state sector pay system are shared by those in the private sector which remain difficult to reconcile. One most noted set of tensions is the lack of real say from employees in the formal wage determination on the one hand and their resistance or resentment of wage differentials among themselves on the other. Another set of tensions is the widening wage gaps between different groups of employees which have more to do with their varying bargaining power in the market than with their competence. It is under this unique context that pay reforms and new pay initiatives are implemented in both the state and private sectors.

Judging from the development of the pay system in China, it may be argued here that it is becoming increasingly more sophisticated, evolving from the earlier (Soviet style) narrow grading system to a variable pay system with more emphasis on performance and profit sharing aimed to motivate (long-term) performance of employees. The shift from an egalitarian ideology of distribution to a performance-oriented motivation–reward strategy, the withdrawal of direct state intervention on pay at organizational level, the shrinkage of the state sector and the expansion of the private one, the influence of Western management techniques, and the need to compete increasingly at the international level have all formed part of the driving force for organizational leaders to (re)design pay schemes that aim to secure the co-operation of their workforce. Given the diversities of enterprise ownership, their varying levels of performance and different focuses in their management strategy, it is not unreasonable to predict that pay strategies in China will be more diverse in the future, as organizational leaders continue to search for more effective initiatives of pay to stimulate their employees' performance.

Finally, it must be pointed out here that the discussion of pay in this chapter has largely fallen within the formal sector where wage levels may be relatively higher, compared with those who are disadvantaged in the labour market, and where employees still have a role to play, although not necessarily formally institutionalized or strongly supported by official collective mechanisms, such as the trade unions, in influencing patterns of distribution. However, there is a large and expanding force of workers whose wage levels are determined primarily by their employers in the informal sector or sweatshop factories, who are in danger of a downward-driven spiral in part due to severe competition in the labour markets. These workers consist mainly of laid-off workers from SOEs, women and rural migrant workers who are the least protected and lowest paid. Issues related to their employment and pay will be discussed in Chapters 7 and 8.

5 Vocational and enterprise training systems

Introduction

'The most valuable of all capital is that invested in human beings' (Marshall 1920: 564). Human capital, according to its proponents (Schultz 1961; Becker 1964; Lucas 1988; Romer 1990), is a major ingredient for high productivity and quality performance, and the most important investments in human capital are education and training. Indeed, a well-trained, educated, hard-working and conscientious labour force is considered to be a major contributor to the remarkable economic performance records of the four Asian Tigers (Japan, Korea, Singapore and Taiwan) during the late 1970s and up until the mid-1990s. These governments' policy of post-secondary education technical skills training focusing on vocationally and techno-logically sophisticated disciplines has created a broad and technically able human capital base well suited to rapid economic development (The World Bank 1993). 'Human resources and the training to upgrade them have been important to [these economies'] successful export drives, despite the high degree of labour intensity in their manufactured exports' (The World Bank 1993: 200).

China, which possesses one of the largest labour forces in the world, has however often been criticized for the low quality of its labour supply (see Table 5.1 for educational levels of the population), so much so that its perceived competitive advantage lies in its abundance of cheap unskilled labour.

It is true that the vast majority of Chinese workers aggregate at the lower end of the skills level, even after taking the huge force of rural workers out of the equation. Among the 140 million urban workers (not including workers in TVEs), only about half were classified as skilled workers by the end of 1998. Only 3.5 per cent were in the senior skilled level and the majority were at junior levels (60 per cent at Level 3 or lower, Level 8 being the highest). Seventy per cent of the rural migrant workers working in the urban areas only possessed qualifications at junior secondary school level or lower (Wu 1998).

Low skill levels of the workforce seem to be a phenomenon even in large enterprises where skills requirement should be relatively high and training

Table 5.1 Educational attainment of the population aged 6 and over in China in 2000 (end-of-year figures)

Educational level	Subtotal	Per cent of population aged 6 and over
No schooling	89,629,436	7.75
Eliminate illiteracy class	20,767,295	1.80
Primary school	441,613,351	38.18
Junior secondary school	422,386,607	36.52
Senior secondary school	99,073,845	8.57
Technical college	39,209,614	3.39
Polytechnic college	28,985,486	2.51
University	14,150,726	1.22
Graduate student	883,933	0.08
Total population aged 6 and over	**1,156,700,293**	

Source: adapted from *China Statistics Yearbook* 2002: 106–9. The data came from the tabulation data of the 5th National Population Census in 2000 (original note).

provision tends to be more abundant. For example, Lai Steel Corporation Ltd, a super-large state-owned enterprise, had 35,358 employees in the year 2000, nearly 66 per cent of whom were below the age of 35. Over 60 per cent of all workers were at medium skills level or below, including those without any grade. Only 515 employees were in senior professional ranks. Since most of them worked in the Corporation's educational institution, hospital and design departments, this meant that only a minority of these people would be working in managerial positions in the actual plant (Xu, Z. 2000). The situation may be worse in smaller and less well-resourced enterprises. According to a nation-wide survey carried out by the State Education and Development Research Centre in 2000, over 60 per cent of the 1,920 graduates surveyed had not received any off-the-job training since their employment after their graduation in the 1990s (The Project Team of the State Education and Development Research Centre 2002).

What are the factors contributing to this skills shortage problem and low level of enterprise training at a macro level? To understand the extent and depth of the skills shortage problem in China, one needs to look beyond training practices at enterprise level and investigate the vocational training system and workplace training in China through a historical lens. This is the task for this chapter. It first critically examines the vocational training system in China, including its size, scope, ownership and governing structure, and problems such as difficulties of student recruitment and employment, inadequacy of training facilities and quality. The chapter then turns to the training provision at workplace level. In particular, the role of the state is reviewed in terms of training regulations and initiatives. This is followed by an analysis of the characteristics and problems of enterprise training. It needs to be pointed out here that many of these characteristics and problems bear considerable similarities to those manifested in other countries. The chapter then contemplates the prospect of training in China, focusing on the role of large enterprises and multinational corporations, and the influence of international standards as a result of China's WTO accession and the adoption of quality initiatives such as the ISO quality series. It concludes by highlighting a number of issues from the more practical aspects of training practices to the more analytical dimensions of the topic. The purpose of this chapter is to provide a broad overview of the training system in China to complement the existing empirical studies on HRM and enterprise training in various ownership forms (e.g. Ding and Warner 1998; Bjorkman and Lu 1999a, 1999b; Cooke 2000, 2002; Ding *et al.* 2001).

Vocational education and training institutions in China

Like many countries in the world, formal education and vocational training in China are two separate systems, leading to two different career prospects for the individuals concerned and with strong implications for their earnings and social class positions. Vocational education and training is normally carried out after the completion of the first nine years of state education. It needs to be pointed out here that China favours the use of the word 'education' rather than 'training' which reflects its long-standing cultural tradition of elitism that treats (manual skills) training as inferior to formal education. The word 'education' is used even when it really refers to 'training'.

As in many other countries, vocational skills training in China is usually provided from two sources: vocational education and training institutions, and employing organizations. This section focuses on the former, which include a range of ownership: state-owned, collectively owned and privately owned. The sources of trainees for these training institutions consist mainly of self-funded individuals prior to their employment, and trainees sent by their enterprise and public sector organization employers. Training qualifications from these institutions range from vocational certificates and advanced diplomas to university degrees.

At a general level, there are two types of schools that carry out vocational education and training in China: vocational school and technical college. They usually offer a three-year training period, although some provide two years' training. Both types of school focus on technical/vocational competency training with a small proportion of basic theoretical knowledge in the curriculum.

Vocational and technical schools/colleges may be classified into three broad categories (in descending order), based on their vocational orientation and sectoral background. The first type are those technical colleges which recruit students in a planned mode and are controlled by the regional/local educational authorities. They specialize mainly in qualifications such as nursing, nursery teaching, banking and accounting (banks have been largely state-owned and controlled in China). The second type are the technical schools established by large SOEs and industrial departments. They are accountable to the Ministry of Labour which is responsible for the annual recruitment of students. These schools specialize mainly in technical skills training for manufacturers. The third type are schools which were turned into vocational schools as a result of the reforms of secondary schools in the 1980s. Usually these poor performers (relatively speaking) were converted into vocational schools because students in these schools had little prospect of going to university. By turning them into vocational schools, it was believed, students could at least gain some occupational skills and qualifications which would give them a better chance of gaining employment. These schools specialize mainly in skills for the light manufacturing and service industries, such as tailoring and apparel manufacturing, cooking and equipment maintenance. Their skills provisions are more tailored to the demands of the informal sectors than the first two categories.

Size of the training schools and scale of the training provision

Under the command economy system, vocational education was centrally controlled by the state in its recruitment, training and employment allocation. During the mid-1980s and early 1990s, the state relaxed its control and encouraged the growth of training schools of different forms of ownership. As a result, training schools mushroomed and more or less reached their peak by 1995 (see Table 5.2). In addition, millions of training places were offered each year by local authorities and other training bodies for adult trainees. The rapid growth of these training institutions contributed to the disorganized situation of the current state of vocational education and training, with many schools having student numbers lower than the state's specified target of 600 (Ma 1999).

In general, large, developed cities have a more established vocational training system than smaller and less well-developed cities. For example, Suzhou, a city once famous for its silk production and one of the flagship cities for vocational training, had eighty-five approved vocational training bases by 1999, offering a capacity of 20,000 training places per year. This has been facilitated largely by its ability to attract a high volume of foreign investment and its rapid development of light industries since the 1980s. There were ten assessment centres and some 530 assessors in the whole city (Wei 1999).

Vocational training institutions have shown signs of declining since the 1990s. For example, in 1997, there were 4,395 polytechnic colleges in the whole country, 543 of which (12.4 per cent) were suspended (Wu 1998). Many others encountered problems in recruiting students. Graduates from these colleges also faced difficulties in finding employment (see discussion below). Educational funding received by vocational schools has been decreasing each year since the mid-1990s. They could not benefit from the favourable tax policies and subsidies granted by the state and which were enjoyed by

Table 5.2 Pre-employment vocational education and training in China (1980–2002) (end-of-year figures)

Year	Technical colleges			Technical schools			Vocational secondary schools		
	Total no. of colleges	Total no. of students at college	Total no. of graduates	Total no. of schools	Total no. of students at school	Total no. of graduates	Total no. of schools	Total no. of students at school	Total no. of graduates
1980	3,069	1,243,000	410,000	—	—	—	3,314	454,000	79,000
1985	3,557	1,571,000	429,000	3,548	742,000	226,000	8,070	2,295,000	413,000
1988	4,022	2,052,000	596,000	3,996	1,161,000	311,000	8,954	2,794,000	810,000
1990	3,982	2,244,000	661,000	4,184	1,332,000	413,000	9,164	2,950,000	893,000
1993	3,964	2,820,000	736,000	4,477	1,717,000	497,000	9,985	3,626,000	1,025,000
1995	4,049	3,722,000	839,000	4,521	1,886,000	681,000	10,147	4,483,000	1,240,000
1998	4,109	4,981,000	1,293,000	4,362	1,813,000	682,000	10,074	5,416,000	1,628,000
2000	3,646	4,895,000	1,507,000	3,792	1,401,000	646,000	8,849	5,032,000	1,763,000
2001	3,260	4,580,000	1,503,000	3,470	1,347,000	477,000	7,802	4,664,000	1,665,000
2002	2,953	4,564,000	1,442,000	3,075	1,530,000	454,000	7,402	5,115,000	1,454,000

Source: adapted from *China Statistics Yearbook* 2003: 718-23.

formal educational institutions such as universities, secondary and primary schools.

There are a range of interrelated problems encountered by the vocational educational and training institutions, which need to be discussed separately.

Administrative problems

One of the fundamental problems faced by the training institutions is that of intertwining ownership and governance, leading to the absence of strategic planning and co-ordination. There is generally a lack of independence of these training institutions. Many are offshoots of large SOEs and sectoral administrative departments, which are rooted in the traditional manufacturing industries and control all the decision making of the colleges. Since most of these owner organizations are in the state sector, they lack sensitivity to market signals. The long chain of command also reduces the polytechnic and technical colleges' flexibility to respond to the market swiftly (although skills training should not rely solely on market forces). The decline of heavy manufacturing and the rise of the light manufacturing and service industries also mean that these SOEs and administrative departments are facing the very problem of being displaced by the economy and need to revitalize themselves to survive.

Since training institutions have developed from a variety of origins, there is a lack of state intervention in forecasting and co-ordination. Although there has been a relatively tight level of control on the polytechnic and technical colleges from their state sector parent organizations, they have neither the expertise nor the information necessary to give strategic direction to these colleges. Moreover, parochial interests inevitably cause conflicts between training institutions in the same geographical locations. Market segmentation, small-sized, all-round service, repetition of capacity building and low efficiency are all part of the associated problems, which further reduce each other's long-term capacity. For example, even in Shanghai, one of the economically and educationally most advanced cities in China, the average student number was only 930 in 1997 (Wu 1998).

Student recruitment problems

A second set of problems is to do with difficulties of recruiting students. All three types of vocational education and training institutions – technical colleges, technical schools and vocational senior secondary schools – are competing for the same student pool, whereas the majority of students want to go to normal senior secondary school and university (because of the elite culture). Some training schools use unhealthy recruitment tactics to attract students, such as exaggerating the school's achievements and giving unfulfilled promises (of guaranteed employment) to students and their parents (Wu 1997).

There is a high level of inconsistency in fee charging, in part because some schools are subsidized by their educational authorities or parent organizations whereas others are self-financed. Training places for popular subjects can be disproportionally more expensive (and in some cases, several times more so) than those for the not so popular ones (to reflect market forces). In order to solve the problem, some city authorities are combining the three types of training institutions for synergy to make them more competitive.

Training resources and provision problems

A third set of problems is related to the training provision itself in terms of training methods and resources. There are considerable variations in the length of training and the number of teaching hours. The same goes for teaching materials, some of which are out-of-date. There are also considerable variations in technical skills training. Some schools lack technical facilities to carry out the necessary training. Many trainees have to practise their technical skills in small basic workshops set up by their training schools and may never have the chance to go to a real workplace to experience how those skills may be applied and developed. Training investment from the state has been limited. The 1996 national fiscal budget for vocational training was 10.93 billion yuan, an increase of 22 per cent from the previous year. However, over 64 per cent of the increased fund was spent on staff (Ma 1999) instead of being used to modernize training facilities. In 2000, the government budget for technical colleges, technical schools and vocational schools was 19.40 billion yuan, representing 9.3 per cent of the total educational budgetary funds. The budget for 2001 was 20.7 billion yuan, or 0.8 per cent of the total educational budgetary funds, an actual reduction of support compared with that received by other segments of the educational sector (*China Statistics Yearbook* 2002, 2003). As a result, an increasingly large proportion of the funding came from social organizations and individuals, donations and fund-raising, tuition and miscellaneous fees, and other educational funds.

Not surprisingly, few stakeholders are content with the current state of the training provision. According to a comprehensive survey carried out by the Vocational Education Institute of Anhui Province (located in mid-China) in 1998 on the agricultural vocational training situation in the province, 64 per cent of employers surveyed felt that employers should participate in the design of the training curriculum in order for the training to reflect employers' skills requirements. Fifty-five per cent of students felt that although what they learned in school was useful, it did not equip them sufficiently for their employment. Likewise, 60 per cent of employers said that the knowledge base of graduates from vocational training schools was too narrow. Eighty per cent of employers also felt that the practical operational skills of the trainee graduates were not sufficient for their posts (Xiao 1999). In the same study, over 80 per cent of teachers surveyed believed that the existing training mode was too outdated to reflect current trends of skills requirements in the labour market. Eighty-five per cent of the heads of training schools also felt that the lack of resources and poor quality of teachers were responsible for the difficulties they had experienced in their attempts to modernize the training system.

There is an insufficient supply of training staff in both quality and quantity. For example, there was a total of over 220,000 staff employed in the various technical schools in 2001. Among them, 100,000 were classroom teachers, and 34,000 were practical training teachers. This meant that nearly 40 per cent of the staff employed were in administrative functions rather than in teaching (*China Statistics Yearbook* 2002: 678).

There is also a shortage of teachers with specialist subjects. For example, according to the statistics published by the State Commission of Education in 1997, only 45.5 per cent of teachers were specialists in the subjects they taught, and a significantly smaller proportion of 2.6 per cent could supervise practice training. By the end of 2000, only 44 per cent of teachers in vocational senior secondary schools possessed a first university degree or above. The situation in technical colleges was considerably better, with about 73 per cent of teachers holding a first university degree (*China Education Statistics Yearbook* 2001).

Employment problems for graduates

A fourth set of problems is to do with the (lack of) employment opportunities for trainee graduates. The prioritization of recruitment candidates in large SOEs and public sector organizations is as follows, in descending order: university graduates (with degrees), polytechnic college graduates, graduates of senior secondary school, laid-off workers, technical college graduates, technical school graduates, and finally, vocational secondary school leavers (Yu, Q. N. 1998). For instance, according to a survey, in 1997, only five out of the 500 graduates of the Vocational School of the Grain Industry in Tianjin City (one of the largest cities in China) gained employment on completion of their training. Similarly, only six out of the 600 graduates from the Vocational School of the Smelter Industry were offered jobs by employers (Niu 1998).

A number of reasons contribute to this situation. First, the decline of SOEs and traditional industries makes it difficult for these former 'patrons' of technical schools to absorb a new supply of graduates. These 'patrons' also reduce funding and other support to the technical schools, as they are facing survival problems themselves. Second, the perceived poor quality of graduates is to be blamed. Poor training facilities, poor quality of trainers and an out-of-date curriculum are seen as major factors contributing to the poor quality of the final 'product'. This is often made worse by the low morale and motivation of the trainees during their training period, because going to vocational training school may be their last choice. Third, these graduates are inexperienced in job hunting. They still rely on official channels (e.g. the local authority and their school) to find jobs for them instead of going out to the labour market themselves to seek employment. Training institutions often fail to provide any training or labour market information to assist those students seeking employment.

Fourth, there is a strong mismatch between graduates' employment expectations and what is available in the job market. Graduates still see large private enterprises and state- or collectively owned organizations as the 'ideal' employer and are unwilling to contemplate employment in small and medium-sized enterprises and township and village enterprises, where skills are needed and employment opportunities may be available. This puts them in the disadvantaged position of having to compete with university graduates. Most graduates also aim for popular or socially prestigious occupations rather than settling for an ordinary job. For instance, Liu and Liu (1999) carried out a survey of nearly 1,000 students of all years who specialized in nine subjects in seven vocational secondary schools in Tianjin City at the end of 1997. They found that 45.5 per cent of students surveyed only wanted to seek employment in the finance, telecom and insurance industries, and tax and commercial bureaux. Some 27 per cent would choose governmental and public sector organizations and only 11.3 per cent wanted to work in enterprises, but they had to be international joint ventures. No students wanted to consider employment in the rural areas.

The four sets of problems identified above form a vicious circle of difficulties encountered by the training institutions from bringing the students in (recruitment) to sending them out (employment). It is unlikely that the unpromising employment prospects for these graduates will change for the better in the near future, given the current large-scale unemployment problems and strong labour market competition in China. Ironically, many enterprises are encountering shortages of technicians at advanced level. For example, Guangzhou (one of the most economically advanced cities in China) currently needs 100,000 senior technicians but fewer than 10,000 are available. Even in Shenzhen, China's pioneer city with its rapid economic development where talent abounds, only 5.6 per cent of its skilled workers are at the advanced level, whereas 75 per cent are at the junior level despite the fact that 28.8 per cent of its labour force is classified as skilled workers (*Yangcheng Evening News*, 26 June 2002).

Enterprise training in China

The workplace provides the other major source of skills training in China. Before we discuss the policy and practice of enterprise training, it is important to have an overview of the legislative role of the state in shaping its training system.

Training regulations

Enterprise training has for decades been guided by a number of regulations issued by the state. This framework of training regulations includes the Constitutions of the People's Republic of China (1951), the Labour Law of China (1995), the Education Law (1995), the Vocational Education Law of China (1996), the Enterprise Law (1988), the Corporation Law (1993), the Enterprise Employee Training Regulations (1996), the Enterprise Management Training Plan (1996), and the Higher Education Law of China (1998). These laws are supplemented by regional and local training regulations and training policies of employing organizations.

Most of these regulations were introduced after the Cultural Revolution when education and skills training again became a top priority for the country (see further discussion below). The 'Reform and Development Plan for Education in China' issued by the State Council in 1993 emphasizes that continuous education and on-the-job training should be the main methods for adult education. The Labour Law of China (1995) states that the state specifies the technical standards for its nominated occupations and implements the vocational qualification system. It emphasizes the necessity of job training and stipulates that 'an employer shall establish a job training system, set aside funds for job training and use them according to the regulations of the State, so as to be able to train its employees systematically in the light of its circumstances'. The Education Law (1995) specifies for the first time that all professionals and technical staff have the right as well as the obligation to undertake continuous training.

The Vocational Education Law of China (1996) was the first piece of legislation on vocational education in China. It specifies the scope of responsibility of governments at all levels. It stipulates that all job holders of skilled occupations must undertake relevant training and tests, and obtain the qualification(s) before taking up their posts. In theory, the Vocational Education Law of China provides scope for local governments to integrate the provision of vocational training with better planning and resource allocation. However, the problem is that, while some provincial and local governments proactively implement the law, others continue to treat vocational education and training as a low priority and make little effort or investment in improving the service. There is no inspection and monitoring mechanism in place to ensure a consistent implementation of the law across the country. Further inconsistencies of practices also arise from the varied details in the local regulations of vocational education and training, as the Vocational Education and Training Law of China only provides a broad framework for local governments to design their own details (Hu 1998).

The 'Temporary Regulations on Continuous Education for Professional and Technical Personnel in China' ('Temporary Regulations' hereafter) was introduced by the state in 1995. This is seen as an important policy document for national continuous training, which marks the beginning of the formalization of continuous training for professional and technical staff. The 'Temporary Regulations' lays down basic rules for provincial and local governments to design and implement their local training regulations. It specifies that all senior and middle-ranking professionals and technical staff should receive at least forty hours of off-the-job training per year, and junior ranking staff no less than thirty-two hours. This is coupled with the 'Plan of Continuous Education for all Professional and Technical Staff in China' aimed to improve the quality of the existing 44.65 million professional and technical staff through training and development. Each industrial ministry is also required to formulate its own regulations for continuous training and development for professionals and technical staff. For example, the 'Civil Servant Training Plan' is aimed to increase the quality standard of the 5.28 million civil servants in China. However, whereas these regulations provide some framework of reference, they are not compulsory in the sense that no penalty will be extended to those enterprises which do not observe the regulations. None the less, these regulations have provided the necessary impetus for enterprise training in China in the past two decades.

History of enterprise training

The history of enterprise training in China in the past five decades may be divided into three periods. The first period was from 1949 to 1955 characterized by the Anti-illiteracy Movement during which all workers who were illiterate or semi-illiterate had to undertake state education in their spare time. By 1955, over four million urban workers (more than 30 per cent of the workforce) had participated in the workers' education programme. Over 1.7 million of them became literate (i.e. knowing at least 2,000 Chinese characters). Meanwhile, 'key' workers were selected and sent for higher education to prepare them for their state cadres' role on their return (The Specialist Team 1999). This practice was interrupted by the 'Big Leap Forward' Movement in the early 1960s and then again by the ten-year-long Cultural Revolution begun in 1966. Meanwhile, by 1965, there were a total of 62,891 vocational and technical colleges/schools in China with 4.98 million students in all (Wu 1999).

The second period began in the early 1980s during which employee training became a top priority of the state again, as was education in the country as a whole. In 1981, there were nearly 110 million shopfloor workers in urban China, 60 million of whom were below the age of 35. Many of them had received little proper education during the Cultural Revolution period. It was decided in a State Congress on employees' education in 1981 that by 1985, all workers (about 30 million at the time) who did not possess a junior secondary school qualification should attend courses organized by their enterprises and that 60 to 80 per cent of them should obtain the qualifications on completion. Younger workers (below the age of 35) were expected to undertake two types of courses: general education (e.g. Chinese and maths), and technical knowledge training related to their jobs. By August 1985, 75.9 per cent of the 30 million workers receiving training had passed their general education exams and 74.4 per cent had passed their technical knowledge exams (Wu 1999), although the true quality of these qualifications was questioned by some. At the same time, the government built nearly 200 new higher educational institutes (known as 'Management Training Institutes for Cadres') where younger managers and managerial candidates were sent by their organizations (mostly public sector organizations and SOEs) for training and development. It was estimated that over 100,000 managerial workers had received training in these institutes in the first half of the 1980s (Wu 1999).

The third period began in the mid-1990s, with the launch of a number of administrative regulations on education and training in China, as was discussed above. Two major state-driven training initiatives play an important role in much of the training and assessment carried out during this period: positional training and vocational competency tests. The state specifies that all job holders must carry out pre-post training before being allowed to work in the post. In addition, a 'dual-certificate' system was introduced in which each individual worker was required to possess both an occupational and a positional qualification certificate to be allowed to work in the post (The Head Project Team 1998). Therefore, for many employees, undertaking positional training is now compulsory, and obtaining vocational competency certification is a necessity to remaining employed.

Positional training

It was estimated that between 1991 and 1995, over 178 million persons had participated, some more than once, in positional training and continuous education, accounting for 85 per cent of all training undertaken by employees in China. In 1996, some 35 million workers underwent positional training and continuous education in the whole country. There were 214,000 cadres (managerial workers) and 240,000 teachers/trainers working in the field of employee education and training (Chu 1998).

Vocational competency test

Between 1993 and 1997, more than 14 million workers in China had participated in the skills competence tests and over 11 million of them had obtained their occupational skills level certificates (Liu 1998). In 1999, 3.38 million workers participated in the vocational competency tests set up by the labour and social security authorities at all levels. Over 2.9 million of them (86.5 per cent) obtained the qualifications. However, 90.2 per cent of the qualifications were at intermediate and junior levels. Over 63 per cent of the participants came from the top ten provinces in China. There were 6,916 assessment centres in the whole country with 73,068 assessors. Over 4,200 assessment

Table 5.3 The top ten occupations which had the most participants awarded qualifications in 1999 (end-of-year figures)

Number	Occupation	No. of participants	No. of people awarded qualifications	Pass rate (%)
1	Computer processor	209,920	182,395	86.9
2	Chef for Chinese food	169,842	148,911	87.6
3	Automobile driver	154,060	145,187	94.2
4	Electrician	151,793	133,787	88.1
5	Computer operator	147,515	127,418	86.3
6	Fitter	110,476	96,002	86.9
7	Automobile maintenance technician	86,584	74,509	86.1
8	Waiter/waitress	81,689	73,687	90.0
9	Beautician	69,606	59,701	85.7
10	Machinist	69,444	61,023	87.9

Source: adapted from *China Statistics Yearbook* 2000: 134.

centres were at the state level. A total of 62.6 per cent obtained qualifications in ten occupations which had the most successful participants among the fifty occupations which are classified and assessed by the state, as Table 5.3 shows. In 2000, 4.42 million workers participated in the vocational competency tests and over 3.72 million of them (84.2 per cent) obtained the qualifications (*China Trade Union Statistics Yearbook* 2001: 187).

By 1997, there were 22,000 enterprise training centres offering a training capacity of 30,000 persons per year to their own employees (Liu and Liu 1999). Since the late 1990s, retraining of redundant workers has formed a large part of the training activities (see Chapter 3 for further discussion). In 2000, there were 3,751 employment training centres and 15,000 community training bodies in the country. Nearly 3.6 million unemployed and laid-off workers participated in re-employment training, and about 2.3 million of them found employment as a result of training (*China Trade Union Statistics Yearbook* 2001: 187).

Management training

As we can see from the discussion above, management training forms a significant part of enterprise training in China. It is recognized that the shortage of qualified managers is a serious problem. The shift from a centrally planned economy to a market-oriented economy accentuates the inadequacy of the old management style of direct administrative control. There is an increasing demand for professional managers with expertise in HRM, finance, marketing and strategic planning. As a result, training Chinese managers has become an urgent requirement for all enterprises concerned. More and more universities are now offering part-time and full-time training courses for middle- and senior-level managers to make them familiar with modern management techniques prevalent in developed countries.

Management training in China has attracted considerable attention from academic researchers from the West. This has resulted in a temporary flourish of Western literature on the nature and extent of management training in China in the 1980s and 1990s (e.g. Walder 1989; Warner 1988, 1990a, 1992; Borgonjon and Vanhonacker 1994; Bu 1994; Child 1994; Branine 1996). Much of this literature points to the fact that the shortage of managerial skills has been a major barrier to China's endeavour to modernize, a deficit of which the Chinese government was well aware and which it has taken measures to address.

It is also worth pointing out here that there has been a general decline in the management training market in China since 1988, with many factory directors considering training to be a waste of time (Borgonjon and Vanhonacker 1994). This has resulted in the insufficient recruitment of management trainees from enterprises to undertake formal management education with formal qualifications. Another reason contributing to the decline is the fact that by the 1990s, the vast majority of the younger generation of managers and management candidates already possessed university degrees in the first place. Management training has also become more industry- and firm-specific, and is often carried out at the workplace and for short periods, delivered by external specialists.

Characteristics and problems of enterprise training

Despite the absence of detailed training statistics to capture a precise picture of workplace training in China, the training landscape so far displays a number of characteristics and problems (Liu, L. X. 2000), which necessarily reflect the 'societal effect' specific to China's historical, political, social and industrial context (Warner 2000). The first is the generally low level of provision across different industries (see Table 5.4). For example, by the end of 1996, only 14.6 per cent of enterprises had established a skills training system; only 11.1 per cent of enterprises had allocated and spent the training fund in accordance with that specified in the training regulations; only 16.7 per cent of employees had taken part in the positional training, and the vast majority of enterprises and employees had little to do with enterprise training. According to statistics published by the Ministry of Education, about 2.13 million professional and technical staff in SOEs and COEs received training from their employers in 1996, comprising 7.6 per cent of the total number of professional and technical staff.

According to the 'Chinese Workers' Situation Survey 1999' conducted by the All-China Federation of Trade Unions, 38 per cent of the 30,421 workers surveyed in the state-owned companies were undertaking training and learning at the time. Among them, 11.39 per cent were receiving training organized by their companies, 7.09 per cent were undertaking training which was self-funded and organized externally, and the remaining 19.43 per cent were carrying out self-study. These figures suggested that enterprising training was limited. The same survey also revealed that only 31.27 per cent of workers in the state-owned sector had received training once since their employment, and another 18.69 per cent had received training twice. While 25.22 per cent had received training three times since their employment, 24.83 per cent had received none. This meant that over half of the employees did not receive training continuously and systematically (Liu, L. X. 2001).

A second characteristic is the significant inter-sector difference between the secondary industrial and the third industrial sector, with the former paying considerably more attention to training than the latter (see Table 5.4).

A third characteristic is that there are considerable variations of training provision between different forms of enterprise ownership in descending order as follows: foreign ownership, share ownership, state ownership, collective ownership, co-operative ownership, Hong Kong, Taiwan or/and Macao investment, small private and self-employed businesses (see Table 5.5). For example, Cooke's study (2002) found that the change of ownership of a brewery from state-owned to Sino–Hong Kong joint venture has resulted in many more training opportunities for its employees, whereas the privatization of a state-owned motor manufacturer has seen worsening practice of HRM in general with little, if any, training provision. Ding *et al.*'s study (2001) of TVEs found that the level of training provision varied among the TVEs studied but was generally low. Knight *et al.* (1999) also revealed that migrant workers generally received only brief training and were poorly rewarded for their training. This is in spite of the fact that migrant (rural) workers have become an indispensable source of labour for many enterprises that should have an interest in training and retaining these workers. In a study of twenty-four small private and self-employed commercial businesses carried out by myself, it was found that while some employees received a moderate amount of induction training from their employers, the majority received little training afterwards (see Chapter 8 for further discussion).

A fourth characteristic is the regional difference in training provision, with enterprises in the wealthier areas (i.e. the east and southeast regions) faring better in general than those in the north and west. Only seven of the thirty-one provinces and autonomous cities in the whole country had issued the 'Continuous Education Law' by 2000 and its implementation was less than stringent (Li 2000).

A fifth characteristic is the two-tier system of management and professional training and development versus mass workforce training, with the former being given a far higher priority than the latter. In other words, it is an elite system in which the more education and training one receives, the more one will (be expected to) have. This official emphasis may be seen in the introduction of the 'Temporary Regulations on Continuous Education for Professional and Technical Personnel in China' by the state in 1995. Continuous training and development focuses mainly on those already

Table 5.4 Statistics of enterprise training in different industries in China in 1996 (end-of-year figures)

Industry	No. of enterprises	Skills training system in place		Training fund allocated and used in accordance with regulations		No. of	Employees participating in positional training employees	
		Enterprise	Proportion (%)	Enterprise	Proportion (%)		Employees	Proportion (%)
Total[a]	2,051,000	299,000	14.6	228,000	11.1	148,453,000	24,856,000	16.7
Mining	11,000	5,000	45.5	4,000	36.4	8,860,000	1,587,000	17.9
Manufacturing	247,000	73,000	29.6	56,000	22.7	52,930,000	9,882,000	18.7
Construction	38,000	9,000	23.7	8,000	21.1	10,350,000	1,158,000	11.2
Transport, post and telecom	44,000	17,000	38.6	14,000	31.8	8,300,000	2,121,000	25.6
Wholesale, retail and catering	365,000	48,000	13.2	40,000	11	18,070,000	2,393,000	13.2
Finance, insurance and real estate	87,000	12,000	13.8	10,000	11.5	3,700,000	717,000	19.4
Social services	78,000	9,000	11.5	7,000	9	4,580,000	735,000	16

Source: adapted from *China Statistics Yearbook* 1997.

Notes

[a] Figures including industries such as agriculture, forestry, fishery, utilities, education.

Table 5.5 Statistics of enterprise training in different forms of enterprise ownership in China in 1996 (end-of-year figures)

Forms of ownership	No. of enterprises	Skills training system in place		Training fund allocated and used in accordance with regulations		Pre-post training provided for workers in skilled posts		No. of employees	Employees participating in positional training	
		Enterprise	Proportion (%)	Enterprise	Proportion (%)	Enterprise	Proportion (%)		Employees	Proportion (%)
State-owned	1,502,000	231,000	15.4	176,000	11.7	241,000	16	109,494,000	20,076,000	18.3
Collectively owned	485,000	55,000	11.3	43,000	8.9	63,000	13	29,542,000	3,271,000	11.2
Co-operative	5,000	500	10	300	6	500	10	485,000	27,000	5.6
Private and self-employed	27,856,000	1,000	0.004	700	0.003	1,000	0.004	61,882,000	41,000	0.007
Share-ownership	18,000	4,000	22.2	2,000	16.7	4,000	22.2	3,573,000	753,000	21.1
Foreign-owned	20,000	4,000	25	4,000	20	5,000	30	2,679,000	538,000	20.1
Hong Kong, Taiwan and/or Macao investments	20,000	1,000	5	900	4.5	2,000	10	2,591,000	116,000	4.5

Source: adapted from China Statistics Yearbook 1997.

possessing (higher) qualifications as compulsory requirements for their promotions.

At the enterprise level, training practice displays a number of problems characterized by the lack of strategic planning and low priority of training in organizational activities. In particular, employee training is often seen as part of the non-core business for companies, and the training department is often used to accommodate cadres who are deemed unsuitable for front-line production. Enterprises often carry out training without any strategic planning, costing or taking into account what their training needs are. Training departments usually operate in a reactive mode to 'fulfil the task given by the higher authority'. While training officers complain that senior company managers neglect training, criticisms often levelled at the training provision are that it is irrelevant, out of touch, a formality to tick the training box, and an opportunity for individuals to gild their qualifications (Xu, L. 2000). While many organizations find it difficult to release their key staff for off-the-job training, on-the-job training remains an infrequently used method for training apart from the traditional apprentice system in SOEs.

For trainees, training is often considered to be boring, irrelevant and a necessary chore. Tests are not strictly administered, and people can prepare their answers in advance or copy answers from each other during the exam. Training is seen as an opportunity for employees to obtain more (and higher) qualifications for promotion and pay increases. Training which does not provide any credentials will find it difficult to attract trainees unless it is compulsory (Li *et al.* 2000). Training is also seen as a company perk that is to be shared by all concerned. A large proportion of the training fund is usually spent on banquets for employees as part of the benefits associated with training.

Finally, training is used as a substitute for workplace downsizing. Since the state requires all downsizing companies to provide retraining for their laid-off workers in order to help them regain employment, enterprises may put people on the training schemes and claim that they have been made redundant while in fact they have not. This practice was more common in the late 1990s and was considered to be a 'one stone many birds' tactic which not only kept the authority happy (for meeting the downsizing target and fulfilling the training task), but also kept the workers happy (because their jobs were safe and they had been 'trained').

Training prospects in China

Despite the problems identified so far in China's vocational and enterprise training, there are signs of improvement and increase in training, at least in quantity if not so much in quality, in part because of the state's intervention through regulations and in part due to other factors summarized below.

Adoption of training models and collaborations

In recent years, policy makers and academics in China have been exploring training models of other countries in an attempt to learn lessons from them. For example, the NVQs and GNVQs system in the UK is considered to be a good example, in spite of the criticisms that this system has attracted back home (Marshall 1994; Eraut *et al.* 1996; Sutherland and Rainbird 2000). The 'dual system' of Germany was hailed as the best model, and some large cities have set up vocational educational centres to experiment with the model. In fact, thirty-two Sino–German collaborative training entities were established in China in the early 1980s. However, this dual system proved to be too expensive for China and the single-discipline nature of the trainers/teachers in China also made it difficult to adopt the system (Liu 1998).

The Chinese government is also adopting a more strategic position in collaborating with international organizations for skills training. One example of this is that China is collaborating with multinational information technology organizations in software training to ease the growing demand for senior software professionals. The China International Talent Exchange Foundation announced in early 2003 that it would introduce a development programme by United States-based Oracle Corporation to train 4,000 software professionals each year. From 1998 to 2001, colleges in China had trained 165,000 people specialized in computers and software, a number far from being sufficient for the demand. To bridge the gap between supply and demand, the Foundation has implemented at least 100 projects introducing foreign professional bodies and carried out co-operation in the industry (*China Staff*, March 2003).

The role of large enterprises

Large blue chip (state-owned) enterprises tend to play a positive role in implementing the training regulations. For example, it was reported (Liu 1999) that in the Capital Steel Corporation (Shougang) in Beijing, all subsidiaries must meet their training targets measured by the number of people being sent for off-the-job training and by the number of training hours, or 5 per cent and 3 per cent of its wage bill would be deducted respectively. Those who were sent for training (on full wages) would receive a training scholarship equivalent to 80 per cent of the monthly average bonus (per person) issued by the company. Those trainees who failed their tests at the end of the training would be given a laid-off wage only and would not be allowed to work in their post until they had passed their tests after retraining. In addition, a competition in technical skills would be held every three months. Winners (the top three candidates) would be given a substantial monthly bonus until they were overtaken by the new winners in the following season. Zhao and Wu's survey (2003) of thirty-one large enterprises (67.6

per cent of them manufacturing firms, 77.4 per cent SOEs, 26 per cent employing between 800 and 1,500 employees and 60 per cent employing 1,500 or more employees) in nine provinces also revealed that these enterprises paid considerable attention to training. Over 90 per cent of them had a formal written training policy in place, although the priority tended to be new employee training and management training, followed by the training of technical staff.

The role of MNCs and JVs in China

While some multinational corporations and international joint ventures in China may operate on a low-cost and low-skilled basis, a number of them are 'blue chip' corporations operating with advanced technology and at the upper end of the business market. Training appears to be a key component of the human resource strategy for these firms. For example, Ding and Warner (1998) found that career development was often mentioned by HR managers interviewed in foreign-invested firms in Shanghai as one of their major responsibilities. This indicates a proactive stance rather than a reactive one, as is typically found in SOEs. The increasing appearance of these firms in China will undoubtedly play a positive role in skills training and development of the country.

In addition, training provision in these corporations tends to be more formal and systematic. Bjorkman and Lu (1999a) found that training programmes of the MNC establishments in China which they studied shared great similarities with those used in other parts of the MNC. For example, MNCs such as Motorola, Ericsson, Siemens and Procter & Gamble have even established their own internal 'universities', 'business schools' or 'management training centres' in China, where courses offered were similar to those offered in other countries. These courses focused on standard business topics such as effective supervision, marketing, financial management, business strategy and human resource management. In addition, several MNCs offered three to four weeks' junior management development programmes similar to those offered elsewhere by the corporation.

The role of training organizations

The rapid growth of commercial training organizations with an expanding range of training service provisions serves as a pulling factor for firms to spend more on training their employees and rely more on external training bodies to provide the training. For example, in 1996, only 1.7 per cent of domestic Chinese firms used external trainers who were mainly academics from universities. By the end of 2001, some 85 per cent of domestic Chinese firms were insourcing training services and most had switched from university lecturers to professional training bodies (Wang, D. 2002). It must be pointed out here that this rapid development of training courses and expansion of training suppliers may not guarantee the quality of training, and client companies need to develop their knowledge about the market to differentiate good training providers from shoddy ones, and to identify precisely what training services are needed for the firm.

Globalization and the need to match international standards

The increasing globalization of business in China has prompted organizations to recognize the need to converge with international norms/practices. For example, we have seen, in the past few years, a tidal wave of applications for ISO 9000 and 14000 quality series accreditation by many business organizations in China. This has led to an increase in training in some enterprises in order to fulfil the accreditation requirements.

The accession to the WTO likewise brought another surge of training. One of the main reasons for the increase in training provision in the past few years has been to do with the WTO-related legal framework. Many business and governmental organizations offered emergency training for their staff to deal with WTO legal matters in order to, for example, clarify the specifications for product ingredients, and to deal with customs and excise. However, this training is far from being sufficient for the Chinese organizations to deal with the surge of demand for WTO-related knowledge. Many businesses have encountered heavy losses as a result of not meeting the WTO requirement standards. For example, between 2000 and 2001, a total of 70 billion US dollars of China's exports has been negatively affected as a result of technical barriers (*Hong Kong Commercial Daily News*, 17 March 2002: A10).

More broadly, China's accession to the WTO provides opportunities as well as challenges for its skills training. The entrance to the WTO inevitably causes sectoral changes, thus rendering certain skills obsolete in some (old) sectors while at the same time creating skills gaps in the new sectors. In particular, the creation of new sectors such as telecom, banking and insurance, and computing, causes skills shortages in these fields not only for trainees but also for trainers. In addition, China's further opening up to world business means that it needs to adapt to the international standards of quality and legal framework.

Conclusions

This chapter has reviewed the policy and practice of vocational and enterprise training in China over the past fifty years, with a focus on the past two decades. The main picture is that formal qualification education and pre-employment training remain the dominant practices. Greater emphasis is given to pre-employment training than to in-employment training, although increasing attention is being paid to the latter. The former has been fuelled by the relatively high unemployment rate and the prevalence of vocational and technical training institutes. While considerable achievements have been made, mainly as an outcome of state intervention, there are still many problems in the skills training system that warrant further discussion here.

First, in terms of vocational education and training, there should be a clearer division of responsibilities between the state, the employer and the training institution. There is a need for the state to formulate and implement a nation-wide long-term training plan and to increase the training budget. The government should promote training through the intervention of policy and legislation, and at the same time through the encouragement of an incentive system instead of participating directly in the training business as do some local educational authorities. There is a need to simplify and integrate the ports of control from various authorities in order to reduce segmentation and repetition of training provision and to increase efficiency through the scale of economy. Training institutions should be given more autonomy to manage their training business.

There should be a closer collaborative relationship between training institutions and enterprises to take advantage of the resources of enterprises. This includes batch training of students for large enterprises based on their 'order' of skills requirements. Work placement opportunities should be offered by enterprises for students to experiment with what they have learned in training school. More importantly, there should be a closer collaborative relationship between the training institutes and the community. 'Community' here refers to other educational institutions, families, governmental organizations and other social support bodies. Stronger ties with this community will facilitate the flow of information and channel resources to the training function to eliminate parochial interest, as vocational and technical training should serve the broader purpose of the development of regional economies.

Second, at enterprise level, although there has been an increase in training activities, there is little evidence to suggest that training forms part of the human resource strategy pursued proactively by the majority of employing organizations in China. Instead, training is carried out mainly by larger enterprises and is concentrated on those who are already privileged with a higher level of skills and qualifications. Whereas large private firms may carry out training as part of their management strategy driven by competitive pressure, technological investment and quality initiatives, training provision in SOEs largely remains a response to the state's intervention. There is, therefore, a need for the state to replace command and directive mechanisms with economic, legislative and administrative mechanisms to promote enterprise training, although there are encouraging signs that this appears to be the trend. There is also a need for a more comprehensive qualification system to formalize skills training and assessment. For instance, by 1998, there were only fifty-five types of occupational qualifications which were approved by the Ministry of Labour whereas there were thousands of occupational posts in practice. In addition, the dual system of occupational qualification and position certification has been implemented mainly by SOEs and public sector organizations, resulting in the issue of positional certificates to several millions of workers. However, it is unclear to what extent this dual system specified by the state has been taken up by private enterprises.

Third, there are some huge gaps in the training targets at national level that deserve higher priorities from the state (as shown in Table 5.6) if China is to gain international competitive advantage from a more skilled workforce. There are currently three main targets of trainees: new labour supply, redundant workers and the unemployed, and workers in formal employment. However, there are another two categories of workers who make up an increasingly large proportion of the total labour force of the country and who are in need of skills training more than the existing three groups – the rural migrant workers and urban workers in small private businesses. (The size of these two groups of workers has been outlined in Chapter 2 and their employment characteristics will be discussed in detail in Chapters 7 and 8.)

The rural migrant workers generally have low educational qualifications and the vast majority are low-skilled. For example, in 1981, professional technical staff made up only 0.03 per cent of the total workforce in TVEs, which generated 20 per cent of the industrial output of China (Zhong *et al.* 1999). Two decades on, this situation has somewhat improved, but was still grossly underpresented by college and university graduates (see Table 5.6). The majority of people working in these sectors cannot afford to fund their own skills training and fall largely outside the scope of state intervention, a situation worsened by their long working hours and minimum rest days. The majority of local authorities have no system in place to target these workers for training. Their employers will only provide training sufficient for them to perform their immediate tasks and rely on them to learn the rest on the job. Yet these are the people whose training will have wider social and economic impacts not only because of their sheer numbers but also because of the tendency for them to go back to their home village to set up their own business and to impart skills that they have acquired to their fellow villagers. These people are already playing an important role in bridging the urban and rural divide which has been a result of the decades-long dual administrative system of China to the severe disadvantage of the rural population (Cooke and Rubery 2002). So far, rural skills training has largely focused on dissemination of knowledge on agricultural technology. Investment in training of broader skills and knowledge for rural migrant workers will also help speed up the process of industrialization of rural areas.

Another group of workers who have fallen outside the formal scope of training provision are those who are employed in the informal sector or in informal employment; for example, those working in private small businesses and self-employed businesses. As pointed out above, training provision appears to be rather limited for workers in this category where both the state influence and the workers' collective power are the weakest. As this category of workers have formed an increasing proportion of the total employed in China since the 1980s and reached 16.5 per cent by the end of 1999

Table 5.6 Composition of urban employment status by educational attainment in 2002 (end-of-year figures)[a]

Educational attainment	Total	Urban units employment	Township and village enterprises employment	Agriculture employment	Private sector employee	Private employer	Self-employed	Others
Total	100.0	44.1	3.7	17.2	14.1	6.2	12.8	1.8
Illiterate or semi-illiterate	100.0	5.4	2.4	64.3	6.3	3.4	15.6	2.6
Primary school	100.0	9.5	3.9	46.8	12.9	6.3	18.4	2.2
Junior secondary school	100.0	28.9	4.7	19.5	19.5	8.1	17.3	2.0
Senior secondary school	100.0	63.1	3.5	3.5	13.1	6.1	9.1	1.6
Polytechnic college	100.0	87.4	1.7	0.3	5.1	2.2	2.0	1.2
University	100.0	91.8	0.9	0.1	3.3	1.6	0.8	1.5
Postgraduate	100.0	93.5	0.8	—	2.0	1.5	0.9	1.4

Source: adapted from *China Statistics Yearbook 2003*: 70.

Note
[a] Figures in percentages.

(Dahlman and Aubert 2001), training intervention for this expanding category of workers will undoubtedly benefit the overall skills level of the labour force.

Currently, the costs of attending formal vocational education and training are largely borne up-front by individuals and their families and that of enterprise training mainly by employers. This semi-voluntary funding system is far from being sufficient to increase the skills level of the country, where an increasingly large proportion of the workforce come from economically disadvantaged family backgrounds (e.g. rural workers) and work in sectors where voluntary training provision is low down in employers' priorities. It is therefore vital that the state should increase its moderate funding of skills training and devise some sort of two-tier system to ensure that those in disadvantaged positions may benefit more directly from the training system. However, it is beyond the scope of this chapter to discuss in detail how this is to be achieved. Indeed, state intervention is needed in a wide range of aspects of employment in order to provide a level of protection to those who are disadvantaged. It is to the issues of inequality and discrimination in employment policies and practices that the next two chapters turn.

6 Gender equality policy and practice in employment and management

Introduction

There are more than half a billion women in China, over 50 per cent of whom are in full-time employment. The female workforce as a whole contributed 38 per cent of the country's GDP (8,940 billion yuan) in 2000. However, knowledge about these Chinese women's employment conditions in general and women's management careers in particular remains limited. Although a series of equal opportunity legislation has been introduced by the state, the fairness of these regulations and the effectiveness of their implementation are highly debatable (e.g. Dicks 1989; Lubman 1995; Warner 1996b; Keith 1997; Potter 1999). At the same time, China has experienced two decades of rapid social, political and economic change. In particular, the changing nature of the labour market and the shift from a workplace-based welfare to a social welfare system have had a direct impact on the state's ability to safeguard the rights and interests of female workers in workplaces where the state influence is weak or weakening.

The aim of this chapter is to review the positive role of the state in promoting women's participation in employment since the founding of Socialist China in 1949. It identifies patterns of gender inequality which exist throughout the process of employment such as recruitment, promotion, lay-off and retirement. The chapter analyses major reasons for the occurrence of this gender discrimination, which range from inadequate social security for child-bearing, ineffective legislative monitoring mechanisms, and gender bias in the employment legislation itself, to unequal educational opportunities and social values. It explores the political, social and economic factors that influence women's upward career mobility. The intention is to identify barriers to women's career progression. Some of these barriers may be unique to organizations in China and so will require special attention if they are to be eradicated, whereas others may be more generic, transcending differences of occupational sector or society. The chapter concludes that recent radical economic and social reforms in China have disrupted the context within which a level of equal opportunity has been achieved in the past five decades. This new situation demands a new institutional framework under which greater equality between men and women in employment may be achieved. The chapter intends to add to our understanding of the prospects for women's management careers in China and to address what needs to be done to open up more career opportunities for them. The chapter will also highlight how barriers to career progression for women in China may resemble and differ from those faced by their counterparts in developed countries, and the extent to which theories advanced in the Western literature are applicable in explaining the patterns of discrimination and the difficulties encountered by women in China in advancing their careers.

Equal opportunity legislation and women's participation in employment in China

Protecting women's employment rights and interests has long been seen by the Chinese Communist Party as an essential measure for realizing equal opportunity in China, at least in principle. In order to promote women's participation in employment, the state has intervened, over the past five decades, through legislative, administrative, economic and media educational mechanisms. Significant investment was made in childcare facilities to relieve the burden of working mothers. This intervention has provided considerable scope for significant advances in pay and social equality for female workers.

Legislation and official policies

Since the founding of Socialist China, the Chinese governments have gradually established a legal system which aims to protect the rights and interests of female employees. This legal system consists of a series of legal and administrative regulations based on the Constitution of the People's Republic of China. Major pieces of legislation include:

- Labour Insurance Regulations of the People's Republic of China (1953);
- Announcement on Female Workers' Production Leave by the State Council (1955);
- Female Employees' Labour Protection Regulations (1988);
- Regulations of Prohibited Types of Occupational Posts for Female Employees (1990);
- The PRC Law on Protecting Women's Rights and Interests (1992);
- The Labour Law of China (1995).

In addition, China has agreed and signed up to a number of International Labour Conventions related to the protection of women and equal opportunities in employment; for example, the UN Convention on the Elimination of All Forms of Discrimination Against Women; the ILO Convention No. 45 concerning the Employment of Women on Underground Work in Mines of All Kinds (1935); and the ILO Convention (1951) No. 100 concerning equal pay for men and women workers of equal value.

This framework of legislation is supported by a number of official policies for increasing the participation of women in employment. In drawing up the legislation and official policies, special attention was paid to protecting women both in finance and in working arrangements during pregnancy, maternity or while breast-feeding. In 1995, the State Council issued 'An Outline of Chinese Women's Development 1995-2000' (*Xinhua Monthly* 1995) which stipulates: '[China should] more or less realize social security for female workers' childbearing costs in urban areas [in that period].'

Women's employment and career characteristics

In general, state intervention in promoting women's participation in employment in China in the past 50 years has seen considerable benefits for women. Today, China has a far higher women's employment rate (see Table 6.1) than the world average of 55.2 per cent in 2001 (United Nations Development Programme 2003). According to official statistics, around seven million new workers have been employed each year since the mid-1990s, about 40 per cent of whom are women (Guo 2000). The scope of industries in which women find employment is expanding into new sectors such as computing, communication, environmental protection, engineering design, estate property, finance and insurance, legal institutions, etc. The number of women employed in these sectors has grown by five to ten times of that before 1980 (Guo 2000). This is closely related to the rising education level of women. As Stockman observes, 'crude measures of gender inequality in urban China reveal no greater inequality than in industrial capitalist societies, in fact possibly greater equality, and a marked reduction in inequality over the period of the building of the communist regime, up to the mid 1980s' (Stockman 1994: 771).

Meanwhile, unlike their counterparts in the Western economy who are likely to drop out of the labour market during their childbearing and childrearing years, women of childrearing age in China have the highest participation rate in employment (see Table 6.2). Career breaks for women to have children appear to be the exception rather than the norm, although some may argue that this is not necessarily beneficial to women, as it increases the social and family pressure on women when they are in their childcaring period. In addition, most working women are full-time workers because there are no established arrangements for part-time work in China to accommodate working mothers. The consequence of these two facts is the complete contrast between the pattern of economic activity of Chinese women and that typically found in the capitalist industrial societies (Stockman *et al.* 1995). The one child per married couple policy implemented in the early 1980s in China also serves to reduce the childcare burden of working women.

These employment patterns show that women have played an increasingly indispensable part in modern China's economy. However, half a century's

Table 6.1 Proportion (%) of female employees by ownership and sector (end of 1995 and 2002)

Item	Total		State ownership		Collective ownership		Other ownership	
	1995	2002	1995	2002	1995	2002	1995	2002
National total	38.6	37.8	36.1	36.7	44.6	38.9	48.3	40.4
Farming, forestry, animal husbandry, fishery	37.6	37.1	37.8	37.3	31.9	29.0	37.2	36.7
Mining and quarrying	25.9	25.3	24.4	25.2	42.1	37.4	22.8	23.2
Manufacturing	45.2	43.0	40.9	37.3	53.1	47.4	49.7	45.6
Electricity, gas and water production and supply	31.4	31.6	31.5	31.8	32.1	32.8	28.8	30.5
Construction	19.4	17.1	20.7	19.6	17.8	16.7	14.2	14.2
Geological prospecting and water conservancy	25.0	27.0	25.0	27.1	26.5	24.5	38.3	22.9
Transport, storage, post and telecom	26.5	28.3	25.9	27.6	29.4	31.4	24.2	31.3
Wholesale and retail, trade and catering	46.3	44.9	44.9	41.5	47.5	44.3	56.4	51.1
Banking and insurance	40.0	45.9	39.3	45.1	41.9	42.5	46.0	52.8
Real estate trade	33.7	34.2	34.1	35.0	33.2	34.8	31.9	33.1
Social services	46.7	41.7	45.8	42.3	49.4	45.3	46.8	38.8
Health care, sports and social welfare	55.6	58.0	56.6	58.6	49.5	53.1	55.9	52.8
Education, culture and arts, radio, film and TV	40.4	45.5	40.4	45.5	42.7	46.3	45.1	44.4
Scientific research and polytechnic services	33.9	33.5	34.1	33.9	31.5	29.7	30.9	31.0
Governmental and Party agencies, social organizations	22.6	25.2	22.5	25.2	35.0	41.2	30.0	N/A
Others	37.2	36.2	32.3	35.2	45.9	41.7	42.8	35.3

Sources: adapted from *China Statistics Yearbook* 1996: 101–2; *China Statistics Yearbook* 2003: 142–3.

Table 6.2 Women's participation rate (%) in employment at different ages

Age	15–19	20–24	25–29	30–34	35–39	40–44	45–49	50–54	55–59	60–64
Participation rate in 1990	70.50	91.22	91.38	91.21	91.20	88.28	81.10	61.80	44.94	27.21

Source: adapted from the Fourth Census of China 1990.

Note
I have been unable to locate equivalent statistics from the Fifth Census of China conducted at the end of 2000.

state intervention in women's employment has focused largely on protecting women's labour rights and increasing their share in employment quantitatively, whereas little provision exists which aims to ensure and improve the quality of women's employment prospects. Statistics on occupational segregation show that a lower proportion of women are professionals or managers, and that a higher proportion are in clerical and lower-level manual work (see Tables 6.1, 6.3 and 6.4). Women professionals and managers tend to be relatively concentrated in the service sector and public sector organizations where a higher proportion of female workers are also found (see Table 6.5). This is despite the finding that China has 'the least occupational gender segregation' in Stockman *et al.*'s comparative study (1995: 73) of China, Japan, the UK and the USA. Many jobs that are available for women in the service industry (e.g. hotel, catering and entertainment) are relatively short term and targeted at women specifically for their youth and good looks. Despite significant changes in cultural attitudes towards the roles of women and men in China, sex stereotyping and gender segregation persists in educational, vocational and work choices. Men make up the majority of employees in most of the occupations and in state-owned sectors where average earnings tend to be higher with relatively greater levels of job security and workplace welfare benefits. For example, in 1997, 65.3 per cent of males worked in the formal sectors of the economy compared to only 34.7 per cent of females (*China Statistics Yearbook* 1998). Among the 60 million workers who worked in informal, private and individual businesses, over 50 per cent were females (Jiang 2000). Working for the informal sectors is often associated with lower wages, reduced job security, lower employment welfare, reduced training opportunities and even fewer promotion opportunities (see further discussion in Chapter 8). An investigation conducted by the Ministry of Statistics in 1999 shows that the earning gap between men and women is increasing year by year (Jiang 2000). This situation has been exacerbated in recent years as a result of the rapid growth of private companies where wage rewards tend to be kept confidential by employers, adding further difficulties for women to claim for equal pay.

Despite decades of equal opportunities legislation and administrative policies, women have not made significant inroads in management careers

Table 6.3 Percentages of female teachers by level of education

	1980	1985	1990	1995	2000	2002
Percentage of female teachers of total teachers	**32.4**	**35.2**	**38.4**	**42.0**	**46.3**	**48.2**
Institutions of higher education	25.5	26.7	29.1	32.9	38.2	40.7
Specialized and technical colleges	26.6	32.8	38.0	41.6	44.9	47.2
Secondary schools	24.8	28.1	31.5	35.8	41.4	43.3
Vocational secondary schools	13.0	24.8	31.5	37.0	42.9	44.2
Primary schools	37.1	39.6	43.2	46.6	50.6	52.9

Sources: adapted from *China Statistics Yearbook* 2002: 680; *China Statistics Yearbook* 2003: 726.

Table 6.4 Percentage of female managers in governmental organizations in 1990

Level	Total (persons)	Men	Women	Percentage of women
Central	17,546	14,261	3,285	18.7
Provincial	66,795	59,837	6,958	10.4
Municipal	324,197	287,741	36,456	11.2
Township	624,068	582,386	41,682	6.7
Community	324,783	306,052	18,731	5.8
Total	1,357,389	1,250,277	107,112	7.9

Source: adapted from the Fourth Census of China 1990.

and remain concentrated in lower level jobs in all sectors. The distribution of women managers in the management hierarchy takes the shape of a pyramid, with the majority occupying only low-level positions within the organizations. The statistics in Table 6.4 show that only a small proportion of women are in managerial positions in governmental organizations at all levels. The higher proportion of women in central governmental organizations than those in the lower levels of governmental organizations is necessarily a result of the direct state intervention to promote (token) women in order to be seen championing the gender equality policy. The reality is that very few women (fewer than 10 per cent) are in ministerial positions or above. The proportion of women in the lowest levels (township and community) of governmental organizations is even lower where state influence is weak. Women managers are also most likely to be allocated to areas of responsibility which have traditionally been women's realms, such as health, education, culture and welfare.

Table 6.5 Number and proportion (%) of female technical personnel by sector in 2002

	Total technical personnel[a]	Female technical personnel[a]	Female technical personnel as % of total	% of female employees in the total workforce
National total	30,893,045	13,084,009	**42.4**	37.8
Farming, forestry, animal husbandry, fishery	738,259	221,500	30.0	37.1
Mining and quarrying	816,055	287,905	35.3	25.3
Manufacturing	4,329,100	1,477,743	34.1	43.0
Electricity, gas and water production and supply	655,858	203,218	31.0	31.6
Construction	1,545,995	359,891	23.3	17.1
Geological prospecting and water conservancy	291,476	83,864	28.8	27.0
Transport, storage, post and telecom	1,081,954	341,547	31.6	28.3
Wholesale and retail, trade and catering	1,187,674	490,309	41.3	44.9
Banking and insurance	1,617,069	718,150	44.4	45.9
Real estate trade	283,987	101,499	35.7	34.2
Social services	768,052	293,022	38.2	41.7
Health care, sports and social welfare	3,493,546	2,161,382	61.9	58.0
Education, culture and arts, radio, film and TV	11,948,261	5,592,369	46.8	45.5
Scientific research and polytechnic services	869,647	300,032	34.5	33.5
Governmental and Party agencies, social organizations	999,334	344,327	34.5	25.2
Others	266,778	107,251	40.2	36.2

Source: adapted from *China Statistics Yearbook* 2003: 142–3, 238–41.

Notes

[a] Figures in persons.

Gender discrimination in employment and barriers to women's career progression

To a large extent, the long-term state intervention in gender equality in China has been 'positive actions' based upon the recognition of gender differences, with measures devised to address the disadvantages that women experience as a result of those differences (Rees 2000). So far, this has been the predominant conceptual framework underpinning the making of equal opportunity regulations and policies. The extensive provision of equal opportunity legislation and the high female employment rate mask a very central problem in women's employment – barriers to career progression. Although women already make up nearly 40 per cent of those employed in China, few play a part in management, even when defining management in the broadest possible way. State-owned organizations are no exception, where the state is the employer and has a direct responsibility to demonstrate its commitment to gender equality in employment as part of a wider effort towards gender equality in society (Cooke 2003a). Due to the limited data available, we have not been able to obtain meaningful statistics on the private sector in China to enable us to compare practices between the state-owned sector and those of the private sector. More generally, women encounter discrimination at all stages of their employment, from recruitment and promotion, to redundancy and retirement.

Gender discrimination in recruitment

Recruitment is perhaps the most difficult barrier that women face in employment because of the current downsizing of state-owned enterprises, the mass migration of rural labourers and the high unemployment rate. Many employers are unwilling to recruit women because they are deemed 'inferior' to men and because of the 'fuss' and cost associated with women's physiological conditions. To eliminate the problem, the state has issued a number of laws, notably the PRC Law on Protecting Women's Rights and Interests (1992), and the Labour Law of China (1995) which emphasizes the equal rights of men and women in all aspects of employment. However, discrimination of different forms widely exists and is often overtly against women who are at the higher end of the labour market as well as those who are sought for their low-pay and low-skill labour.

Prior to the 1990s when personnel quotas were allocated to the enterprises by the state authority, enterprise managers complained of being forced to take on a much larger proportion of women than they would wish, even in cases where work was not heavy (Granick 1991). In the 1980s and early 1990s when the allocation of graduates was carried out by the state, the reluctance of employers (many of them state-owned organizations) to accept women graduates was already apparent. This problem became much more widespread in the mid-1990s when the state withdrew its role in the allocation. Female university graduates now face more difficulties in obtaining employment than their male counterparts. They often encounter embarrassment, discrimination, degradation and rejection in the process of job seeking, mainly (if not simply) because they are female. No legal mechanism is available to these female graduates who are discriminated against to seek justice.

Although, back in 1951, the Ministry of Personnel issued 'The Announcement of Abolishing the Practice of Rejecting Pregnant Women in Recruiting Workers or Students', women today may not get as far as being pregnant before they are rejected by employers. Many job advertisements (especially in the private manufacturing and service industries) openly specify that women candidates should be single and below the age of 25. Female workers may have to sign an employment contract that contains an unlawful clause: 'The (female) employee will not get married in the period of employment and the employing unit can terminate the contract once she is pregnant.' Despite media exposure and the introduction of administrative regulations to halt these widespread discriminatory practices, they show no signs of ceasing.

Gender discrimination in promotion

As we have seen in the statistics above, a disproportionally small number of women work as senior or middle-ranking state cadres, or in managerial positions in industries (see Cooke (2004d) for further discussion on women in management in different sectors). The lower level jobs in occupations of higher skill/knowledge and higher social status (e.g. doctors, scientists, university lecturers) are usually filled by women who are already the minority group in these occupations. Although a relatively high proportion (about 30 per cent) of women graduates are recruited into governmental organizations annually, women in these organizations, as well as in other types of organizations, progress more slowly than men from the same entry point. Women graduates often have lower status jobs, more limited promotion prospects and earn significantly less than men. Statistics show that women fall behind men in their careers quite early – certainly far too early to put the blame on having children. Even when women find the right track to a management career, they still fail to be promoted as quickly or as frequently as men.

While men who enter the mixed-gender governmental organizations are promoted in accordance with their seniority of age and tenure and eventually rise to the top, women tend to remain in the lower echelons. Men in China also experience greater upward mobility when they change jobs (Bian 1994). So far the majority of women in political careers end up in their positions by coincidence or by default (of being a woman) rather than by their own deliberation. They have little autonomy in determining what they want their career to be, reflecting, perhaps, a directive culture of the state in which 'want me to do' rather than 'I want to do' remains the norm. Government pressure for affirmative action has induced governmental organizations to put more women in managerial ranks, sometimes helping them to break through the glass ceiling. But affirmative action has also led to other kinds of ghettoization: giving women titles without authority (Reskin and Ross 1992). Over 60 per cent of women in managerial positions in governmental organizations were appointed by the higher level of authorities and only about 4 per cent of them won their position through leadership campaigns or recruitment assessment (Yang 1999). For those who have been elected for promotion, the proportion failing to be re-elected in the following session appears to be higher than that for their male counterparts.

Gender discrimination in selection for redundancy

Women are also disadvantaged in the selection for termination of employment. Employment statistics show that the number of women in employment has been declining since 1995 with the proportion of female workers in the whole workforce in 1998 (37.9 per cent) 7 per cent lower than that in 1995 (*China Statistics Yearbook* 1999). This is largely a consequence of the recent state-led initiative of SOE restructuring in which thousands of workers have been laid off or forced into early retirement.

In the waves of redundancy in SOEs and COEs, women rather than men have disproportionally borne the burden of job losses. According to the result of a random survey conducted by the Ministry of Statistics in 1997, the proportion of laid-off female workers was higher (59 per cent) than that of male workers while female workers made up only 39 per cent of the workforce of those enterprises surveyed (Zhang and Zhao 1999). Most of the laid-off women are middle-aged (above 35 years of age). Childrearing responsibility has been one of the main reasons for women (between the age of 25 and 35) being laid off. A significant number of managers responsible for redundancy admitted that they would be inclined to lay off female workers rather than their male colleagues (Wang 2000). Laid-off women are more likely than men to encounter age and gender discrimination in seeking re-employment, with a lower re-employment rate than men. Low pay has also been widely reported as the main reason for laid-off female workers who regained employment to leave their new jobs.

According to a survey carried out by the All-China Women's Federation (ACWF) and the Ministry of Statistics at the end of 2000, 72 per cent of women between the age of 18 and 49 in urban areas were in employment, 16.2 per cent lower than that of 1990. Nearly 50 per cent of laid-off female workers from SOEs believed that they had encountered gender and age discrimination in seeking re-employment whereas about 30 per cent of men felt this way. As for employment status, while almost 100 per cent of women were in full-time formal employment under the state planned economy, this figure had dropped to about 60 or 70 per cent by the end of 2000. There is an increasing proportion of women who are engaged in informal employment with low pay and low employment security such as hourly and temporary work (Lu and Zhao 2002).

Gender discrimination in retirement

Since 1951, China has followed a retirement policy in which female workers in general retire five years earlier than their male colleagues in the same occupations (at the age of 50 for manual female workers and 55 for non-manual). In addition, men and women could take early retirement five years earlier during the 1980s to make room for the young unemployed, many of whom were their offspring. More women, especially those in manual jobs, than men took early retirement under these circumstances. This legislative discrimination against women exists not only at the mass level but also at the elite level where there are obvious incentives for the state to amend the regulations.

In order to retain and use the expertise more effectively, the Ministry of Personnel has, over the past two decades, issued a number of documents (e.g. Document 153/1983; Document 141/1983; Document 5/1990) which stipulate that professorial experts may carry on working till the age of 60 if they wish and if their health permits. These documents also stipulate that a minority of female experts may carry on working after they are 60 if they are needed by their organization (Luo 2000). Although these documents have provided legitimacy for intellectual women to extend their working lives, their opportunity to do so is controlled largely by their employing organizations, which tend to say that their expertise is no longer required. If work is viewed as a right rather than an obligation, then in this case, a female professor or senior engineer is disadvantaged not only relative to her male counterparts, but also to the male clerical workers whose employment right is guaranteed until they are age 60. At an aggregate level, this is a huge waste of expensively trained skill and knowledge for the country.

The situation is worse for female managers and cadres who have to step down from the front line of command at the age of 50 unconditionally, irrespective of their rank (with the exception of ministers). Those who are below a certain rank have to retire at 55, while those who are above may stay until they are 60. This means that few female managers and cadres make it to the top level and, if they do, they are not likely to stay there for long. Again, rare skill and knowledge may be lost as a result of this discriminative policy against female workers. It is exactly for this reason that women are less likely to be trained and promoted by their employers.

More unfairly, at least for the women and their families, women have to endure a substantial reduction in their retirement income since their pension is proportional to their final wage and to their length of service (e.g. 88 per cent for 35 years of service; 82 per cent for 30 to 34 years of service; and 75 per cent for 20 to 29 years of service for civil servants). Therefore, a woman who takes early retirement may have a working life ten years shorter than her male colleague, and her lifelong earnings are likely to be heavily reduced. The statutory regulation of an earlier retirement age for women provides employers with economic incentives to lay off women rather than men because this enables the enterprises to pay them laid-off allowances for a shorter period of time than men before they are eligible for the public pension. Therefore, this policy may carry a double penalty for women.

Causes of discrimination

It is clear that despite the fact that recent laws clearly state that women should have equal employment rights and benefits to men in terms of pay and conditions, promotion opportunities, pay rises and housing, these regulations have not been adhered to in practice. A number of factors are responsible for this state of affairs. These include employers' economic concern, the absence of an effective enforcement mechanism of equal opportunity legislation, gender bias in employment policies, unequal educational opportunities between men and women, traditional social values, and the mentoring system. These are further discussed below.

Employers' economic concern

Gender discrimination in recruitment arises due to employers' economic concerns, a problem that is exacerbated as a result of economic reform. Since the late 1980s, the state has allowed (the state-owned) employing organizations to gradually roll back their extensive employee welfare provisions, such as housing benefit, medical care and pensions, in favour of a tripartite social security system in which the individual employee, the employer and the insurance company all have a financial stake (see Croll (1999) for more details). This decision is an attempt to lighten the crippling financial burden for employers, many of whom would otherwise become bankrupt. However, the development of the social welfare system is severely lagging behind the rapid pace of the externalization of workplace welfare, in part due to insufficient funding from the government. A direct impact of the commercialization of the social security services is the increased cost both for the women themselves and their employers arising from childbearing.

In general, the cost of childbearing borne by the employing organizations is proportional to the number of female workers they employ, since most people entering formal and standard employment are relatively young and tend to stay with the same organization for a relatively long period of time. Therefore, the more (young) female workers an organization employs, the higher the costs it may have to bear. Without the support of an effective social security system to reimburse the reproduction costs, incentives will be understandably low for employing organizations to recruit female workers who have yet to go through their childbearing period. Discrimination against childbearing-age women in their entering employment and later in their exiting employment (as discussed above) will continue, preventing women's participation in employment and career progression.

The introduction of the employment contract system in the mid-1980s and its wide adoption in the 1990s has opened up the opportunity for employers to design their employment contracts with women workers in ways which enable them to avoid employing women during their childbearing period when the costs of keeping these mothers are perceived to be high. This is particularly the case for those sweatshops which thrive on the low-skilled and low-earning young female workers who work excessively long hours. This in turn opens up the possibility of involuntary discontinuity of employment for women throughout their working lives, which further reduces the incentives for employers to recruit, train and promote female workers.

Lack of effective legislation enforcement mechanism

As we can see, state intervention of equal opportunities in women's employment has relied as much on the introduction of administrative policies as on legal regulations which were then (expected to be) implemented by the employing organizations largely owned by the state itself. Legal enforcement of the legislation and policies rarely took place in this employment context. Those organizations which failed to implement the state's instructions properly were to be put right by their supervising departments. This harmonized chief–subordinate relationship between the state which initiates regulations and policies and the employing organizations which carry out orders has been increasingly strained since the 1980s by the growing autonomy of organizations in managing their own business and the changing nature of enterprise ownership. This means that employing organizations are much less controlled and subsidized by the state on the one hand and have to be more responsible for their own finance and business survival on the other. As Tanner points out, '[legislation in China] can no longer be considered as a unified top-down policy making system. Instead it is better thought of as a multi-stage, multi-arena system' (1995: 39). This system is further complicated by the lack of credentials of the Chinese legal intellectuals (Potter 1999), the inability of the courts to enforce their decisions (Lubman 1995), the co-existence of mediation institutions outside the court hierarchy and the various *ad hoc* methods of dispute settlement (Dicks 1989).

The rapid growth of the private sector over the past two decades has created new types of industries with a large number of job opportunities which require a range of skills. Recruitment to these posts is a two-way selection process between the employer and the applicant. These newly emerged businesses, to a great extent, have helped to create, and are in turn affected by, a labour market system in which a higher proportion of women work and where the power of law and order has not yet been able to permeate. While it is not suggested here that the non-state-owned organizations and the more autonomous state-owned enterprises have now all brushed aside the state orders and ignore social justice, they are, none the less, more difficult to reach through the conventional administrative means if they choose to do so. This is largely due to the absence of an effective legal monitoring system.

To a large extent, discriminatory practices intended to avoid the (extra) cost of hiring women (during their reproduction period) are facilitated by the absence of specifications in employment laws in terms of what constitutes discrimination against women, what monitoring mechanism is in place for handling potentially discriminatory actions, and what the penalty is for offenders. Punishments for violating the regulations mainly apply to those unlawful actions which occur during employment and/or in dismissal. Even so, methods of punishment are largely restricted to administrative rather than legal actions, in which violating employers are given official warning, demerit recording and administrative penalties, while victims are awarded financial compensation. This situation is worsened by the low level of awareness of employment regulations by both employers and workers. For example, a survey carried out by the Women's Studies Centre of Fudan University and Shanghai Trade Unions Headquarters showed that only a minority of women workers could correctly identify incidents which violate the employment regulations such as delayed payment of wage and bonus and social insurance. In addition, 40 to 70 per cent of managers did not know how to follow the legal procedures in handling labour–management disputes arising from these incidents (Wang 2000). Lack of legal enforcement and a low level of awareness of employment regulations are characteristic of the employment system in China (see Chapters 7 and 8 for more discussion).

Gender bias in legislation and policies

Two extreme misconceptions of equal opportunity seemingly exist in the way the state has promoted women's working rights and protected women's interests in order to elevate women's position in society as a whole. One is guided by the (mis)belief that what men can achieve can equally be achieved by women, hence Mao's once widely popular motto 'Women hold up half the sky'. Women were once encouraged to perform strenuous tasks which were conventionally carried out by men, such as working at height, in mines and under cold water. In sharp contrast, the other misconception of equal opportunity is based on the firm belief that women are physically and physiologically a weaker sex than men and therefore policies are geared towards accommodating this 'weakness' in order to demonstrate the state's consideration for women.

As such, there is a strong element of gender bias in two aspects of the employment policies – promotion selection and retirement – which discriminate against women directly and indirectly and effectively close off women's access to the top management ladder. Since the 1990s, the state employer has implemented an age-related policy for management training and development with the aim of injecting new blood into its vast management team. Young talent of below 35 years old is selected for management training in succession planning. Any potential candidates above the age of 35 will not be considered for their first promotion. This means that women in their thirties who are ready for career progression when their childrearing responsibilities have eased off may not have the chance to progress as they have passed their 'sell-by date'. For those who are in the junior ranks of management, once they are above the age of 40 for women and 45 for men, they will not be nominated for further promotions. This 'anti-ageing' policy of promotion to keep the management force young results in a decrease in the proportion of women managers over age 45. For example, over 82.6 per cent of female cadres in governmental organizations in 1999 were below 45 years of age (Liu, Y. 2001), compared with about 60 per cent in 1990.

As for the retirement policy, it was first implemented in 1951 as a preferential treatment for women when most jobs involved physical work. As science and technology progressed, manual labour has gradually given way to mental work. Yet the discriminative retirement policy has remained unchanged but is now under serious challenge from pressure groups such as the All-China Women's Federation (Deng 1998; *Guangzhou Daily* 27 August 2000). According to Pan (2002: 130), a motion was proposed in the National People's Congress held in 2001 to extend the retirement age for women. A policy recommendation was also put forward to eliminate the difference in retirement age between women cadres (currently 55) and women manual workers (currently 50) by allowing them to retire at 55. The time frame for its implementation is five years (2006 to 2010). A longer term strategy (2011 to 2020) aims to eliminate the difference in retirement age between men and women, allowing both groups to retire at the age of 60.

Unequal educational opportunities between men and women

To some degree, the disproportional presence of women in the less advantaged sectors and their low presence in the management hierarchy may be explained by their marginally lower levels of education compared to those of men in general. This is true particularly in rural areas and contributes to the much lower proportion of women in management than men and their municipal female counterparts. But women's education levels have been rising at a faster rate than, and approaching, those of men (see Table 6.6).

Similarly, the participation of women in higher education has been increasing at a faster rate than that of men. As the younger generations of women are becoming increasingly well educated and well qualified, (inferior) education level may not be a convincing reason to justify the lack of women on the management ladder, at least for organizations where university degree qualifications have been the requirement for job entry.

Table 6.6 Women's educational levels in China[a]

	1980	1985	1990	1995	2000	2002
Female students as % of total students	43.0	43.4	44.9	46.5	47.1	47.1
Higher educational institutions	23.4	30.0	33.7	35.4	41.0	44.0
Specialized/technical secondary schools	31.5	38.6	45.4	50.3	56.6	56.6
Regular secondary schools	39.6	40.2	41.9	44.8	46.2	46.7
Vocational secondary schools	32.6	41.6	45.3	48.7	47.2	47.6
Primary schools	44.6	44.8	46.2	47.3	47.6	47.2

Sources: adapted from *China Statistics Yearbook* 2002: 680; *China Statistics Yearbook* 2003: 726.

Note

[a] Figures refer to female students as percentage of total students in education in given year.

However, discrimination against women starts in the recruitment selection to higher education institutions, which will have a cumulative effect on their subsequent career advancement. For women to enter the same courses as men in the same universities, they may have to demonstrate better performance records. For example, science, engineering and medical courses are traditionally considered to be subjects for men and dominated by male students. Fewer women apply for those subjects and if they do, they need higher scores than men because it is believed that women's 'abstract thinking ability' will slow down once they are in their late teens. This form of discrimination against women continues when female graduates seek employment, as discussed above.

Traditional social values

There remains a lack of social expectation and, to a certain extent, tolerance that women should be above men, or a wife should be more advanced than a husband in her career. Traditional values in China emphasize that a man should be talented while a woman should be pretty. Women's responsibilities are essentially to be carried out within the family. The centuries-old perception that the man should be the smarter and more successful partner in the (marital) relationship still prevails. A wife's primary duty is to support her husband's career and share the glory of his success. Couples may decide, as many in China do, that the man's career takes precedence (Korabik 1994). This may act as a disincentive for women to seek career advancement. Those who break away from the deeply ingrained normative foundation for gender segregation and subordination may have to pay a price (although it must be stressed here that there are Chinese husbands who give strong support to their wife's work and career, as is found in all societies). 'China's growing ranks of career women are facing increasing difficulties in attracting the country's eligible men, whose idea of the perfect wife is a homemaker, not a breadwinner' (*Sunday Telegraph*, 24 April 2001). The media has also been blamed for casting a negative image on women because it tends to under-report women leaders' achievements and to stereotype women leaders as being unfeminine (Jin 2002).

In addition, women in China have been criticized for their lack of motivation in career progression, lack of confidence, narrow-mindedness, lack of leadership charisma, fear of success, dependence on men, and preference of family over career (e.g. Korabik 1994; Zheng *et al.* 1995; Wang and Du 1999). For example, Wang's survey (Wang, C. 1999) of over 200 women cadres in governmental organizations in Zhejiang Province in 1997 reveals that considerable differences exist in the way men and women weigh up their career and family life balance. Women tend to put their family interests before their careers. These findings in some ways echo Hakim's argument (1996: 119) that the majority of women 'accept the sexual division of labour and treat market work as an additional, secondary activity, to be fitted in with the demands of domestic life'.

All these may be reasons that form part of the difficulties in women's career progression. However, there are other factors at a deeper level which have been little explored as reasons to explain gender inequalities in employment and careers in China. Some of these may be sensitive issues which have been avoided so far in public debate. In particular, social norms which inhibit a mentoring system between men and women may be a strong reason why women have had limited success in moving upward.

Mentor system incompatible with social norms

Mentoring is often seen as a necessary route to career progression in Western literature, a system which many authors (e.g. Kram 1985; Vinnicombe and Colwill 1995) believe is to the disadvantage of women. Kram (1985) defines a mentor as an experienced, productive manager who relates well to a less experienced employee and facilitates his or her personal development for the benefit of the individual as well as for the organization. Although mentoring may either be formal, as part of the formal organizational policy for career development, or informal, as a private arrangement between two individuals which does not necessarily have organizational approval, most mentoring relationships tend to be informal (Klauss 1981).

Kram (1983, 1985) and Burke (1984) suggest that mentors provide both career and psychological benefits to their protégés. They claim that, in career terms, a mentor may advance a career by nominating the protégé for promotion (sponsorship), by providing the protégé with opportunities to display their talent (exposure and visibility), by suggesting strategies for achieving work objectives (coaching), by minimizing involvement in controversial issues (protection) and by the assignment of challenging work. In psychological terms, the mentor may enhance the protégé's sense of competence and identity by giving performance feedback; mentors may serve as role models and they may encourage protégés to experiment with new ideas.

Both formal and informal mentoring is practised in China, far more so the latter. Like many Third World societies, informal social relationships, or '*guanxi*' as they are called in Chinese, provide the lubricant for the Chinese to get through life. 'The Chinese put considerable effort in *guanxi* construction and *guanxi* evasion' in order to obtain 'the kind of convenience and benefit that is often not available through official systems' (Chen 1997: 898). Understandably, in a society where (employment) laws are too 'tentative and inadequate' (Warner 1996b: 782) to ensure fairness at work, people depend on their personal relationships, particularly their contacts with those in power, to get things done and to advance their careers. As Butterfield (1983: 80) observed,

> It was a form of social investment. Developing, cultivating, and expanding one's guanxi became a common preoccupation. The advent of the Communists has not fundamentally changed that. As a result, the

Chinese have turned the art of personal relations into a carefully calculated science.

This presents particular difficulties for women in China. Since few women are in senior management positions to act as their role model or mentor, female managerial candidates may have to look for men to be their mentors. The problem is that the pairing of men and women into mentor–protégé relationships is a gesture prone to accusations of sexual liaison, given the level of intimacy that the relationship naturally engenders (Vinnicombe and Colwill 1995). The potential damage to the pair tends to be far more severe in China where it is almost taboo for a man and a woman to form a close working relationship. Adultery has never been tolerated in the history of China, even in the modern era. The road to success has been littered with talent destroyed by (rumours of) illicit passion, many stories of which were dramatized for moral teaching. An intellectual entrepreneur interviewed by Yang (1996: 20) summarized the pitfalls in career progression insightfully:

> There are many talented women around me, but I can't promote any of them no matter how capable they are. In China, at least for now, men need to be extremely careful of two things if they want to have a successful career. That is money (corruption) and women (adultery or prostitution). This is a lesson drawn from many people's experience.

A typical woman tends to maintain a distant and solely work-based relationship with her peers and subordinates, especially after she is engaged or married. Any indication of friendship beyond a working relationship may be considered improper. This acts as a disincentive as well as a disadvantage for women in seeking career progression.

Women entrepreneurs

Thus far we have discussed women's careers using examples mainly from governmental and public sector organizations. This section will provide a brief summary of women entrepreneurs mainly in the private sector in China. It is difficult to capture precisely the total number of women entrepreneurs in China, given the current radical restructuring of ownership and the rapid growth of the private and self-employed economy (see Chapter 2). An added problem is that national statistics often fail to detail gender differences, especially in the employment-related data, making gender statistics study extremely difficult (Zheng 2001). Nevertheless, we can make a reasonable assumption that the number of women entrepreneurs is growing, albeit not at the same rate as the growth of employment in the non-state sectors. According to the Second National Sample Survey (taken on 1 December 2000) of Women's Social Position in China (The Project Team 2001), 6.1 per cent of women, compared with 8 per cent of men, in urban employment were in managerial positions. This was an increase of 3.2 per cent from that of 1990. Among the women entrepreneurs surveyed who were in the senior managerial positions in enterprises, 95 per cent have been promoted to the managerial positions since the 1980s. In addition, 57 per cent were promoted to their senior managerial positions in the 1990s, a figure close to that of men. Among the women entrepreneurs surveyed, 58 per cent have made investments and established their businesses successfully since the 1990s. This indicates that more and more women are becoming entrepreneurs in the non-state sectors at an increasing speed.

In addition to the lack of statistics, few in-depth studies have been carried out to explore the profiles of women entrepreneurs in China, with the exception of a small number of survey studies. One of these was the ACWF's postal questionnaire survey (ACWF 2000) carried out at the end of 1999, targeting 1,750 women entrepreneurs in non-public sectors in the whole country (with 1,124 returned valid questionnaires, 61 per cent of them from large and medium-sized cities). The survey found that the majority of the entrepreneurs were younger women (90.3 per cent below 50 years of age and 49.3 per cent between ages 36 and 45) and had higher educational levels than the national average for women. The vast majority worked in private-owned enterprises (74.4 per cent), whereas others worked in share-ownership companies including joint ventures (18 per cent) or were self-employed (5 per cent). The majority of the companies in which they worked had between eleven and fifty employees, while less than a quarter of the companies had fewer than ten employees. Over 30 per cent of these companies were in commercial businesses, 16.4 per cent in catering and entertaining, 14.6 per cent in clothes manufacturing, 11.7 per cent in social services, and 11.5 per cent in other light industries. Over 89 per cent of the respondents were married (82.9 per cent were in their first marriage), 84.4 per cent felt that their husbands were a great source of support in their career and 52.7 per cent operated the business together. These respondents felt that they were inferior to men in their physical strength (60.3 per cent), determination (36.9 per cent), readiness to challenge (28.8 per cent), strategic decision making (27.4 per cent), analytical ability (20 per cent) and innovativeness (18.9 per cent). They also believed that quality deficiency of women themselves and social bias were the major causes for the lack of women entrepreneurs in China.

Shi (2002) also conducted a nation-wide survey of over 1,000 women entrepreneurs in November 2001 on the eve of China's accession to the WTO. The study found that the majority of them had little knowledge of the WTO and had done little to prepare their companies for it, although over 50 per cent of them believed that China's accession to the WTO would benefit its economy. About 74 per cent of them were unfamiliar with the labour standards of the International Labour Organization (ILO) and only one-third of those surveyed exported their products directly or indirectly to the international market. It has to be pointed out here that it is unclear if male entrepreneurs would be in a better position were they also surveyed. Shi's survey also revealed, perhaps unsurprisingly, that the majority of women entrepreneurs were relatively young, with one-third between 30 and 40 years old and about half between 40 and 50 years of age. Many of their businesses were registered in the 1990s, indicating that they have had some years of experience in the business. In addition, the majority worked in non-state sectors, with 41 per cent working in private enterprises, 13 per cent in share-ownership firms, 15 per cent in COEs and 28 per cent in SOEs.

Conclusions

This chapter has reviewed the role of the state in improving equal opportunities in employment for women in China. Important legislation has been introduced in the past two decades which is necessarily part of a wider agenda of the Chinese government in promoting social equality between men and women. These innovations have potentially far-reaching effects (Dicks 1989) largely due to the unprecedented political priority of the legal system in China since 1978 (Keith 1997). However, these regulations have not yet brought real equality for the majority of women in China, because it is in precisely the same period that China has been through dramatic political, economic and social changes that have fragmented the employment environment under which the legislation could be enforced relatively effectively.

Moreover, these regulations have not been supported by broader equal opportunity initiatives at organizational level as part of the human resource management strategy. Initiatives to support the career progression of women have been limited to a number of state-sponsored high-profile public campaigns from time to time. More practical initiatives to support working women come from company policies on childcare arrangements. These company policies, however, have largely not been adopted in the private sector. Neither have the majority of employing organizations been promoting, according to public knowledge, gender equality initiatives to remove barriers to women's career progression. One notable exception has been Shell, one of the largest investors in China, which employed about 500 workers. Shell has hard targets for promoting women to senior positions and allows women to work up to the same age as men, thus enhancing the opportunity for their career progression (*China Staff*, June 2002). Current high unemployment rates and the relatively low level of human resource management knowledge may be accountable for the situation. In addition, women have not been able to form a pressure group to exert influence at all levels to advance their case for gender equality in employment and career progression.

To a large extent, the employment pattern of Chinese women reflects the global tradition of female predominance in the lower levels of jobs with fewer promotion opportunities. Women still face considerable challenges in climbing up the managerial ladder. Direct or indirect gender discrimination widely exists explicitly and/or implicitly throughout the process of employment. Certain patterns of gender inequality emerging in China appear to share great similarities with those of Western economies (Stockman 1994). For example, quite often, employers are not discriminating against women in favour of men, but are discriminating among women on the grounds of their childcare responsibilities (Curran 1988).

What tends to be different in China is that Chinese women tend to have a continuous working life without being interrupted by their childcaring responsibilities. This is especially the case for urban younger women who are affected by the one-child policy and where childcare facilities are highly accessible. This provides a context within which women in China with young children may not find themselves confronted with the dual burden of employment and family life to the same extent as women in other countries. It is argued that, for historical reasons, management jobs in the West are designed specifically for married men who are able to cope with the long hours and dedication that management careers demand because they have the support of their full-time home-making wives. If long hours, continuous employment, significant geographical mobility and a series of highly challenging jobs are the price that women in Western countries have to pay for their managerial positions, then the Chinese women candidates for managerial jobs are handicapped by more ideological and organizational factors, at least in the state sector organizations. Like their counterparts in developed countries, Chinese women who are in managerial positions tend to have 'second-class' careers which advance more slowly and disjointedly than those of men (Liff and Ward 2001). The same applies to women in professional occupations such as university lecturers (Cooke 2004d).

Finally, marketization of the economy may bring new opportunities for women to develop their entrepreneurship and managerial careers, in spite of the adversarial situation identified in this chapter. Already, we are seeing a steady increase of women entrepreneurs in the private sector, although the majority of them are in smaller businesses. Equally, China's entry to the WTO will undoubtedly bring new product markets into the economy and therefore new employment opportunities for women. It is predicted that the service sector will be a new focus in China's economic development for which women may be in an advantageous position. However, new skills will be needed if women are to benefit from these career opportunities. There is also a compelling need for further research on the career prospects for women in the private sector in order to compare and contrast their situation with that of their counterparts in the state sector.

7 Minimum wage and implications for equality in employment

Introduction

So far, the discussion of employment and HR practices in this book has focused mainly on those who work in the formal sector and in mainstream employment, although the situations of various disadvantaged groups, such as rural migrant workers and laid-off female workers, have also been discussed to some degree. This chapter takes this discussion further by looking at one of the most important employment aspects – the minimum wage – for workers who may be in a disadvantageous position and at the periphery of the labour market. However, the chapter not only focuses on the minimum wage per se. Rather, by investigating a range of issues concerning the formation, implementation and enforcement of a minimum wage, it reveals a wider picture of inequality and discrimination in employment and organizational policies and of labour segregation along the lines of the urban/rural divide.

The formal introduction of the minimum wage regulations in 1993 by the Chinese government has so far been met with only modest enthusiasm by academics, employers and local governments, measured by the limited public debate it has attracted and the considerable variation in its implementation across the country (Cooke and Rubery 2002). The intention of a minimum wage policy is to enforce social justice through legal intervention. In theory, the introduction of a minimum wage policy should have far-reaching implications for a large developing country such as China by providing a wage floor for the majority of its workers who are clustered at the lower end of the job ladder. In practice, however, the context against which the minimum wage policy is introduced may be complex, and its introduction may serve multiple purposes other than that of providing an acceptable wage level for the low-paid workers and the associated reduction of wage discrimination in the labour market (Rubery 2003). This objective may also be circumscribed by other priorities such as that of increasing employment (ILO 1988).

There has been a moderate debate among academics in China on the plausibility and implications of the introduction of the minimum wage regulations (e.g. Chen and Wang 1994; Li 1995; Sai and Yin 1995). Opinions are inevitably divided between those who support the regulations and those who are against them, echoing the views expressed in Western literature (see review by Rubery 2003). Supporters (e.g. Sai and Yin 1995) argue that, in the transitional period in which non-state-owned organizations are growing rapidly and market competition is intensifying, a minimum wage system can play a positive role in:

- regulating employers' behaviour;
- protecting workers' interests;
- improving the quality of labour supply by raising labour standards;
- improving the management of enterprises and productivity by increasing labour costs.

Others believe that a relatively high minimum wage level can benefit the economy in the long term by forcing those sectors which rely on intensive labour with outdated technology and low productivity to invest in production improvement. However, there are other Chinese scholars who contend that minimum wage regulations are contrary to the development of a market economy. For example, Chen (2001) argues that under a process of moving to a market economy, wages cannot be an outcome of 'regulations' but must be determined by the market forces of 'demand and supply'. Minimum wage regulations, according to this perspective, will only lead to the unemployment of low-waged workers, reductions in China's international competitiveness, or substitution between other elements of the total remuneration package. Such approaches fail to identify the importance of rules and regulations in developing fair and efficient markets and assume that, even in a context of excess labour supply, wages can be determined purely by the forces of demand and supply.

This chapter first examines the pressure for the introduction of a minimum wage policy and which groups of workers are in need of wage protection in the transition to a market economy. It then explores the potential implications of a minimum wage policy for employers and different groups of workers. This is followed by a discussion of the barriers to and attitudes towards the implementation of the minimum wage regulations. The chapter then focuses on the tensions between groups of low-paid workers in the labour market and how certain groups may actually be disadvantaged should the minimum wage policy be enforced. The chapter highlights the gender implications of the implementation of a minimum wage policy as well as the urban–rural divide in the labour market, two thorny issues that cannot be easily resolved in the employment system.

Pressure for minimum wage regulations

The pressures for the introduction of minimum wage regulations come from the need to protect the basic living standard of several groups of workers who emerged as new groups of working poor as a result of China's deepening economic and social reform in the past twenty years. In particular, three groups of workers have attracted the most attention for their low pay and/or poor working conditions (see Table 7.1 for a summary of their employment conditions).

First, there are the rural migrant workers who flood into town to make a living for themselves and their family in the country. They concentrate in the private and informal sectors where both employment security and wage levels are generally low, as outlined in Chapter 2. These undemanding workers are largely unorganized and unaware of their labour rights. This grossly excessive supply of labour has provided employers with every opportunity for exploitation in terms of wage levels, working hours, working and living conditions, health and safety, and other employment benefits and protections.

A second group are the workers whose enterprises (many of them state owned or collectively owned) are in bad debt and/or no longer engaged in production activities. For example, in 1993 the Labour Bureau of Beijing City carried out a survey on sixty-three enterprises which were still in operation but with poor financial returns. Of the 23,000 employees surveyed, 4,658 of them (20.3 per cent) had a monthly income of less than 200 yuan, whereas the minimum monthly income required for a worker and his or her family was, according to the guidelines of the Beijing Statistics Bureau, about 200 yuan (Wang and Niu 1996).

The third group are the laid-off workers whose employment relations with their employers still exist but who are no longer needed for work by their employers. This group of workers grew considerably during the late 1990s as a result of the far-reaching restructuring of the ailing SOEs (see Chapter 3 for further discussion). This group of workers experience considerable differences in the benefits they receive from their employers. Those who belong to profit-making enterprises have relatively few problems in getting their laid-off wage and health insurance from their employers, whereas those whose employers are in bad shape do not have guaranteed income or benefits. An additional problem faced by this group of workers is that they tend to encounter problems in seeking re-employment. This is particularly the case for those laid-off men who are above 50 years of age and laid-off women who are above 40 (known as the '4050 phenomenon'). It is estimated that there are over three million unemployed who are in this category who make up nearly one-third of the laid-off workers (*Yangcheng Evening News*, 14 August 2003). Even if successful, their new jobs are likely to be of poor quality because this group of workers tend to be low-skilled (or possess skills which are not marketable) and middle-aged. For example, the re-employment rate for laid-off workers was 50 per cent in 1998. This figure dropped to 42 per cent in 1999, and decreased further to 35 per cent in 2000. In the first six months of 2001, only 10 per cent were re-employed (the Project Team of Social Situation Analysis 2002). In many cases, this

Table 7.1 Employment conditions of major groups of workers on low pay

	Urban enterprise workers	Laid-off workers	Migrant rural workers[a]
Employment regulation protection	Labour law	Labour law	Labour law
Social welfare coverage	Extensive social welfare (e.g. health, pension, unemployment, and minimum living standard insurance) provision but may not be enforced by employers due to poor financial health	Extensive social welfare (e.g. health, pension, unemployment, and minimum living standard insurance) provision but may not be enforced by employers due to poor financial health	Little social welfare coverage, if any. Tendency of employers not to observe legislative requirements even when they are applicable
Workplace representation, labour organization and source of protection	Trade unions Workers' Representatives Congress Local labour authority Women's Federation	Trade unions Re-employment centre organized by employer or local labour authorities Women's Federation Local community committee	Trade unions (low level of union recognition and even less in strength) Collective bargaining in *ad hoc* manner Local administrative authorities
Cost of living	Higher than migrant rural workers because of independent housing and catering arrangements	Higher than migrant rural workers because of independent housing and catering arrangements	Relatively low with collective catering and living accommodation provided by employers

Priority of policy maker and enforcer	Dependent on pressure exerted by the workers	Relatively high because of political implications as a result of the collective outcry of discontented laid-off workers	Relatively low because of urban–rural divide in which rural workers are considered second class to their city counterparts
Cost of hiring	Higher than migrant rural workers because of higher wage demand and social security duty	Higher than migrant rural workers because of higher wage demand and social security duty	Lower than urban workers because of lower wage, economies of scale in catering and accommodation provision to subsidize low wage
Advantages in the labour market	Relatively more skilled, with higher educational qualifications	Relatively more skilled, with higher educational qualifications	Generally younger and physically stronger
	More social network	More social network	More willing to accept hard work and longer hours
	Higher priority given by the government	Higher priority given by the government	More willing to accept low wages
			(Potentially) higher productivity for like work

Note
[a] Refer to those workers who are permanent city residents and work in state-owned or collectively owned enterprises.

group of workers are in competition with rural migrant workers in the job market (see further discussion below).

In addition to these three large groups of workers, there are other groups whose minimum wage may not be guaranteed. For example, as a result of the withdrawal of the direct state intervention in the wage determination in SOEs since the 1980s, enterprises have introduced an increasing variety of reward packages in order to link individual performance and reward more closely with organizational performance. There were also enterprises which deliberately suppressed workers' wages through random fines and penalties related to their production activities.

Minimum wage regulations in China

In 1984, the Chinese government announced its recognition of the 'Minimum Wage Treaty' implemented by the ILO in 1928. But it was not until 1993 that the first piece of administrative regulation on minimum wage (the 'Enterprises Minimum Wage Regulations') was drawn up and issued by the Ministry of Labour. This administrative policy was taken up by local governments which have been given the autonomy to formulate their own policy tailored to the local economy and employment situation. The minimum wage policy was ultimately legislated in the Labour Law of China (1995).

According to the Labour Law, employing organizations must pay their workers a minimum wage set by their local governments, usually at municipal level. 'Minimum wage' refers to a wage which should be sufficient to cover basic living costs for the workers themselves as well as their family members, usually based on the minimum cost of living for the worker plus 50 per cent (for half of each family member). The Labour Law asserts that employers should not include subsidies such as canteen and travelling supplements, benefits in kind, nightshift premiums and overtime as part of the wage when calculating the minimum wage. The Labour Law also specifies that the level of minimum wage of each local area should be co-determined through negotiation between the local government, the trade unions and the representatives of the enterprises. When determining the level of the minimum wage, the parties should take into consideration the local standard of the minimum cost of living for the worker and the average number of family members whom the worker needs to support, the average wage in the area, the level of productivity, the employment rate and other economic conditions. Employers are also required to pay workers their minimum wage during their statutory rest and holiday periods.

Local governments are given the power to increase the level of minimum wage to match the rising costs of living, usually on an annual basis and no more than once a year. For example, in 2001, Beijing local authorities increased the minimum hourly rate from 2.4 yuan to 2.6 yuan, and the minimum monthly wage from 412 yuan to 435 yuan. Guangdong Province carried out similar adjustments in 2001, which saw a minimum of a 7 per cent increase of its minimum wage. As a result, the content and coverage of the minimum wage regulations vary from area to area in the country.

Enforcement mechanisms

As is the case with the design of the minimum wage policies, the ultimate responsibility for enforcing them lies with the local governments. Local labour authorities of all levels (from township to province) are responsible for the monitoring and inspection of the implementation of minimum wage policies by local enterprises. They are also responsible for dealing with specific problems which emerge in the implementation and for modifying the policies based on the local situation. In addition, trade unions of all levels are given the power to monitor the implementation of minimum wage policies within the legal framework. In theory, minimum wage regulations provide a legal weapon for trade union officials in their role of protecting workers' interests.

Those workers who receive less than the minimum wage from their employers can also submit applications to the local labour administrative and monitoring authorities for the labour tribunal. Employers who are found guilty of violation will be ordered to backdate the pay and provide an additional 25 per cent by way of compensation. Some local governments (e.g. Henan Province) even require the guilty employers to pay an additional penalty of between one and five times the actual amount owed to the workers and/or the authorities.

Employers tend to violate the minimum wage policy in one of two ways. One is to include subsidies in the wage calculation; the other is to set unachievable performance targets in the labour contract so that the worker can only earn a wage less than the minimum wage threshold. This normally happens to workers who are on a piece rate or on a deduction wage system (i.e. wage proportional to tasks completed).

It was reported that, as a result of the efforts made by the employment legislation monitoring organizations, 3.9 million rural migrant workers were issued employment permits (without which their employment status would not be recognized) by their employing organizations in 1998. Five million workers were issued their employment contracts, and 2.4 million workers were paid their retroactive wage in total of 0.67 billion yuan which were illegally withheld by their employers (The Ministry of Statistics 1999).

Problems in the formation and implementation of the minimum wage policy

The introduction of the minimum wage regulations has met with a number of problems both at the policy formation level and the implementational level. At the policy level, the Labour Law (1995) asserts that the minimum wage regulations are applicable to enterprises of different economic nature and the workers who receive their wages from these enterprises, including the self-employed businesses. However, it does not provide any details on the minimum wage regulations in term of who should pay, who should be paid and at what level, and how it should be calculated. Instead, local governments are given the power to determine these details based on their local economic characteristics. Grey areas and inconsistencies thus exist in the minimum wage policy statements manifested by local governments, which are often written in ambiguous terms and are therefore open to (mis-) interpretation, leading to legal caveats. At the implementation level, the caveats created by the ambiguity of the policy offer considerable scope for discretion by employers to decide whether they should meet the minimum wage requirements. This discretion is further accommodated by labour regulation inspectorates who, for various reasons, may be more sympathetic to employers than the workers.

Who should be covered by the minimum wage?

It is not always clear who should be covered by the minimum wage. Although some governments specify in their policy statements which groups of workers are not covered by the regulations, the majority of the governments do not provide any specific guidance. For those which specify beneficiaries of minimum wages, no explanation may be given as to why certain groups should be excluded, nor is there any mechanism for the affected workers to challenge the fairness of the decision. Although not legally clarified, some people suggest that disabled workers and live-in nannies should be excluded from the protection of the minimum wage regulations (Liu 1999). They claim that enforcing a minimum wage for disabled workers will have a negative effect on their employment opportunities, as employers will prefer to employ able-bodied workers given the same conditions. Such belief is at odds with the objectives of the minimum wage policies which aim to protect the weaker groups of workers against employers' opportunistic behaviour. As for the live-in nannies, it is believed that their work content and intensity vary considerably and it is therefore difficult to specify their wage level.

Who should pay a minimum wage?

It is not always clear which employers should implement a minimum wage policy. For example, enterprises in financial difficulties are temporarily exempt from the minimum wage regulations during their restructuring period. Those enterprises deemed to be 'in grave operational difficulties' are allowed to delay their wage payments to their workers, even though these 'difficulties' do not necessarily mean the enterprises' inability to pay wages. However, no specifications are made to quantify these terms. Nor is there any clarification as to whether those enterprises unable to pay minimum wages should be classified as 'in stoppage' or 'bankrupt' (see further discussion below). A major problem associated with this ambiguity is that only those enterprises which are in profit are required to implement the minimum wage regulations. This means that about 60 per cent of the SOEs do not have to comply with the regulations (Chen and Zhang 1999).

The greatest ambiguity and debate in terms of what kinds of enterprises should pay the minimum wage is perhaps that concerning the TVEs. It is argued (e.g. Fu 1995) that TVEs, small private enterprises, enterprises organized by the street community, and self-employed businesses which employ workers should be exempt from the minimum wage regulations. Among these forms of economic entity, TVEs are the most debated as to whether or not they should implement the minimum wage regulations, even though the size, level of technology and productivity in some TVEs surpass that of SOEs. Those who argue against the enforcement of a minimum wage in TVEs maintain that TVEs play a crucial role in providing employment opportunities for a large number of unskilled rural workers whose wages in the TVEs will almost certainly be higher than what they can earn by undertaking agricultural work (Fu 1995; Sai and Yin 1995). A wage intervention may force these enterprises out of business or reduce their scale of production, ultimately causing unemployment to the rural workers (also see Chapter 2).

At what level should the minimum wage be set?

The impact of the minimum wage policies on the workers, the employers, the labour market and the economy of the country is dependent on the level of the wage set by the state. This is a particularly important issue for China due to its vast geographical spread with considerable differences in the cost of living and the level of economic activities between different regions.

It is argued (Sai and Yin 1995) that there is a danger that the minimum wage, if set at too high a level, might trigger an upward wage spiral in enterprises who currently pay well above the minimum wage, as they may feel under pressure to maintain differentials. Therefore, a high minimum wage level will lead to a vicious circle of wage growth and price growth and trigger inflation (Sai and Yin 1995). At a national level, a high minimum wage level may also reduce China's global competitiveness since many foreign investors are attracted to China primarily for its low labour costs (Sai and Yin 1995).

Another issue in the determination of the level of a minimum wage relates to what the optimal level of wage should be for each geographical/administrative area in order to reflect the living standard of the area without overwhelming the area with rural labour on the one hand and deterring (potential) investors on the other. In general, the minimum wage in China is approximately 30 per cent of the average wage (full-time and mixed gender) of the whole country (Lu 2000). The average wage is calculated based on the basic wage which makes up only between 50 to 80 per cent of the total work-related income of the worker, depending on the financial performance of a company (see Chapter 4 for wage compositions).

There are significant differences in the average wages between the poor and the rich provinces in China. The gap between the highest and the lowest average is even more striking. For example, the national average wage in 2001 was 10,870 yuan. Shanghai had the highest average wage of 21,781 yuan (over 200 per cent of the national average) among the thirty-one provinces and autonomous cities, whereas Anhui Province (an adjacent province of Shanghai City) had the lowest average figure of 7,908 yuan (less than 73 per cent of the national average) (*China Statistics Yearbook* 2002). These differentials in the average wages between provinces inevitably have implications for the level of minimum wages.

How should the minimum wage be calculated?

A further issue related to the varying levels of minimum wages across different regions in the country is the lack of consistency between governments as to how the minimum wage should be calculated (see Table 7.2). Wages are normally calculated and referred to on a monthly basis in China. Some local

Table 7.2 Minimum wage levels of selected cities and provinces

City or province	1995		2000	2001
	Average wage^a	Minimum wage$^{a, b}$	Average wage^a	Minimum wage$^{a, b}$
Tienjin (city)	542	210	1040	412, 402
Jiangsu	495	210, 175, 140	858	430, 360, 250
Anhui	384	180, 150	582	340, 320, 310, 290, 260, 240
Hunan	400	170 (adjustable ± 20%)	677	325, 305, 285, 265, 245, 225
Guangxi	425	200, 190, 180, 170	638	275, 260, 235, 210
Hainan	445	280, 230, 180	617	400, 350, 300
Shanghai (city)	773	270	1544	490
Shenzhen (city)	1023	380	1920	574, 440
Shandong	345	170 (adjustable ± 20%)	731	370, 340, 310, 280, 260

Sources: adapted from Wang and Niu 1996; *China Statistics Yearbook* 1996, 2001 (end-of-year figures); Market (Newspaper), Internet version 13 September 2001.

Notes
[a] Figures in yuan and refer to wage per calendar month.
[b] Each province may have several grades of minimum wage due to varying living costs in different parts of the province. The most notable difference is that of Guangdong Province which has the biggest gap.

governments specify the number of days in a month on which the calculation of the minimum wage should be based whereas other local governments provide few specifications for guidance. Some specify hourly rates based on the minimum daily rate divided by eight hours, whereas others do not regulate the number of rest days in a given month.

Regional inconsistency also arises due to the fact that labour authorities apply different criteria in their calculation of the minimum wage level (Fu 1995; Lin 2000). For example, the minimum wage in Shanghai City in 2001 was set at 490 yuan per month, i.e. 27 per cent of the monthly average wage of all workers in Shanghai (1,815 yuan). In Tienjin City, the minimum wage of 2001 was 412 yuan per month, 35 per cent of its workers' average wage (1,192 yuan) of that year (*China Statistics Yearbook* 2002).

A related problem is that some local governments do not specify how frequently they should review and adjust (upgrade) their minimum wage policies. Some do not make an adjustment for several years whereas others upgrade their minimum wage level annually, albeit at small margins. In the year 2000, fifteen regions in the country adjusted their levels of minimum wage (*Market* 2001). Some governments grant only a small margin of increase which is not sufficient to compensate for inflation (Diao 2000).

Impact of and attitudes towards the minimum wage policy

The dilemma of the state towards minimum wages

Since the mid-1990s, the Chinese government has been facing increasing pressure to create employment opportunities for the large number of urban workers who have been made redundant and an even larger number of rural workers surplus from the land. A minimum wage will benefit those workers made redundant by their SOE employers, since the majority of them are semi-skilled 'older' workers (i.e. above 35 years of age, by the Chinese standard). It will also benefit the rural migrant workers whose earning will undoubtedly be lower if they remain in farm work. Private businesses, foreign businesses and joint ventures are the likely employers to absorb these workers. Recognizing the link between poverty and agricultural work, Premier Zhu announced in 1997 that towns and small cities would be allowed to expand to provide more job opportunities for China's farmers. With an urbanization rate of only 30 per cent, there is a huge potential for further urbanization given the right policy conditions. However, it is here that the tension in the balance of the social policy is at its highest between the demand for the absorption of rural workers into the city and the need to provide a wage floor to protect a minimum work and living standard.

Employers' attitude towards minimum wages

It is not clear to what extent the minimum wage policy has impacted on employers and workers due to the absence of detailed labour statistics and relevant reports. However, given the lack of bargaining power of the low-wage workers (unorganized and excessive supply in the labour market), the significant policy loopholes and the slack enforcement mechanism, there is plenty of scope for enforcement to improve the effectiveness of the regulations.

It is not uncommon to find private enterprises which can afford the minimum wage but are unwilling to do so because of their profit drive. These employers only implement the minimum wage regulations reluctantly in order to avoid heavier costs which may fall upon them as a consequence of violating the regulations (e.g. fines). There are also those who violate the regulations because they disagree with the principle, at least so they claim. According to a recent investigation conducted by the labour authority of Nanjing (one of the largest cities in northeast China), some of the employing organizations ignored the minimum wage regulation, believing that it was irrelevant to the market competition (www.molss.gov.cn 2001). One contractor of a construction site was reportedly shocked when, asked about the minimum wage in an interview, he said that workers should be paid only when there was work for them. Another interviewee, a marketing manager of a medical company, argued eloquently that there was not, nor should there be, an upper limit or minimum wage protection for his salespeople. 'Those who were capable could earn more than 10,000 yuan a month and those who were incapable might earn nothing. How could it be called market economy if there were a minimum level?' (www.molss.gov.cn 2001)

In other cases employers might have difficulties in paying wages at all if their factories were out of production or in debt, a typical case for the collectively owned enterprises (Cooke and Rubery 2002). In principle the introduction of the minimum wage regulations offers a safety net for workers whose enterprises are in a poor financial situation and provides a legal document to support workers to bargain their (minimum) wage with their employers. However, these measures are not always effective, as enterprises in financial difficulties may still find it difficult to implement or will be unwilling to implement the minimum wage regulations.

The non-adherence to the minimum wage regulations may also be a result of the employers' (and the workers') ignorance of the labour regulations in general.

Tolerance of employers' unlawful behaviour by affected workers

It is not only the case that many workers have a low level of awareness of their employment rights but also, even when they are aware that their employers have not paid them a minimum wage, most workers choose to put up with it rather than seek legal protection because of their fear of job losses as a consequence of their complaint. More particularly, low wages tend to be more tolerated by two groups of workers who need the protection, perhaps more so than other groups – young workers and rural migrant workers. Although the Labour Law (1995) does not specify any age limit in the application of the minimum wage regulations, it is likely that reduced wages for young workers would be quite acceptable in China for two reasons. First, China is a society which has a long tradition of respecting and rewarding seniority (Cooke 2002). Second, most young single people live with their parents who are keen to see their offspring in employment in order to prevent them from going astray. The living costs for these people are therefore lower than if they lived on their own, allowing for the payment of low wages. In addition, being in employment is seen as an opportunity for young workers to receive training and gain experience of both work and life. The reasons why rural workers are willing to accept low wages will be discussed later in this chapter.

Attitude of local labour regulation inspectorates

The implementation of the minimum wage regulations by the local governments was somewhat slow when they were first introduced. Chen *et al.* (1996) found that the labour authorities appeared to be reactive and sympathetic to employers in enforcing the minimum wage policies. They were also guilty of a slippery interpretation of the regulations and had little institutional back-up when enforcing those regulations. They only dealt with the violating employers if the affected workers reported them.

One reason for the lax enforcement of the minimum wage regulations may be to do with the rural migrant workers. The majority of beneficiaries of minimum wages would be rural labourers if the minimum wage policy were to be implemented in its broadest sense. However, municipal officials may be less sympathetic towards them and design social policies in favour of city residents. This is in part because city administrators see rural migrant workers as an additional source of urban disorder who cause administrative problems in the city, such as birth control, environment protection, increased crime rates and traffic problems. In addition, it has been noted that some developing countries accommodate lower labour standards as part of a conscious strategy to attract foreign investments into export processing zones (Rubery 2003). This is most possibly true in some areas in China where sweatshops exploiting rural migrant workers with long working hours and below-minimum wage rates are endemic in TVEs and foreign investments.

Minimum wages and tensions between groups of low-paid workers

Minimum wage legislation in principle should provide a floor to the labour market, thereby reducing differentiation among labour market groups, and aiding the reduction of wage discrimination – whether based on gender, place of origin (rural migrants versus urban workers), race, age or other factors. However, where minimum wage regulation is neither comprehensive nor fully enforced, as is the case in China, the outcome may be also to increase competition and tension between labour market groups (Cooke and Rubery 2002).

The biggest tension and the greatest difficulty in the implementation of the minimum wage policy is perhaps that to do with the two largest groups of workers who may benefit from the policy – the laid-off workers and the rural migrant workers. These two groups of workers are in some ways highly substitutable and homogeneous in the labour market, although it has been argued (e.g. Meng 2000) that rural–urban migrant workers are not responsible for urban unemployment in China. Their situation has been discussed in general earlier in this chapter, but their labour market positions will be further discussed here.

Rural migrant versus laid-off workers: competition across the urban–rural divide

The large-scale migration of rural workers to the cities for work is a relatively new phenomenon emerging in the past two decades, although there have been previous waves of migration since 1949. There are now somewhere between 80 and 120 million migrants linking the urban to the rural and who are transforming both landscapes (Saich 2001). According to national statistics, the average age of these rural migrant workers is 33.6 years. About 70 per cent of them are between the ages of 15 and 49, with 30.7 per cent between 25 and 34 (Hu 2001). Women constitute a relatively high share of rural migrants but they tend to be migrants before marriage, the majority between the ages of 18 and 25.

The push from the decline in farming incomes and the pull of better paid work in the cities have led many younger people to abandon the harsh conditions of rural labour for higher wages in the cities. While still some 75 per cent of China's population are registered as living in the countryside, farming families are increasingly reliant on non-farm sources of income. This may come from remittances from migrants, or from wage labour in TVEs, or from household businesses. In 1996 over three-quarters of the basic incomes of agricultural workers came from this latter source (Benewick and Donald 1999). As the saying goes in the rural communities: 'The earlier you go to town, the earlier you become rich. The later you go to town, the later you become rich. But if you don't go to town, you will never get rich.'

Low pay is necessarily a relative concept (Rubery 1995). Whether rural migrants should be considered low paid depends in part upon the reference point for comparisons (Cooke and Rubery 2002). If a comparison were made between migrant rural workers and other urban workers, this would indicate that rural labourers are very low paid. But if the comparison were between migrant rural workers and rural farmers, or between rural families with and without migrant workers, the result would be very different. For example, the national average income of migrant rural workers was 240.3 yuan in 2000 (The Hunan Team of the Agricultural Research Team of Ministry of Statistics 2001). In Hunan Province, the average income of migrant rural workers (including seasonal migrant workers) was 4,339 yuan in 2000, more than double the average net income of farmers in the same province. There were considerable income differentials between rural households which did not have migrant workers (with an annual average of 6,256 yuan) and those which did (with an annual average of 7,508 yuan) (Hu 2001).

Moreover, the process of rural migration is having varying regional affects. According to China's first national agricultural census published in 1998, 'there were five times as many farmers engaged in private ventures in the east than in the west (of the country), and four times as many individual household enterprises. Thirty-three per cent were engaged in non-agricultural production in coastal areas, compared with 15 per cent in the east' (Saich 2001: 152).

It has been widely noted by Western scholars on China (e.g. Croll 1999; Saich 2001) that China is pursuing a highly non-egalitarian development strategy at the expense of the rural population. For the past five decades, the social welfare provision for rural China has been a separate and much more restricted system with no social insurance, few subsidized services available to farmers and their families and little more than a minimal safety net guaranteed for the childless elderly and other vulnerable categories of lone persons (Croll 1999).

While in theory the minimum wage policy covers those who are in low-paid employment, many of whom are migrant rural workers, the largest group which benefits from the minimum social insurance benefits are those who have been made redundant by their (state) employers. Rural workers have yet to gain their social recognition and status from their municipal 'big brothers' and gain equal social welfare protection from the state. According to the 1999 national survey on the basic situations of urban residential households, the average income of members of urban households in the month of August was 400.2 yuan, whereas that of rural households (living in the city) was 300.1 yuan. In addition, a respective 37.4 per cent, 12 per cent and 14.2 per cent of urban household heads had taken up pension, unemployment and medical insurance respectively, whereas only 9.9 per cent, 2.2 per cent and 3.1 per cent of their rural counterparts had done so (Huang *et al.* 2002).

Are rural migrant workers competing with laid-off workers in towns?

The differences in standards of living between rural and urban on the one hand and between rural families with and without migrants on the other highlight the potential for pressure on wage levels at the bottom of the Chinese labour market, associated with rural migration. These workers are acting as a very large reserve army of labour, supported in part by access to an extended family but also conditioned by their experience in the countryside of a low standard of living without access to social security. This competition for low-level jobs in the urban areas comes from both rural migrant men and rural migrant women, although the types of low-level jobs taken by these two groups are likely to conform to sex-role stereotyping. Moreover, some of the jobs that the rural migrants are taking are not necessarily jobs that urban laid-off workers would be willing to take due to their low pay and low social status. Thus the competition between rural migrants and urban laid-off workers intersects urban/rural social distinctions as well as gender divisions (Cooke and Rubery 2002).

There are three scenarios in the relationships between the rural workers, the laid-off workers and the enterprises or urban residents who require domestic services (Zhang and Huang 2000):

1   Jobs where there is genuine competition between the two groups, insofar as rural workers are doing jobs which the laid-off workers are willing to do, and whose demand for higher wages (than what the rural workers ask for) is within the affordability of or willingness to pay by the enterprises or urban residents.
2   Jobs which are laborious and dirty and which the laid-off workers are not willing to do. For example, street cleaning is considered to be a laborious job which enjoys a very low social status. Many urban workers will prefer to remain unemployed rather than take up such a job. In these situations, rural workers are hired at relatively high wage levels to perform the tasks.
3   Jobs which both groups of workers are willing to do, but the demand for higher wages by the laid-off workers (due to their higher living standards and therefore costs) makes it difficult for enterprises or urban residents to afford to employ them and they will therefore give the jobs to rural workers. These are predominantly jobs in the community and domestic services. These jobs are highly sensitive to wage price and will disappear as rural workers leave the posts. For example, urban residents may decide to outsource their housework because it is cheap to hire rural workers to do it. Once the rural worker leaves the post, the tasks may be taken back in-house to be performed by household members.

There is a wide difference in labour costs for employers in China between hiring an urban and a rural worker. According to the calculation of the Beijing Labour Bureau, to employ an urban worker, an employer in Beijing has to pay 1 per cent of the wage bill on unemployment insurance, 6 per cent on health insurance, 19 per cent on pension insurance and 5 to 10 per cent on administration fees for temporary work. This amounts to a total of 31 to 36 per cent of the wage for hiring an urban worker, whereas the employer merely needs to pay an administration fee of 15 yuan for hiring a rural worker (Zhang and Huang 2000). The higher employment costs as a result of increased labour standards cannot be borne by consumers in the form of higher prices (Lee 1997), since the general level of purchasing power in the country is still low and sensitive to price changes. This is especially the case for employers engaging in the production of low value-added products. In the absence of a nation-wide co-ordination of full implementation of the minimum wage regulations, most of the immediate costs of adherence to the regulations would have to be borne by individual employers. In China it is also difficult for employers to offset the cost of the minimum wage through work intensification by reducing the number of hours given for set tasks such as cleaning. The conveyor belts for these workers have already been switched to their maximum speeds, with or without the minimum wage. Many work twelve to sixteen hours per day with few rest days throughout the year. Further work intensification is therefore not a practical option in order to recoup costs.

In general, rural migrant workers have comparative advantages over urban workers because they are cheaper to hire, more willing to work longer hours and in a poor working environment. The cost of living for rural migrant workers tends to be low and is usually provided by employers. It is not unusual for employers to provide uniforms, transport, meals and accommodation for the workers to subsidize their low wages. The employers benefit from the economies of scale and from minimizing time allowed for the workers' production capacity, whereas the workers benefit from the convenience that the provision brings and can work longer hours to maximize their earnings. According to the employment statistics of 2000, 56.9 per cent of migrant workers worked more than fifty hours a week and another 37.6 per cent worked between forty and forty-nine hours a week. In comparison, only 17.8 per cent of urban residents worked more than fifty hours a week and 78.6 per cent worked between forty and forty-nine hours a week (Hu 2001). On the whole, the total disposable income of the rural workers who are on a lower hourly rate and not protected by the minimum wage regulations may be higher than those low-wage urban workers who are covered by the minimum wage but have to bear higher costs of living.

In some senses, the rural migrant workers are not in direct competition with the laid-off workers. Rather, they are taking jobs that their urban 'big brothers' would not consider in addition to those jobs which are specifically created for them. To a greater extent, what these rural migrant workers demand is a job with a wage and not so much job quality or (higher) wage level. It is the combination of low wages and poor working conditions, with high productivity coupled with the suppression of basic labour rights (e.g.

collective bargaining) by the employers, that creates the rich opportunities for offering employment to this group of workers. However, inequality in pay in specific work and in employment in general not only expresses itself in the urban and rural divide, but also in the gender divide.

Wage regulations and gender implications

It has been noted in Chapter 1 that gender-related statistics in China are very limited; nevertheless, we can make reasonable assumptions from the sporadic data that there are strong implications of low pay for gender, mostly to the disadvantage of women, especially those in labour-intensive manual occupations and those in the low-paid service industries. The disadvantaged position of women as compared to that of men in their employment characteristics in terms of the types of jobs they do, the hierarchical positions they take and the wage levels at which they are paid have been discussed in detail in Chapter 6. Even when men and women are doing the same jobs, men tend to get higher wages than women, as is shown in Table 7.3.

As was discussed in previous chapters, the restructuring of the state sector has undoubtedly led to a deterioration of women's position, since women have been disproportionately subject to lay-off. As a consequence female

Table 7.3 Average wage for selected occupations for October 1998 (figures in yuan)

Industry and occupation	Average wage (m and f)	Average wage for male	Average wage for female
Coal-mining	549.6	562.5	422.4
Clothing industry	568.9	680.2	539.8
Tailor	632.6	842.0	541.3
Operative	555.0	622.9	539.5
Wood processing	680.9	668.4	710.5
Chemical industry	847.3	864.3	819.0
Operative	756.0	736.6	784.0
General worker	709.3	719.7	693.0
Construction industry	849.9	896.3	691.8
Retail industry	710.8	761.4	685.3
Cashier	697.3	436.2	776.5
Shop assistant	709.3	772.7	673.9
Catering industry	907.7	1054.7	788.3
Waiter	876.7	1111.0	782.3
Hotel industry	868.6	1089.3	721.9
Room cleaner	640.5	686.7	623.8
Total average		953.9	805.2

Source: adapted from *Labour Market Wage Prices in Large and Medium Sized Cities* 1999.
Note
Occupations selected here are from among the lowest paid occupations. Wages are normally calculated by calendar month in China.

workers are increasingly concentrated outside the state sector in the informal sector such as TVEs and private small and self-employed businesses where labour regulations either may not apply or are not effectively enforced due to lax enforcement and lack of inspection. Many are urban workers, not just rural migrant workers. Again, there are very few official statistics on the employment situation for this group of workers. However, since a large proportion of workers in this informal sector are females, employers' non-observation of labour regulations may have a disproportional negative impact on female workers in general.

This problem is particularly prominent in the private service industry where pay tends to be lower than that in other industries and where more women than men are employed. For example, by the end of 1999, a total of 79.4 million workers worked in private and self-employed businesses. Over half of them (50.6 per cent or 40.2 million) worked in the wholesale and retail trade and restaurants, and 86 per cent (34.7 million) of these workers were working for employers who were classified as self-employed (*China Labour Statistics Yearbook* 2000). While the total wage of these workers may not necessarily be low, this may be achieved through long working hours and the absence of rest days. This is particularly the case in small commercial businesses where the majority of workers are younger females (below 30 years old) who tend to drop out of the labour market at their motherhood, even though this is an unusual practice for Chinese women, especially for those in the state- or collectively owned sectors. The quality of work and employment for (female) workers in the informal sector will be discussed further in Chapter 8.

Finally, low pay is also the main reason for those laid-off female workers who regain employment to leave their new jobs. According to a survey carried out by Shanghai All-China Women's Federation (1997) on 1,166 females in local job centres in May 1996, 22.8 per cent left their new jobs within the first three months because of the low pay. Among them, 29.6 per cent were earning less than 201 yuan per month, 55.6 per cent earned between 201 and 300 yuan, and 7.4 per cent between 401–500 yuan, whereas the minimum wage of Shanghai in 1995 was 270 yuan and its average wage 773 yuan (see Table 7.2). The majority of 55.7 per cent of the women surveyed felt that a wage between 401 and 600 yuan was acceptable for a general post. Another 27 per cent would accept a wage of below 400 yuan and only 17 per cent set their acceptable minimum wage at a rate of over 600 yuan. Urban women workers appear still to be expecting to receive a wage more comparable to the relatively equal urban wages at which they were employed in the state sector and are not yet ready to accept wages at the level commonly set for rural migrants. However, over time, if urban women continue to face discrimination from urban employers *vis-à-vis* male urban workers and to face competition from rural workers in the informal sector and are eventually forced into taking jobs at migrant wage level, a new gender divide in pay could emerge even within the urban sector (Cooke and Rubery 2002).

Conclusion

This chapter has summarized the pressures for the introduction of the minimum wage regulations in China and the potential implications for different groups of workers, such as those who work for the SOEs, TVEs, and those who are employed in the low-paid industries and the informal sectors. The problems encountered in the implementation of the minimum wage regulations in China are manifold, from the determination of the wage level to its enforcement, and from the ideological conception to the more practical matters. Not only are we faced with the issues of who should pay and who should be paid a minimum wage, we also have to deal with the problems of policy inconsistency and incoherence at both intra- and inter-regional levels. As such, the significance of a minimum wage policy in China is different from that in the developed countries due to the unique social, economic, political and legal characteristics of the country under which the policy is to be enforced.

To a large extent, the problem of tackling low pay in China is not so much the lack of minimum wage regulations as the lack of an effective enforcement mechanism. This is largely a result of the excessive labour supply, the low level of legal awareness, the lack of workers' bargaining power, the low voice of the disadvantaged groups in the society, and the willingness of the low-paid groups to accept low wages. In this case the group most likely to accept low wages is rural migrants – both male and female (Cooke and Rubery 2002). In addition, Chinese society tends to take a generally lenient attitude towards low-paying employers and believes that rural workers are in any case better off working in the industries at a given wage level than in agriculture. China is a society which has been cultivated by an egalitarian ideology for centuries. Low wages have been the chief mechanism to ensure a minimum living standard for the majority of the people (see Chapter 4 for further discussion). This is so much so that the fact is often overlooked that there has to be a minimum wage floor somewhere to prevent the already very low wage from slipping even further down at the risk that all will end up having very little to live on (Cooke and Rubery 2002).

Although achieving social equality by eliminating the gap between the wealthy and the poor has been a key part of the agenda of China's revolutionary philosophers and policy makers in its contemporary history, the objective of increasing wage levels through the minimum wage regulations has paradoxically tended to be circumscribed by other priorities and has met with limited enthusiasm at the implementational level. There is the overall tension between continuing economic development, high employment rates and social stability, and maintaining or increasing levels of job quality. The expanded roles of local governments in social welfare in general and in the minimum wage in specific cases force/enable the central government to take a back seat in overseeing the formation and implementation of the policies.

These problems are compounded by the fact that only a small proportion of the total low-paid labour force is employed within the organized sector where these policies can be more readily enforced. A large proportion of the labour force is employed in the unorganized sector, both in rural and urban areas, where the application of these laws cannot be guaranteed. Indeed, the very existence of the unorganized sector depends upon the fact that it falls outside the scope of labour regulations. The low-paid workers are at the mercy of the market and uncertain growth. It may be argued that if these tensions remain unsolved by the central state, then further decentralization and diversification of welfare support could lead to a policy and resource vacuum at the centre (Saich 2001) and worsening employment conditions for a large proportion of the labour force. More state intervention is therefore needed to co-ordinate and police the formation and implementation of policies at the regional level. This is essential to the formalization of the expanding unorganized sector, so that the unorganized sector shrinks with growing demand for labour from the organized sector.

To conclude, it would seem that the demand for enforcing the minimum wage regulations from workers and their pressure groups, the willingness of employers to adhere to the regulations, and the readiness of the state to police their observance will require a new social contract which will involve a shift in the perception of individuals, employers and the state towards welfare rights and obligations. Until such a social contract is developed, the prospects both for reducing gender pay discrimination and providing more general protection against low pay and hard-working conditions remain extremely poor (Cooke and Rubery 2002).

The next chapter will provide further discussion on employment conditions for those who work in the informal sector, through the examples of a small group of (urban) workers employed in private small commercial businesses.

8 Employment relations in private small firms

Introduction

Small firms constitute the bulk of enterprises in all economies in the world, making a major contribution to private sector output and employment (Storey 1994). It has been noted that the growth of small firms since the 1980s is an international trend in which large firms shed jobs while smaller ones create them (Stokes 1998). For many commentators and policy makers, small businesses are well placed to play important economic, social and political roles in employment creation, resource utilization and income generation (Nelson 1987). They are dynamic, efficient, competitive, and perhaps most importantly, a source of new jobs. Others highlight the fact that small businesses are a major source of exploitation and a 'sweatshop' (Rainnie 1989; Scase 1995). Private small firms are often associated with relatively poor quality of work and employment, which are often the reasons for their existence and growth in the first place. Still others draw our attention to the heterogeneity in this sector with personalized informality being the key feature (Ram 1994; Matley 1999; Wilkinson 1999). More importantly, it is now recognized that informality and familial ideologies often evident in small firms can mask the highly exploitative nature of work (Holliday 1995) and that the informality of small businesses cannot 'smooth away the power relations that shape the management process' (Ram *et al.* 2001: 846). Instead, the nature of employment relations in small businesses hinges on the dynamic balance between conflicts and harmony as well as control and consent shaped by a web of social and economic relationships in which small firms are embedded (Ram *et al.* 2001; Barrett and Rainnie 2002).

Writers on HRM in small firms also observe the fact that HRM in small firms differs from that in larger firms (e.g. Golhar and Deshpande 1997; Kinnie *et al.* 1999) and that informality in the management of human resources issues appears to be characteristic of many small firms all over the world with the degree of formality increasing as firm size grows. For example, Wager (1998) found that firm size appeared to be a major determinant of a number of HRM practices in that very small firms were significantly less likely to have adopted eight of the ten practices examined in the study. Amba-Rao and Pendse's (1985) investigation of the compensation practices of seventy-eight small firms in north-central Indiana revealed that small business compensation and maintenance practices lacked a systematic and rational approach. Similarly, Verser's study (1987) found that the twenty-five small business owners studied often dealt with subordinates arbitrarily and did not perceive that this arbitrary behaviour contributed to employee morale or productivity problems. McEvoy's study (1984) likewise observed the fact that small businesses lacked creative staffing practices. Many small businesses are set up by the owner-managers who enjoy or derive some satisfaction from what they do while also generating an adequate income. They may not be interested in unlimited growth for various sound reasons (Gray 1992), and therefore, once a level of activity that provides the adequate income is reached, management becomes routine and tactical. There is probably little thought given to strategic management unless things start to go wrong (Burns 2001). More importantly, as Marchington *et al.* (2003) observe, small business employers may have to adopt astute and largely informal HR strategies as part of their survival strategy. On the other hand, Becon *et al.*'s survey (1996) of 560 firms in the UK revealed that there was a surprisingly high take-up and awareness of new management ideas among small business managers, with a change in ownership being the driving force for reorganization. Current interest in small businesses in developing countries stems largely from the widespread concern over unemployment (Nelson 1987). Since the early 1980s, private small businesses have been growing rapidly as a new or revived form of ownership in China (see Table 2.2, p. 27).

However, the growth of private businesses in China has been heavily influenced by the ebb and flow of political support in the past two decades and small business owners tend to keep a low profile and to remain cautious in their expansion. There are in general three sets of ideology concerning the existence of private business. One position in the debate is taken by those who see private business as a necessary supplement to the public economy. They argue that private business can stimulate production, enliven markets, expand employment, provide a source of income for those whose livelihood has been destroyed by the broader economic changes, and help to satisfy the needs of the people. A second approach contends that the private economy is already and should be more than just a supplement to the socialist economy, and is a 'necessary component' and an 'organic part' of the national economy and of socialism with Chinese characteristics. A third perspective is dominated by the hard-liners who contest that private enterprise is a 'candy-coated bullet' undermining socialism, which is identified with state-run enterprises. Policies on private business thus drift from side to side depending on the political tides, although the first approach is now becoming the dominant force, as the state is increasingly dependent on private small firms to create employment opportunities (see Cooke (2005) for further discussion).

Despite the growing significance of the private small business sector in the economy and social life, there are few detailed studies on issues related to employment relations in these small firms, as was pointed out in Chapter 1. This chapter aims to address some of the issues raised there by first reporting the findings of a study of twenty-four small and micro commercial businesses in a medium-sized city in southern China. It focuses on aspects that are central to the domain of employment relations, such as recruitment and induction, skills training, working time arrangements, remuneration and motivational incentives, workforce representation, labour rights, and owner–labour relations. This is followed by a discussion section that provides a brief comparison between the findings reported in this chapter and those of other studies carried out both within and outside of China. The chapter also highlights the policy and research implications for employment relations in the private small business sector.

The study

This study consists of two questionnaire surveys (one on employers and one on workers) and interviews of employers and employees from twenty-four small and micro commercial/retail shops in a medium-sized city in southern China in 2002. The two surveys covered similar questions on employment relations but were adapted for employers and employees. All questionnaire forms were distributed and collected by the researcher in person. In all, twenty-one shop owners and ninety employees (out of a total of 191 employed) from these twenty-four shops were surveyed (see Table 8.1). Of the employees surveyed, nineteen were male and seventy-one female. All of them worked full-time. A follow-up sub-sample, comprising half of the owner respondents and thirty-five employee respondents from these shops, were further contacted for informal interviews to obtain more information.

The study deliberately focuses on the small commercial/retail business sector for a number of reasons. First, a single sector of commercial/retail business is chosen in order to control for the heterogeneity of the small firms in different industries. Even so, a level of intra-industry variations still exists, particularly in wage levels, as will be shown below. Second, the small commercial/retail business sector is chosen because it represents a significant proportion in the growth of individual economy in China over the past two decades. For example, by the end of 1999, a total of 79.4 million workers worked in private and self-employed businesses. Over half of them (50.6 per cent or 40.2 million) worked in the wholesale and retail trade and restaurants, and 86 per cent (34.7 million) of these workers were working for employers who were classified as self-employed (*China Labour Statistics Yearbook* 2000).

A majority of 81 per cent of the owners were below age 36 whereas 92 per cent of the workers surveyed were between 20 and 35 years old. Most owners (86 per cent) had qualifications at senior high school level (equivalent to A level in the UK) or above, whereas a considerably lower proportion of workers (57 per cent) possessed the same level of qualifications. This profile

Table 8.1 Survey information

Business	Age of shop (years)	No. of workers employed	No. of workers surveyed	No. of hours worked per day[b]	No. of hours per week[b]	No. of rest days and holidays per year[c]
Computing 1	6	7	6	9	56	38
Computing 2	¼	2	2	12	76	36
Computing 3	2½	1	1	9	57	36
Computing 4	2	2	2	8	47	56
Computing 5	1	1	1	9	54	52
Bookshop	6	38	5	7	41	56
Clothes 1	_	16	3	12	72	52
Clothes 2	4	4	2	9	63	2
Clothes 3	10	13	10	8	54	12
Clothes 4	8	4	4	6.5	44	12
Clothes 5	10	5	5	7	48	7
Clothes 6[a]	4	8	8	13	91	2
Clothes 7[a]	3	3	2	13	91	2
Food 1	2	3	3	8	53	20
Food 2	8	6	2	10	69	7
Food 3	3	8	8	9	61	12
Shoes 1	3	32	5	6	36	52
Shoes 2	2	4	1	6	36	52
Shoes 3	8	4	4	7	49	0
Jewellery	5	16	5	6.5	39	52
Hairdressing	3	4	4	12	76	36
Beauty salon	8	4	3	13	82	38
Telephone equipment	4	5	3	6	30	104
Photocopying and typing[a]	3	1	1	8	52	24
Total		191	90			

Notes
1. Working hours recorded here were mostly based on the employers' report, which may be slightly lower than the workers' report on some occasions, as later discussion shows.
2. There are approximately ten days of statutory holidays in a year.
[a] Owner not surveyed.
[b] Hours not including overtime that may be or are in fact worked.
[c] The number of rest days and holidays per year was calculated by the number of rest days each worker was allowed to have for each calendar month multiplied by twelve months, plus the number of statutory holidays the workers were allowed to have by the employer per year.

is broadly similar to that of the national level (see *China Labour Statistics Yearbook* 2003). If anything, owners in this study tend to be younger and to have a relatively higher level of educational qualifications compared with the national statistics. This is due in part to the relatively high proportion of computer shops in the sample, where skill and qualifications are more essential and where younger rather than older people are more interested in computers, given their recent development in China. A majority of 71 per cent of workers had been working for their current employer for less than two years and 39 per cent had a basic wage of 401 to 500 yuan per month (see Table 8.2).

Employment relations in these firms

Recruitment and induction

Word-of-mouth (reported by 52 per cent of owners) and wall posters (reported by 62 per cent of owners) were the most frequently used methods for advertising job vacancies by the shop owners. This finding accords with that reported by the employees surveyed in that 51 per cent of workers said they came to hear of the vacancy through word-of-mouth, and another 49 per cent said they found out about the vacancy from wall advertisements. A majority of 67 per cent of owners did not feel that they had recruitment problems mainly because of the relatively high unemployment rate. Of those employers who experienced recruitment difficulties, the reasons they cited included: low quality of applicants (bookshop); lack of depth of knowledge (computing); lack of experienced applicants (up-market clothing); poor work attitude (shoes); and work being too laborious (hairdressing). This is despite the fact that each advertised job vacancy often attracts a large number of applicants; for example, nearly 400 applications were received for the two posts of shop assistant advertised by the bookshop in 2002.

The vast majority of owners (76 per cent) reported that they used interview as the main, if not the only, selection method. On-the-job demonstration was the second most used method (29 per cent). This finding is supported by that from the employees surveyed in which 91 per cent said that interview was the selection method for their recruitment and another 24 per cent of employees said they had been through an on-the-job demonstration as part of the selection process. Only the bookshop and the jewellery shop used written tests (set by the owners themselves) in addition to interviews. This is due in part to the nature of their products and in part because they were much larger shops in comparison with most of the other shops. Literacy and communication skills were the most common requirements for job candidates in addition to A level or vocational qualifications. Educational qualification requirements were obviously higher for the bookshop, jewellery and computing shops than they were for the food shops due to the nature of the products they sold.

A majority of owners (86 per cent) claimed that they provided some form of initial/induction training for their new recruits. Training content included company policies and procedures, tasks and responsibilities, product knowledge, sales techniques, and approaches to customer service. Some shops (e.g. hairdressers, beauty salons and food shops) provided on-the-job training for their staff to help them gain the skills necessary to perform their tasks. However, trade secrets such as food recipes would not be passed on and

Table 8.2 General information on surveyed owners and workers

Age	20–25	26–30	31–35	36–40	41–45	46–50
No. of owners	5	7	5	1	1	2
% of total	24%	33%	24%	5%	5%	10%
No. of workers	37	33	13	5	2	—
% of total	41%	37%	14%	6%	2%	—

Qualifications	Primary school	O level	A level	Advanced diploma	University degree
No. of owners	—	3	12	5	1
% of total	—	14%	57%	24%	5%
No. of workers	4	35	42	8	1
% of total	4%	39%	47%	9%	1%

Service length of workers	Less than 1 year	1–2 years	2–3 years	Over 3 years
No. of workers	35	29	16	10
% of total	39%	32%	18%	11%

Basic wage per month[a]	300–400 yuan	401–500 yuan	501–650 yuan	700–800 yuan
No. of workers	32	35	13	6
% of total	36%	39%	14%	7%

Note
[a] Wage in China is normally calculated on the basis of a calendar month.

opportunities for developing key skills which are highly marketable (e.g. computer assembling) would only be provided to key employees whose loyalty would be secured through relatively high wages and performance incentives.

Perhaps the biggest discrepancy between the employer and the employee's report in this study rests in the perception of training. Although many employees reported that they had received some initial training from their employers on product knowledge, sales techniques and technical skills (e.g. IT and beautician), 21 per cent of employees claimed that they received no training from their employers and another 30 per cent did not answer the question. In particular, none of the employees from the bookshop said that they had received any training from their employer, even though their employer said that training was provided on company policies and procedures and tasks and responsibilities. Somewhat surprisingly, over half of the workers from the computing shops also believed that they had not received training from their employers. This is perhaps due to the possibility that most people do not feel that they have had any training unless the training is provided in a formal setting imparting skills which they believe are useful in themselves. However, this finding supports the analysis in Chapter 5 that employees in private and small businesses generally receive little training.

All but one shop had a probationary period for their new recruits, ranging from three days to three months. In general, shops which required higher levels of skills or knowledge (e.g. computing, up-market clothing), the handling of valuable products (e.g. jewellery), or presentation of company image (e.g. bookshop) required a longer probationary period from the staff as a screening process to displace people whom the owners felt inappropriate to retain as a result of their perceived inadequate aptitude and attitude. Some shops also used the probationary period to weed out staff who could not meet their performance target (e.g. clothing). Pay during the probationary period was generally lower than that after the probationary period.

Working time arrangement

All workers worked full-time, as part-time working is not commonly practised, due in part to the need for a full wage to support a reasonable standard of living. Those who are engaged in part-time work, such as domestic services, may need to take on two or three jobs to survive (Cooke 2003c). Nearly 40 per cent of the workers in this study reported that they worked eight to nine hours a day and another 27 per cent worked twelve to thirteen hours a day (see Table 8.1). While the larger shops tended to split their operating hours into two shifts, the smaller shops often staffed their business hours with only one shift. What is surprising is the relatively high total number of weekly hours that these workers worked each week, a situation compounded by the low level of rest days and holidays that were given to the workers.

The majority of shops gave their workers only two or three rest days per calendar month (see Table 8.1). Most owners did not allow their workers to take their statutory holidays because these were the busiest periods for the businesses. The busiest periods for commercial businesses in China are in the evening, at weekends, and statutory holidays when people in other sectors are not working and have the time to go shopping. Most, if not all, commercial shops will be open for business during these periods in order to catch sales revenue. Given the competitive pressure in the sector, these may be the only periods when the business can make a (reasonable) profit.

As a result, 66 per cent of workers reported that they worked more than fifty hours a week, with 12 per cent of them working between seventy-one and eighty hours and 10 per cent between ninety-one and a hundred hours a week. A total of about 88 per cent of workers had fewer than fifty-nine days' rest days/holidays per year, among which 41 per cent had between one and nineteen days. In addition, thirteen owners (62 per cent) admitted that they would ask their employees to work overtime on short notice whereas 62 per cent of workers reported that their employers would ask them to work overtime on short notice. These working time arrangements, even excluding any overtime that the workers may be asked to work, are well below the standards specified in the Labour Law of China (1995). According to the labour regulations, employers can require workers to work eight hours per day, a maximum average of forty hours per week, a maximum of three hours of overtime per day and thirty-six hours per month. In the meantime, employers should give their employees a minimum of one rest day per week in addition to statutory holidays (approximately ten days) (see below for further discussion on employment protection legislation). This finding is similar to that reported by Chan (2001) who found that long working hours and only two rest days per month for migrant workers were the norm in many factories.

One major reason for this long-hour working is the cost of the operation. The majority of employers are making only a marginal profit and staffing costs consist of a significant proportion of the operating cost. The smaller shops can only afford to staff with one shift, often topped up with non-wage family helpers such as retired parents. This makes it impossible for these employers to have any staffing flexibility, especially when part-time work is rarely practised in China. In addition, because wage levels are generally low, workers are willing to work very long hours (and overtime) as a means to top up their wages. This practice is quite common in the peripheral sectors in China as well as in other countries.

Motivational incentives and remuneration

All but three shop owners (Food 1, hairdressing, and photocopying and typing) reported that they used at least one type of bonus or incentive scheme on top of the basic wage to motivate employees in order to increase performance level and/or to elicit desirable behaviour. Most shops adopted some sort of performance/profit-related pay schemes, giving a certain percentage (usually 1 per cent) of turnover or gross profit as bonus. Performance/profit-related bonuses usually made up 30 to 50 per cent of the worker's total wage income. This means that a relatively high level of business risk is shared by individual workers. The majority of shops also gave a monthly bonus (usually about 10 per cent of the basic wage) to workers for full attendance, good customer services, or generally good behaviour.

In addition to these incentives, many owners issued festival and/or end-of-year bonuses as a long-standing Chinese tradition to express the owners' goodwill to the workers. The proportion of this type of bonus varied from shop to shop, but in general, the ones that did not have (many) other types of bonuses tended to give a bigger sum to their workers. For example, Food 3 (a downmarket café) did not have any type of bonus other than giving its workers a relatively large bonus (20 per cent of the monthly basic wage) on each of the five major traditional festivals in China. The owner felt that the nature of their business made it difficult to implement a performance/profit-related bonus scheme. She did not see the need to adopt a full attendance bonus as her workers were generally 'quite good' and would not be late for work unless something urgent happened. However, she did see the need to have some mechanism in place to maintain morale of and patronage for her employees. Distributing festive bonuses was considered appropriate (see Chapter 4 for a discussion of the significance of bonuses in Chinese workers' wages).

In terms of annual pay rise, only twelve employers (57 per cent) gave their workers an annual pay rise and 60 per cent of workers reported that they received an annual pay rise from their employers. For those who received an annual pay rise, the level of rise was commonly reported by both the employers and employees to be within 5 to 10 per cent, although some depended on the profit level of the year. On the whole, less than 15 per cent of workers surveyed earned more than 1,000 yuan per month on average as an overall package, while the rest earned between 500 and 800 yuan. This is a markedly lower figure than the average wage of 1,307 yuan per month for workers in the same province in 2001, a figure which would have been higher in 2002 when the study took place, given the continuous trend of wage increases (*China Statistics Yearbook* 2002).

As revealed earlier, 62 per cent of owners said that they would ask their employees to work overtime on short notice. However, only 48 per cent of owners reported that they paid overtime to their employees when they stayed behind at the end of their shift. The same proportion of owners reported that they only paid the normal rate to those workers who had to come to work on their rest days. A majority of fifty-six employees (62 per cent) said that they received the normal rate of pay when they worked overtime on their rest days and 16 per cent of workers said they received 1.5 times of pay. A small proportion of 14 per cent of workers said they were paid double time when they worked on their rest days and statutory holidays. Again, these payment arrangements are generally below what is specified in the Labour Law of China (1995), in which employers are required to pay no less than double time of the normal wage for their employees working on their rest days and no less than three times for statutory holidays. It is to the wider issues of employment protection that we now turn.

Employment protection

One of the most striking features that is found in this study is the extent to which the employment experiences of these workers do not match what are stipulated in the Labour Law of China (1995) and the more recent Individual Solely Owned Enterprise Law of China (issued in 1999 to take effect from 1 January 2000). Few of the workers had a written employment contract with their employers, as specified by the Labour Law (1995), other than verbal agreements at the recruitment stage to lay down a few basic terms and conditions on pay and working time, for example. It should be pointed out, however, that this does not necessarily mean less job security or shorter tenure for the workers compared with those who work in TVEs and FDI factories staffed primarily with migrant rural workers (see Cooke 2004c).

In addition to the long working hours, lack of rests days and holidays, and low rates of overtime pay as identified above, there are also a range of other employment protection terms which the workers have not so far been able to enjoy. For example, while the vast majority of employees working in the state/collectively owned sector enjoy pensions and medical insurance in addition to other fringe benefits, 80 per cent of workers in this study reported that their employers did not pay into any social insurance for them. Only three employers reported that they paid medical insurance for their workers. They were notably the larger employers whose employment policy and practice were apparently more formalized and were under tighter monitoring from the local labour authorities. This finding supports Zhu and Nyland's observation (2004: 872) that 'marketisation has had a negative effect on the security of many employees' and that 'many employers have attempted to evade their responsibilities'.

While the Labour Law (1995) specifies that employers should not delay wage payment to their workers, 38 per cent of employers in this study reported that they sometimes or often delayed wage payment to their workers due to cash flow problems. Similarly, 34 per cent workers reported that their employers sometimes delayed their wage payment and another 3 per cent said that this happened to them often.

Another feature in employment relations is that although most jobs were an open-ended contract, employers could terminate the contract relatively easily without being challenged by the individual personally or through legal channels. Many shops, especially the computing shops where recruitment and induction took longer, required their workers to give one month's notice prior to their resignation, but the same length of notice was not reciprocated by their employers who normally served one week's (verbal) notice in advance of employment termination.

One reason that may explain the lack of employers' input into social insurance and the absence of formal documentation is that shop owners did not wish to disclose the true scale of their business operations in order to avoid higher business taxes and the costs of social insurance contributions associated with the employment of workers. It is common in China for small shop owners to deliberately not register their employees with the local authorities and to report a much smaller sales figure than the actual amount (Zhu *et al.* 1998; Liu and Yang 2001). Some shop owners were reluctant to reveal the actual number of workers they employed during the interviews, claiming that some of the workers were unpaid family members. It is also not uncommon for shop owners and their employees to conspire to foil the labour and tax inspectorates. One shop owner even boasted how easy it was to do so:

> 'Usually, we will receive a message from our contact in the authority before they come to visit the shop. We will then hide anything that we think should not be there and pretend that everything is normal. Sometimes if I am not there, I will caution my staff to be vague or say "don't know" to any questions they ask. If they [labour authority] ask who they [the workers] are, they will say they are my relatives or friends who happen to be there to help me out while I am not there. We do get caught occasionally, but we can usually ask friends to sort out the fine afterwards.'

Another reason for the lack of employment protection for these workers is the low level of awareness of employment legislation by both the workers and their employers. Over 75 per cent of workers reported that they did not know what employment regulations existed to protect them. Four workers thought that they were not protected by any employment legislation. A similar level of ignorance of employment legislation was demonstrated by their employers in that 57 per cent of them did not know what labour regulations they had to comply with and 19 per cent believed that they did not have to comply with any regulations. This level of awareness is much lower than that found in other studies carried out in the public sector and larger private organizations (e.g. Wang 2000), but is similar to that in sweat-shop manufacturing firms in China (e.g. Chan 2001) and small firms in the UK in Ram *et al.*'s study (2001).

However, the lack of employment protection does not necessarily mean that sweatshop-type employment relations prevail in these small and micro firms.

Owner–employee relations

Employment relations in small firms are often reported as being informal with firms labelled as either 'a big happy family' or 'a sweatshop' (Rainnie 1989; Scase 1995; Wilkinson 1999). Owner managers typically play a dominant role in determining how the business is to be run and what employment terms and conditions are to be offered to their workers. Collective workplace representation is often lacking. The findings of this study certainly echo some of these characteristics, although many of the shops are, as perceived by the workers, neither 'a big happy family' nor 'a sweatshop'.

Although 70 per cent of workers believed that their employers had consulted them in making decisions in the management of the business, 29 per cent of employers said that they did not consult their workers in making business decisions. Two-thirds of the employers surveyed said that they determined unilaterally the wage levels of their employees while the remaining third said that wage levels were co-determined with the workers concerned. Employees surveyed accorded the same view in that 74 per cent of them believed that their employers alone determined their wages. A considerable proportion of workers (39 per cent) believed that their employers were paying only the market rate, a view supported by 43 per cent of employers.

In addition, many of the individuals interviewed were not fully aware of their terms and conditions with their employers. For example, two workers from Clothes 2 said during the interviews that they did not know what bonuses they would get or if they would be given an annual pay rise, as they had been working for their employer for less than three months at the time. This example and other incidents found during interviews indicate that employees tended to accept terms and conditions as a given instead of an outcome of bargaining, and that many workplace customs and practices were established on an *ad hoc* basis as the employment relationship evolved.

No workers in this study were trade union members or belonged to any other workers' associations as their representing body, although it has been widely noted that trade unions in China play a very different role from that commonly found in other countries (Ng and Warner 1998; Cooke 2002). Few workers' associations exist in China as a result of a long-term official discouragement of free associations. The only official channel which workers can use to protect and advance their labour rights is the local labour authorities who are not always proactive or sympathetic towards labour, to say the least. In any case, neither the employers nor the workers would tend to choose the labour authorities as their preferred mechanism for resolving their disputes should they ever occur. In fact, a few workers interviewed were obviously surprised by the suggestion and dismissed the possibility of using the labour authority as a mediating body to resolve workplace disputes. Instead, 42 per cent of workers indicated that they would talk it through with their employers. A minority of 17 per cent of workers stated that disputes with their employers would not happen or their employers were always right. It is also worth noting that 29 per cent of workers opted not to answer the question of how they would handle a dispute with their employers. In a similar vein, direct negotiation with the individuals concerned seems to be the way many surveyed employers (48 per cent) would choose to resolve their differences.

Since the majority of shops in this study employed no more than five workers who might have joined the company at different times, under different circumstances and with varying levels of pay, collective action would apparently be difficult to organize given the current high unemployment level and in the absence of a cultural tradition of collective bargaining or open confrontation. However, one example of collective resistance to the owner was reported by the owner of Computing 1 where the majority of six workers did not turn up for work immediately before the Chinese New Year in February 2002 (when it was the busiest period) in protest at their perceived insufficient amount of the end-of-year bonus. The workers did not explicitly express the true cause of their absence from work; instead, each gave individual excuses for being absent. However, they all came back to work the next day as if nothing had happened after the owner gave them an additional bonus, even though the owner felt that the original bonus was already an acceptable one, in addition to the various generous perks and bonuses they received throughout the year. The timing, the relatively high skill level and knowledge of the business operation required for the job all played an important part in the victory of the workers, and their employer had little choice but to give in.

In general, the owner–employee relations in this study appeared to be relatively relaxed, obviously some more so than others, with a noticeable closer relationship in the smaller firms as a result of the owners working alongside the workers. It was quite common for owners of smaller shops to buy snacks for their workers during the day and to issue occasional perks to lubricate relationships or to paste over unhappy events, although there were the inevitable odd cases of strained relations between certain individual workers and their employers. A vast majority (86 per cent) of owners said they were generally happy with their employees, whereas 67 per cent of workers felt that their relationships with their employers were 'good' and 11 per cent said 'very good'.

This neither 'beautiful' nor 'sweatshop' type of employment relationships in many ways reflects the Chinese traditional value in the maintenance of social relationships, in which harmony is emphasized and overt confrontation is the last resort. While rebellion tends to be suppressed with a firm hand, requests expressed in subtle ways are better received and accommodated. Furthermore, these seemingly 'happyish' employment relationships may perhaps be explained by and should not conceal the fact that there was a relatively high level of both labour turnover and dismissal in this study (see Table 8.2 for length of service). A vast majority (89 per cent) of workers had worked for their employers for less than three years but the level of business expansion was low overall. While some individuals chose to quit their jobs (for instance, the beauty salon lost eight workers in its eight years of existence), many were fired by their employers. According to the survey information, 67 per cent of owners said that they have had to dismiss workers for reasons mainly to do with the workers' perceived incompetence and/or poor work attitude. Some shops appeared to have experienced these incidents more regularly than others. For example, Food 1 dismissed six workers in the two-year life of the shop. The bookshop dismissed no fewer than eighteen workers in the past six years because of their 'incompetence'. Clothes 1 dismissed five workers in six months (during their probationary period as a screening process). Clothes 3 had fired at least twenty workers in its ten years in business mainly because 'they violated the rules of the shop'. Food 3 fired five workers in its three years' existence because of their 'poor performance and attitude'. It is worth pointing out here that this was taking place in a broader employment context of the country in which job security and harmony were the social norm and employment mobility was relatively low in the formal sectors, particularly in the once dominant state/collectively owned sectors until the recent mass-scale employment restructuring.

Implications of these findings

Although the findings of this study are based on a relatively small sample of private and self-employed businesses, there is no reason to suggest that these findings cannot be generalized with a level of confidence, since they are located in a typical city, represent typical businesses commonly found in the commercial/retail sector, and most of the employment practices in these small businesses appear to share a considerable level of common characteristics. Based on these findings, there are a number of points that need further discussion here.

First, the findings of this study suggest that the characteristics of employ-ment relations in private small businesses in China are significantly different from those found in the SOEs, joint ventures and larger private organizations, as revealed in this book and elsewhere (Child 1996; Warner and Ng 1998; Ding and Warner 1999; Wang 2000; Cooke 2000, 2002). By comparison, there is a much greater level of formality on employment policy and practice in these larger organizations and the quality of employment tends to be higher for the workers when judged by training opportunities, wage levels, working hours and other employment rights.

The findings of this study also support those carried out by other authors on private (small) firms. For example, according to Tan and Liu (2003), over 90 per cent of private businesses in China had their finances controlled by family members, and about 40 per cent of the senior and middle-ranking management came from family members or friends. More generally, (smaller) private businesses in China commonly face problems of insufficient man-agerial expertise and inability to retain key staff, largely as a result of a lack of systematic human resource management policy.

Similarly, a large-scale survey (with 8,000 valid returned questionnaires) carried out by Lu and Wang (2003) on employment relations in private businesses in Zhejiang Province (economically one of the most developed provinces where private businesses have played an important role) found that there were significant discrepancies in social welfare participation among the private businesses. While 45 per cent of the enterprises took part in welfare provision, only 8 per cent of the workers were covered. In addition, while professional and managerial staff enjoyed a wide range of company benefits and perks, these provisions have not been extended to ordinary workers. Over 70 per cent of the private businesses adopted piece rates for wage reward, with the majority of employees working for at least fifty hours per week on average. Overtime was regularly worked, often on a compulsory basis. In 40 per cent of the businesses, each employee worked on average thirty to fifty hours' overtime per month, with the highest being 180 hours. Over 20 per cent of the employers delayed wage payment. Some employers withheld a proportion of the wage until the end of the year in order to prevent workers from leaving the firm. There was a relatively high level of staff turnover with long working hours, frequent overtime, poor working conditions, and delayed wage payment being the main reasons. Labour–management conflicts were less likely to be in the form of radical confrontation, with exit of employment as the main route to terminating the situation. The majority of employers and workers believed that the management–labour relationship was generally harmonious.

All these findings from various studies suggest that there may be a severe shortage of managerial and entrepreneurial skills in the private (small) businesses and that the intrinsic value of jobs in these firms may be generally low, with direct financial reward as the primary mechanism for motivation.

Second, the findings draw our attention to the fact that there is a high level of similarities between the Chinese small businesses and their counterparts in other countries in terms of their business environment and employment practices, and that there may be some generalizable patterns at the inter-national level. Procedural informality, (owner)-managerial prerogative in employment relationships, and a low level of awareness and adherence to employment regulations appear to be the norm (Rainnie 1989; Scott *et al.* 1989; Keasey and Watson 1993; Stokes 1998). A policy of employment relations is often not formulated in a self-conscious manner and informal routinization plays a large role in the day-to-day running of the business. There is little evidence generally of pre-planning of labour relations in order to avoid potential problems. Further similarities include a relatively high level of labour turnover and the individualized process of pay bargaining between employer and employee, with the employer's unilateral determination often being the outcome (Curran *et al.* 1993; Gilman *et al.* 2002). In fact, the marked similarities of small firms across nations of both developed and developing economies have been observed by other authors (e.g. Ram 1994; Edwards *et al.* 1995). For example, Ram (1994) points out that many of the practices in the small Asian-owned clothing firms in Britain found in his study share considerable similarities with those of what seem to be very different cases in Deyo's study (1989) of small firms in the Far East. In both studies, familial and community links play an important role in the negotiation of workplace relations which are characterized by relational reciprocity and mutual obligation. Edwards *et al.* (1995) likewise observe that small firms in Italy or elsewhere in Kondo's (1990) study share many features with those in Britain, and that the negotiation of interpersonal ties tends to be a common aspect of such firms.

In addition, Chinese traditional values in the negotiation of workplace relations noted in this study appear to be shared more widely in the Asia-Pacific countries. As Dana (1998: 73) observes, 'central to the Japanese belief system are the concepts of obligation, indebtedness, and loyalty, all of which reinforce the very important notion of harmony for the common good.' Similarly, Levine (1997: 10) observes, 'industrial relations in Indonesia emphasizes the traditional Indonesian values of harmony, mutual self-help, and consultations leading to consensus.' However, Chinese values alone cannot fully explain the largely non-confrontational characteristic of employment relations in the small business sector, and indeed in most sectors, in China and, to some extent, in other East Asian countries which share a similar path of economic development. It has been argued that the economic growth of East and South East Asian countries was largely built on the governments' proactive policies in attracting foreign funds and their willingness to suppress labour rights (The World Bank 1993).

To a certain extent, the exploitative nature of employment practices characterized by low pay, excessively long working hours and the absence of employment protection often endemic in small firms in both the developed and developing economies, as observed in this study, may be explained by the insecurity and marginalization encountered by the small business owners themselves. The availability of cheap labour and willingness of employees to work long hours remain the key to survival/competitive advantage for many small business operations. Owner-managers themselves may work long hours too and rely heavily on their family members to manage the long hours. The relatively low skill requirement of most of these jobs and the highly cost-sensitive nature of the businesses also enable/compel most employers to offer low wages and operate in a hire-and-fire mode, drawing largely from workers in the secondary tier of the labour market. The only exception is the computer shop where skills requirements and consequently pay level are far higher and employees tend to stay with the firm longer, a pattern of employment relationships akin to Fox's (1974) 'relational contracting' model.

Third, there are several additional factors to explain why employment relations practices in these small businesses in China are the way they are. One factor is that while small business associations or similar bodies may be available in developed countries such as the UK to provide advisory and support functions to small business owners to make them more aware of good practices and legal constraints, these types of bodies are still largely absent in China. Small business owners often rely on their intuition to manage their business through learning by doing and learning by failing, or relying on their personal network for help. A second factor is that there is still a vacuum of collective mechanism to articulate labour interests in the informal sector in China. Bureaucracy and low credibility of government officials tend to prevent workers from seeking help from official channels (Cooke and Rubery 2002). A third factor is that there is a high level of mutual dependency between the owners and the workers who tend to maintain a co-operative relationship for their own survival. So much so that at times there may be mutual incentives for both owners and workers to muddle through labour legislation and keep official inspections at bay. Most of these shops are very small scale and have operated for a relatively short period of time. Many owners enter business not because they have the cultural flair for entre-preneurship but because of the limitation of real choice to earn a reasonable living, just as Ram (1994) noted that entering small business was the only choice for the ethnic owners and workers in his study in the UK. Given the current labour market situation in China, the type of employment and labour conditions found in the small businesses in this study is likely to remain for the foreseeable future.

Fourth, based on the research evidence, there is a compelling need for greater effort from the state to increase protection of employment rights for workers in private (small) firms, an area which is receiving increasing attention in the EU and America. There *is* employment legislation in place in China to, in theory, provide individual protection for small business employees and to set standards of behaviour for their employers. However, these labour regulations are often not observed by private businesses. Moreover, given the significantly higher proportion of females who work in private small businesses, it is reasonable to suggest that women can be a vulnerable group in this sector where they tend to work extensively long hours and have to drop out of the labour market on becoming a mother (an uncommon practice in modern China). The long working hour culture in the small business sector also explains the relatively young age of the (female) workers who fill those jobs. This may be interpreted as a setback from the considerable level of gender equality in employment achieved under the system of command economy in China (Stockman *et al.* 1995; Cooke 2001). More incentives should therefore be given to small business owners to help contribute to the social insurance on behalf of their workers, in addition to raising their legal awareness and more stringent labour inspection. Support should be given by the state to enhance the entrepreneurship skills and management skills of small business owners. Equally, trade union and other official organizations have yet to find a way to unite workers in this sector and articulate their interests in partnership with employers.

Conclusion

This chapter has described the background under which the growth of the private small business sector has taken place in China. It investigated a number of aspects of employment relations in private small businesses in China. In general, employment conditions in this sector are worse than those of state-owned or larger private firms. Meanwhile, employment relations practices in private small firms in China appear to share considerably similar characteristics with those of small firms in other countries, developed or developing countries alike. However, there are also important differences in the nature of employment relations practices in private small firms in China, compared with those of other countries, because of its unique political, social and economic environment. A number of implications have arisen from discussion, especially in terms of what the state can/should do in order to provide a healthy environment for the growth of the sector.

In addition, more systematic comparative studies are needed on workplace relations and human resource issues of small firms across the developed and developing countries. As we can see, a significant and growing proportion of workers in China, and in the rest of the world, are now working in the private small business sector whose employers play a fundamental role in determining the pay, working and living conditions of millions of workers and in the structuring of labour markets. Further research both at a deeper level and on a broader scale is therefore necessary to advance our knowledge in a fast-growing area where workers are generally exposed to harsher employment conditions. Without these crucial studies we will remain poorly informed, on the basis of sparse official statistics, about the patterns of employment relations, the quality of working life, the quality of entrepreneurship, and other human resource-related characteristics dynamic to the growth of the sector.

9 HRM in China – recent developments

Introduction

After a relatively dispirited discussion on the inequality of work and employment in the previous three chapters, this chapter returns to a more positive and optimistic note on recent developments in HRM in China. In spite of the heavy criticisms of China's personnel policy and practice by (Western) scholars, human resource management is attracting wide attention as a subject in the relatively new management discipline in China since the late 1990s. There has been an unprecedented addition of instruction books and journals prescribing the what, why and how aspects of the subject readily identifiable in the Western HRM literature. More and more universities are developing HRM courses at both undergraduate and postgraduate level, although currently only a few universities have the capacity to provide degree courses on HRM. Organizational leaders also speak in the language of HRM, although it is debatable if such policy and practice truly exist in their organizations.

This chapter investigates the extent to which employing organizations in China have adopted HRM, where the most important changes in their personnel policy and practice have taken place and what types of HR initiatives have been adopted. It is not the intention of this chapter to engage in a philosophical debate of what HRM is in the Chinese context or what impacts HRM may have on organizational performance in China. Rather, it is an attempt to highlight recent developments in HR practices as well as ways in which HR functions are delivered in China based on the existing information. The chapter aims to cover a number of thematic topics (but omitting those that have been dealt with in depth in other chapters, e.g. pay and training) as well as a range of organizations of different ownership structures in order to provide a broader picture on the changing landscape of HRM in China. As such, the chapter may appear somewhat discursive in places, with the added constraints of limited data on the subjects and space available. Drawing largely on secondary data, the remainder of this chapter begins with a brief review of literature on the debate of whether HRM is taking root in China. It then moves on to explore in more depth specific aspects of HRM, namely recruitment, performance management, enterprise culture, HR outsourcing and e-HR. These aspects are selected for discussion here in part because they have not been dealt with elsewhere in the book (e.g. enterprise culture and e-HR), but more so, in my opinion, because they are the areas where important developments in HRM are experienced in China. The role of MNCs and JVs in disseminating Western HR practices is also discussed before the chapter's conclusion.

Is HRM taking root in China?

Early studies on HRM in China (e.g. Warner 1993; Child 1994, 1996) expressed caution in adopting the terminology of HRM to describe its personnel policy and practice. Warner (1993) suggested that while China was changing rapidly, it would still be realistic to 'think more than twice' before perceiving recognizable human resource management practices in most Chinese enterprises. His view was supported by Child (1996: 157), who noted:

> Although definitions of personnel management and human resource management vary considerably, modern Western thinking tends to be predicated upon assumptions such as the primary contribution of competent and motivated people to a firm's success, the compatibility of individual and corporate interests, the importance of developing a corporate culture which is in tune with top management's strategy for the firm, and the responsibility of senior management rather than employees' own representative bodies for determining personnel practices. It attaches importance to systematic recruitment and selection, training and development (including socialization into the corporate culture), close attention to motivation through personal involvement and participation in work and its organization, appraisal and progression procedures and incentive schemes. . . . This concept of human resource management is not found in Chinese enterprises. It is represented neither in the structures of management nor, by and large, in its practices.

A decade on, we are seeing signs of progressive change, with an increasing number of firms becoming more conscious of the need for effective management of human resources. This is a result of the deepening political and economic reforms in the state sector, the influence of MNCs and JVs with their Western HR practices, and the need to compete internationally and to be 'connected to the world', fuelled by China's accession to the WTO.

There is now an emerging consensus among researchers (e.g. Warner 1998; Zhu and Dowling 2002) that many traditional HR policies in China have changed and that there is clear evidence that a more complex and hybrid management model is emerging as the result of an increasing level of marketization and enterprise autonomy. For example, Ding and Akhtar (2001) note that an increasing number of Chinese enterprises are moving towards the adoption of HRM practices that focus on human capital development. This was particularly the case for larger and new enterprises across different ownership structures that were located in relatively developed cities. Zhu and Dowling's survey study (2002) similarly found that over half of the enterprises (with the exception of COEs) had written job analyses which were used for other HR activities, such as HR planning, recruitment and selection, and performance management. Furthermore, enterprises of different types of ownership all placed an emphasis on job-specific information for selection criteria, which demonstrated a positive correlation with the perceived effectiveness of staffing practices. Different external sources, such as advertising and the labour market, were used for recruitment purposes and more workers were employed on a contract basis.

More significantly, Zhao and Wu's survey (2003) of thirty-one large and super-large enterprises (67.6 per cent of them manufacturing firms and 77.4 per cent SOEs) in nine provinces revealed that the vast majority of enterprises had formal HR policies and procedures in place. About 80 per cent had a performance appraisal system and 75 per cent had HR planning, 67 per cent of which were based on job analysis. Most enterprises used a combination of recruitment and selection methods for recruitment. They tended to adopt different methods for different types of jobs.

There are also evident changes in the role of HR managers, as noted by Ding and Warner (1999) whose study of twenty-four SOEs and JVs in four major cities found that the role of personnel managers has changed dramatically in both the SOEs and JVs. They were involved in making decisions in a range of HRM issues such as recruitment and selection, training, promotion, dismissal, reward and discipline. However, personnel management in the JVs exhibited more of the HRM characteristics than those found in the SOEs. While personnel departments in both SOEs and JVs had extensive involvement in training, the former still had less power than the latter in the determination of reward and disciplinary actions.

These findings all indicate a level of resemblance to HR practices used in the advanced economies. However, this should not be taken to imply that HRM in China does not carry its own distinctive features. The remainder of this chapter explores in greater detail some of the aspects of HR practices in China.

Recruitment and labour market trends

A number of factors affect the ways organizations are recruiting their staff in China. First, the gradual withdrawal of the state from direct intervention in the state sector has brought to an end the directive and nepotic mode of recruitment in this sector (see Chapter 3 for further discussion), although a residual element still persists. This has allowed the state sector employing organizations to recruit directly from the external labour market. Recent HR reforms in the state sector in a bid to modernize its workforce and improve its performance also require state-owned organizations to formalize their recruitment procedures. Second, it is now a well-recognized fact that the labour market in China is encountering a paradoxical problem of skills short-ages on the one hand and a gross surplus of unskilled/semi-skilled labour supply on the other. This has forced many organizations to adopt a more sophisticated recruitment strategy to compete for talent from more diverse sources including expatriates and overseas Chinese graduates. Third, the surplus of unskilled (rural migrant) labour has allowed organizations operating at the low-pay low-skills end to continue to rely on word-of-mouth of the existing workforce to advertise their recruitment needs. For example, a survey of recruitment practices in (sweatshop) factories by Hare (1999) indicated that over 80 per cent of jobs were found through family, friends and village networks, with most workers knowing about the factory they would be joining before they even left the village. Similarly, a survey of migrant workers by Knight *et al.* (1999) revealed that the method of recruit-ment for 81.4 per cent of the Shenzhen population surveyed was through relatives or friends. The rest of this section discusses recent developments in recruitment in light of the skills shortages facing employers.

There have been a number of developments in both the state and the private sector in terms of recruitment methods they use and the sources of skilled staff available. First, for the state sector, recruitment and performance management are perhaps the two aspects of HRM that have experienced the most radical changes in governmental organizations (see Chapter 3). Earlier studies on HRM of (foreign) firms in China observed the difficulties of firms to recruit talent due to the unwillingness of their (state) employers to release them (e.g. Tsang 1994). They also reported that local governments in joint ventures tended to interfere with recruitment through nepotism (e.g. Bjorkman and Lu 1999b). These practices are now marginalized as recruitment becomes more professionalized in the state sector and foreign firms assume a more powerful bargaining position in the Chinese economy and the role of local governments is evolving. As we have seen from dis-cussions so far, more and more domestic firms in the public and private sector alike are beginning to adopt more transparent recruitment procedures and more sophisticated recruitment methods, drawing their pool of human resources from the labour market.

In particular, job fairs are becoming a popular recruitment method for graduates who used to wait on campus for employers to visit or for institu-tions to seek employers for them. This is in spite of the fact that, according to a nation-wide survey carried out by the State Education and Development Research Centre in 2000, university remains their main channel for find-ing employment. The survey showed that over 27 per cent were assigned a job by the university, some 18 per cent were recommended to their employers by the university, more than 16 per cent found their job through job fairs organized by their university or local authority, and over 27 per cent found employment by themselves or through the family network (The Project Team of the State Education 2002). Since the turn of the century, the organization of job fairs has become larger in scale and more professional, although there has been bad publicity of irresponsible organizers with pure profit motives. This has led to a number of job fair regulations being introduced recently by the state and regional governments to regulate the recruitment market. Job fairs are also being used by those (professionals) who are already employed to seek new jobs.

Second, there is a worsening skills shortage of professional and managerial staff nation-wide, a problem that has led to retention problems and wage wars. Many firms report that it is getting more and more difficult to recruit the right candidates for management and professional levels. For example, a survey carried out by ASIANET Consultants found that 91 per cent of the firms surveyed in Shanghai felt that it was getting more difficult to recruit senior executives, and 64 per cent felt the same regarding middle managers (*China Staff*, October 2002). Bjorkman and Lu (1999b) noted that retention of managers and professionals was a significant problem for many joint ventures, especially in large cities such as Beijing, Shanghai and Guangzhou. According to a survey conducted by Watson Wyatt in 2001 on HR professionals, the most important HR challenge they have faced has been the attraction and retention of quality staff (*China Staff*, May 2002). As a result of the skills shortage, a new group of working aristocrats is now emerging in China who are called the 'golden collars'. They are typically aged between 30 and 45 years, well-educated (often in the Western countries), and familiar with Western business practices and cultural trends. These people are able to command extremely high wages and other employment benefits that are significantly better than those that the majority of workers can demand. This wage war may also threaten the conformity of a global HR strategy of MNCs and minimize the financial advantage of employing local Chinese instead of expatriates in key posts.

Third and relatedly, a two-way talent flow is being developed in the labour market in China in the twenty-first century in that we are now seeing a reverse trend of talent inflow (back) into China instead of outflow alone, a brain drain phenomenon which has prevailed since the 1980s. In the past twenty years more than 580,000 Chinese went abroad to further their education. A total of 130,000 overseas Chinese students had returned to China (known as '*hai gui pai*') by the end of 2002 and there has been a significant increase since then of 13 per cent each year (Peng 2003). In the past, returned overseas graduates were hot job candidates for employers. This situation is, however, changing. In 2002, over 7,000 returnees to Shanghai could not find suitable jobs. Perhaps a most striking feature in the labour market in the year 2002 was the influx of a large number of job candidates from Hong Kong (and increasingly from Taiwan as well) to improve their employment prospects. Many of these candidates were educated in the West and familiar with the Western culture. They are no less qualified, and perhaps more experienced, than the overseas graduate returnees and are cheaper to hire than Western expatriates. Currently, there are nearly 300,000 Hong Kong people working in mainland China. In 2002, Guangzhou, Shenzhen, Shanghai and Beijing all held large-scale job fairs in Hong Kong to attract talent (Wu 2003). The injection of this pool of a ready-trained skilled workforce from Hong Kong and Taiwan will, to some extent, ease the acute problem of skills shortages in China, but it is only a drop in the ocean.

Fourth, the skills shortage problem, which is experienced in various degrees by different regions in the country, may be exacerbated by the relatively low mobility of the skilled workforce, in sharp contrast to the high level of mobility and flexibility of the low-skilled (rural) migrant workforce. If inter-firm mobility has been restricted in the past in China because of administrative bureaucracy, then recent mobility barriers come from that of inter-city mobility. Whereas administrative constraints have gradually been removed from the authority's role, many key employees are extremely reluctant to move from a first-tier large city such as Shanghai to a third-tier one in the inner mainland, should their (foreign) employers wish to relocate their offices to save operating costs or to develop new market bases. It is not unusual for foreign firms to offer their Chinese key employees a relocation package at a level similar to what they would have to offer to expatriates before they would agree to move. In many cases, Chinese employees would simply refuse to be relocated and find alternative employers (*China Staff*, September 2002).

More generally, turnover rates among university graduates appear to be relatively low, a feature in line with the Chinese tradition of long tenure in employment. For example, according to a survey carried out by the State Education and Development Research Centre in 2000, only 14 per cent of the 1,920 graduates surveyed had changed their jobs in the first five years of their employment. The main reasons for job changes were better opportunities for their careers and higher wages. Over 65 per cent of those surveyed felt 'very satisfied' or 'quite satisfied' with their job whereas 31 per cent were 'not very satisfied' (The Project Team of State Education 2002).

None the less, urban employees in China are changing jobs more frequently than their parents' generation did. According to *China Staff* (July to August 2001), a survey carried out by the National Research Centre of Science and Technology Development and the Norway International Research Centre showed that not only were people changing jobs more frequently but most found new jobs through friends and acquaintances. The study involved a total number of 7,000 residents from Beijing, Wuxi and Zhuhai cities. It looked at urban employment and the workforce distribution levels in these areas for the years 1998 and 1999. The study revealed that prior to the 1980s, workers tended to change jobs after being with the same employer for fifteen to twenty years. In the 1980s, this figure was reduced to ten years and in the 1990s workers typically changed jobs after five years. This finding is supported by a more recent survey on 800 workers carried out by a research centre in Guangzhou City. The survey found that over half of those surveyed intended to seek alternative employment, the main reason being dissatisfaction with their wage level (*Workers' Daily*, 29 November 2002).

Performance management

Another noticeable change in HRM in China has been the use of performance management systems. It has been argued that a major issue in Chinese management has been motivation and labour discipline (Lockett 1988). While state sector organizations are now linking employees' performance much more closely to their reward, promotion and job security, often through performance appraisals and other forms of assessments (see Chapter 3), performance-related pay schemes have become more common in private sector enterprises. For example, Zhao and Wu's survey (2003) found that the vast majority of enterprises used material incentives (e.g. bonuses and profit sharing (mainly for technical and managerial staff)) as the primary motivator at work. However, it has been widely noted by academics and practitioners that implementing performance management systems was a major challenge for HRM. For example, it has been reported that joint ventures in China have encountered difficulties in adopting performance management as an integral part of their HR strategy (Child 1994; Ding *et al.* 1997; Bjorkman and Lu 1999b; Lindholm 2000; Braun and Warner 2002). Lockett (1988) suggested that the Chinese culture was a potential barrier for Chinese enterprises to adopt Western management techniques. An interview survey of twenty Chinese company directors from the construction industry in China also showed that most of these Chinese-owned companies have implemented some form of performance management system. These directors felt generally that performance appraisal was more easily conducted at the shopfloor level but not for professional and managerial staff. They also believed that the performance-related pay and bonus schemes in place did not have sufficient variations, due to people's resistance, to reflect the performance differences among staff. The survey was conducted by myself in late 2003 while staff were on an executive management training programme in the UK.

A recent survey conducted by an HR consulting firm – Development Dimensions International (DDI) – has examined the development of performance management practices in China (*China Staff*, May 2003). The DDI study found that organizations in China (participating firms were all MNCs although domestic firms were invited to participate) have raised their awareness of using performance management systems as a business strategy to drive results. In general, a significant proportion of employees were satisfied with their performance management practices. The survey found that more than half of the organizations surveyed were effective in:

1   Structuring specific performance plans that contain work objectives and behaviours to help focus the efforts of employees.

2   Reviewing performance with employees at least once a year.
3   Linking performance to pay.
4   Holding supervisors accountable for evaluating the performance of their direct reports.

The study also identified a number of areas which the surveyed organizations needed to improve. These include:

1   Developing the skills of appraisers in performance management concepts, roles and skills. This is needed particularly when it comes to feedback and coaching, and sharing performance data openly with employees.
2   Evaluating performance in a fair manner that avoids cronyism, favouritism and bias.
3   Reviewing approaches to differentiate between the performance of employees.
4   Increasing employees' involvement in the performance management process.

More broadly, these studies point to similar problems faced by managers in the implementation of performance management systems in China to those found in Western countries. For example, the design of the performance management system may be flawed; criteria of performance measurement may be difficult to underpin; managers may not be comfortable in delivering appraisals and feel uneasy about providing behavioural data in the appraisal to support the ratings they give their staff. One of the greatest sources of frustration of employees is that feedback from managers is not specific, accurate and clear, and they may feel demotivated after the appraisal (*China Staff*, May 2003).

Enterprise culture management

'Enterprise culture building' is undoubtedly one of the, if not *the*, latest popular management phrases in China. Enterprise culture building is in fact nothing new to China, in spite of its recent propagation as an advanced Western management philosophy to be adopted by Chinese enterprises. Some large and super-large SOEs have long developed their own management philosophy, dating back in the early 1950s when they were often promoted as model enterprises by the state, such as Anshan Steel Factory and Daqing Oil Field. In particular, '*Angang* (Anshan Steel) Constitutions' and 'Daqing Iron Man Spirit' have long played the role of enterprise cultural value and congruence, albeit under different names. Chan (1995) likewise observed that many so-called 'Japanese management techniques' adopted by the Chinese enterprises, such as morning briefings, already existed in China.

Enterprise culture building in China may be broadly divided into three periods since the founding of socialist China (Li and Bai 2000). The first period was from 1949 up until the end of the Cultural Revolution, although the phrase 'enterprise culture' was not used. Enterprise culture of this period was predominantly about setting and following behavioural norms with high publicity of good practices of 'role-model' organizations that were usually super-large SOEs. Honesty, diligence, endurance of hardship and thrift were widely promoted as the guiding values. Employees were expected to treat their enterprise as their own home. The second period was between the early 1980s and mid-1990s when people were given increasing freedom to pursue material wealth in the early years of the deepening economic reforms. Entrepreneurship was encouraged as a new culture. This new-found freedom has led to many organizational leaders pursuing their own interests at the expense of the organization. The third period began in the mid-1990s when Chinese enterprises were under increasing exposure to what were perceived to be 'best practices' of MNCs, JVs and domestic role models. 'Enterprise culture' as a management technique was imported to China together with advanced technology and other management techniques. All of a sudden, there was a heatwave in the adoption of enterprise culture by all types of organizations, if more in name than in substance.

In spite of the enthusiasm of both management and academics in promoting enterprise culture as the new cure for all enterprise diseases, few systematic studies have been carried out to establish what it is; what its characteristics are; how it works in China; and what the problems may be in its implementation, for example. In order to shed light on the practices of enterprise culture in China, I have carried out an analysis of published reports on the implementation of enterprise culture. A key phrase 'enterprise culture' was used to search for journal articles from the *China Academic Journal* (CAJ) network for the period from 1994 to the end of 2003. A total of 421 articles were collected that contained discussions of enterprise culture. After an initial analysis, eighty-two articles were selected for further analysis (see Table 9.1). Others were either too brief or non-empirical speculations. Seventy-three of the eighty-two articles selected were published after 1997. These were case study reports of companies (mostly self-reporting from the case study companies) which have implemented enterprise culture management.

The analysis of these articles shows that there are six core cultural aspects (broadly categorized) which are generally adopted by companies in their implementation of enterprise culture initiatives. These core aspects include:

1   Employee care (material) culture. This type of enterprise culture is welfare oriented and emphasizes on the paternalistic welfare of employees. Attention is focused on improving employees' quality of life by enhancing their living standards and working conditions, usually through bonuses, subsidiaries of all kinds, transportation to work, health care provision and a better working environment. SOEs in China have had a long tradition of extensive workplace welfare provisions until recent reforms when many of these provisions have been rolled back.

2 Entertainment culture. Workplace entertainment provisions range from sports events, arts competitions, theatrical performances, local festive competitions, holiday trips, libraries, games rooms, literary clubs, matchmaking to fashion shows. Again, these activities are aimed at enhancing employees' quality of life to retain and motivate them.

3 Operational excellence culture. This aspect of the enterprise culture includes subsets of culture such as productivity improvement culture, customer service culture and innovation culture. Enterprises may adopt initiatives such as quality improvement schemes (there has been a surge in the application and accreditation of the ISO 9000 series in China in the past few years), problem-solving teams and customer service initiatives. Employee suggestion schemes are often used as a component of enterprise culture building. Similarly, skills and craftsmanship competitions, quality competitions and technical collaborations are promoted in order to raise the skills level of employees and quality standard of products.

4 Procedure culture. This is achieved mainly through the systemization of workplace procedural rules and regulations, including job analysis and description, performance targets, reward and disciplinary procedures, safety procedures and other behavioural norms.

5 Image culture, including product and/or service brand image. This focuses on the promotion of organizational image and public relations through a range of proactive enterprise image-building activities involving participation in local social events and competitions, sponsorships and donations, trade fairs and exhibitions, media publicity, and collaboration with other enterprises. Enterprises also invest heavily in enhancing the physical layout of the workplace through uniforms, badges, logos, trendy refurbishment and well-maintained gardens.

6 Ideology (spirit) culture. This is usually achieved by setting role models, moral teaching of socialist values and briefing meetings about the principles of enterprise culture. It also includes training for employees to raise their skill levels and general educational courses to enhance employees' educational qualification levels. It is believed that these measures will enhance the self-esteem and conscientiousness of workers.

In particular, the analysis shows that a higher proportion of companies in the secondary sector (25 per cent) than in the tertiary sector (14 per cent) have employee care programmes in place (see Table 9.1). Similarly, a higher proportion of companies in the secondary sector (88 per cent) than in the tertiary sector (64 per cent) have skills training, educational courses and role models in place. This reflects the characteristic differences in these two sectors. Traditionally, enterprises in the secondary sector are more oriented towards employee care and have greater need for skills. The analysis also reveals that employee entertainment and operational excellence are the two major focuses of enterprises in cultural management. This is reinforced by

Table 9.1 Enterprise culture management activities – an analysis of case study reports

Sector	No. of articles	% of total articles	Employee care[a]		Entertainment[a]		Operational excellence[a]		Image culture[a]		Procedural culture[a]		Ideology culture[a]	
			No.	(%)	No.	(%)	No.	(%)	No.	(%)	No.	(%)	No.	(%)
Secondary sector (e.g. manufacturing, construction, energy)	68	83	17	25	41	60	46	68	39	57	24	35	60	88
Tertiary sector (e.g. telecom, finance)	14	17	2	14	8	57	12	86	8	57	9	64	9	64
Total	82	100	19	23	49	60	58	71	47	57	33	40	69	84

Note
Five of the companies were foreign-owned or JVs, the rest were SOEs or domestic private firms. All were large or medium-sized enterprises. No suitable articles on public sector organizations were found.
[a] Figures represent the number of articles and percentage in the sector.

Table 9.2 Enterprise culture management activities – level of adoption

No. of cultural aspects	6	5	4	3	2	1
No. of companies that have taken up no. of aspects	3	9	25	25	17	3
%	4	11	30	30	21	4
No. of companies in secondary sector that have taken up no. of aspects	2	8	20	21	15	2
%	3	12	29	31	22	3
No. of companies in tertiary sector that have taken up no. of aspects	1	1	5	4	2	1
%	7	7	36	29	14	7

enterprise/brand image building. However, the general uptake of employee care programmes is markedly lower than that of the other five categories. This suggests that image, productivity and quality other than employee welfare are the primary concerns of enterprises. In addition, the majority of companies take up three or four aspects of the enterprise culture rather than the full range of six categories (see Table 9.2). Some enterprises have a range of sophisticated public relations management initiatives while others have only basic activities in place.

The analysis of the case study articles further suggests that the choice of cultural elements in the enterprise culture initiatives appears to be closely related to the characteristics of the enterprise itself, including its history, ownership, size and product market. More specifically, three types of enterprise stand out in their different focuses on the HR elements as enterprise culture.

The first type are the super-large national model enterprises that have a long SOE history such as Daqing Oil Field. Their new enterprise culture movement is essentially a renewed emphasis on their traditional enterprise values that prevailed in the 1950s and early 1960s. This inevitably gives an impression of 'old wine in new bottles', substituting the word 'spirit' with 'culture'. However, it may be argued that this is what has been proved suitable to their enterprise from their early years of experience and that there is no reason why they should not adopt the same content as a way of revitalizing their enterprise vigour lost in recent decades. But perhaps more importantly, the inherent political mindset of these SOE enterprises implicitly prevents propagation of the jargon of Western enterprise culture because it may be seen as a betrayal of the past and an admittance of internal failure, as these SOEs were once hailed with national pride.

The second type are firms from the new high-tech (private) industry. By contrast, they tend to use more HRM language and are more exposed to Western culture (and technology). They are not afraid of using Western management language because they do not carry the socialist enterprise baggage and are not constrained by an SOE growth trajectory. In fact, they need to use Western management jargon as a symbol of their open-mindedness and modernity. This is because the discourse of modernity carries much disciplinary power in China these days, and those who do not act or speak of adopting advanced (Western) practices are deemed backward and outdated (Cooke 2004c). They are able to borrow Western management notions and reinterpret them with Chinese meanings in the configuration of their management practice. In short, wholly foreign-owned, joint ventures and high-tech domestic firms use more similar management jargon than do traditional SOEs and small domestic private firms.

A third type are those half-way houses that have a combination of some elements of the first two types. They are typically smaller domestic Chinese firms. Depending on the influence that the senior managers subject themselves to, the cultural language in these enterprises may lean towards one type or the other. Some also make use of government organizations and other political bodies, such as the All-China Women's Federation, the trade unions, Party organizations and the Youth League body, to enhance their enterprise image. They participate in events initiated by these organs as the locus to drive their enterprise culture movement.

Many companies reported (perhaps not surprisingly) that the implementation of enterprise culture initiatives has had tangible positive effects on the morale of the workforce and the productivity of the enterprise. They reported that their employees cared about their workplace environment far more than they had in the past. In general, enterprise culture is perceived to carry out the following functions (Yu 1994):

1   A guiding function by providing guidance for employees' behaviour through enterprise value and behavioural norms.
2   A congruence function by uniting employees through a common set of values and norms through communication.
3   A motivational function through a sense of responsibility and pride, reward and punishment.
4   A restriction function through enterprise procedures, rules and regulations.
5   A radiation function through the dissemination of efficient practices of good enterprises.
6   A stability function through enhancing the commitment of employees.

They essentially reflect enterprise management, enterprise entertainment and enterprise spirit. Mu and Bi (1994) argue that procedural culture is at the lowest level of enterprise culture while enterprise entertainment culture is the most visual and vigorous culture. Enterprise ideology/spirit, however, is the highest level of enterprise culture. It is an outcome of the combination of all aspects of culture and it represents the values, norms of behaviour and congruence of the enterprise.

Generally speaking, there are several characteristics in the enterprise culture in China (Mu and Bi 1994; Yu 1994). These appear to be: time-specific (reflecting the political, social and economic environment of the time period); humanity-specific (in the form of employee care); diverse (there is no restriction on what enterprises may include), reflecting the internal and external characteristics unique to the enterprise; mouldability (e.g. moral teaching); normative (procedures); collectivistic (emphasis of congruence); nationality-specific (national spirit); and community-specific (e.g. participation in local events). Enterprise culture in China is therefore a complex and multi-layered system, and its implementation is by no means without problems.

What remains unknown is the extent to which Chinese workers embrace these enterprise culture-building initiatives, in spite of the fact that these initiatives are perceived to be important and championed by some organizational leaders. Few creditable studies, if any, have been found on employees' opinion about enterprise culture management. There is therefore no hard evidence that the implementation of enterprise culture schemes has led to better organizational performance and an enhanced quality of working life of employees. As Rubery and Grimshaw (2003: 61) point out,

> These initiatives mainly involve eliminating unproductive processes and unproductive time, thereby almost by definition increasing work intensity. Question marks are placed over whether other societies' work-forces would be willing to accept continuous improvement techniques if they led directly to more intense work pressures.

In China, covert resistance to imposition may occur but overt forms of opposition appear to be relatively rare, at least in the enterprises where I have conducted my research. This is due in part to the job loss threat and perhaps more so because overt disagreement is not a method that the Chinese tend to use to deal with differences (see e.g. Chapter 8).

New trends in delivering the HR function – outsourcing HR and e-HR

Two recent developments are influencing the ways in which the HR service is delivered in organizations in the Western economies. One is the increasing use of HR outsourcing specialist firms. The other is the adoption of e-HR. The increasing use of HR outsourcing by firms over the past decade is necessarily a management strategy in response to accelerating competitive pressure. Firms outsource (part of) their HR function for reasons such as cost reduction, improvement of service through external expertise, opportunity of keeping the function fresh and up to date, and avoidance of upfront capital investment when attempting to introduce such a transformation (Cooke *et al.* 2004). In addition, outsourcing is seen as one way of liberating the HR professionals within the client organization to perform a more consultative and strategic role. While the growth of HR outsourcing business is to a large extent facilitated by the radical advancement of information and communication technologies (ICT) in recent years, many companies also report an increasing use of e-HR in-house. For instance, in some large organizations, employees are encouraged/expected to use e-HR to update their personnel records. To what extent, if any, are the HR functions in China being influenced by these new practices? This section provides information on whether, and the extent to which, HR functions in organizations in China are experiencing these changes.

HR outsourcing

Based on the available evidence from secondary sources of data, the outsourcing of HR in general appears to be rather limited in China, although there are trends of the increasing use of external providers for their services such as recruitment and training (see Chapter 5 for training). A major reason for the lack of outsourcing and/or shared services of the HR function is, according to the Watson Wyatt's Greater China e-HR survey of 268 firms in the region (*China Staff*, November 2002), the lack of options for outsourcing and shared services. The 'Outsourcing in Asia-Pacific' survey conducted by the HR consulting firm Hewitt Associates (*China Staff*, April 2003) further reveals that many companies in China are either unfamiliar with the processes and procedures of HR outsourcing or are unfamiliar with the players in the market. In addition, it may be difficult for companies in China to justify a decision to outsource on the basis of potential cost reductions because administrative labour is still relatively cheap in China and it may actually cost more to outsource the function than to keep it in-house. The same survey also points out that most outsourcing activities in China come from MNCs.

Given the rapid growth of the number of recruitment and headhunting agencies in China, recruitment is undoubtedly one HR function that makes the greatest use of external services compared with all the other HR functions. Zhao and Wu's survey (2003) found that 25 per cent of enterprises used headhunting or employment agencies for recruitment, although more than half of the enterprises had never used external experts to take part in the selection processes. More and more companies are now using executive search to recruit senior executives. A mixture of executive search, agencies and advertising are also used to recruit middle managers. It is believed that there are at least 1,000 headhunting and employment agencies in Shanghai and several hundreds in Beijing. Headhunting and employment agency firms now provide HR assessment services to user organizations. Influential head-hunting agencies include, for example, Talent – the first independent headhunting firm established in China in 1994. Manpower, a multinational employment agency, established its first China office in Shanghai in early 2000 and later another branch in Beijing to deal with part-time and temporary staffing services.

'Headhunting' agencies first appeared in China in the late 1980s. These organizations initially created a mysterious impression due to their often covert and sometimes illegal operations. Not surprisingly, the vast majority of firms using headhunting agencies have been in the private sector. In recent years, regulations have been issued by local governments to legalize their existence and specify the types of business which they are allowed to operate, especially for foreign agencies. To date, their existence has more or less become accepted by all concerned. They are given more freedom, through legal recognition, to operate in areas where they were not allowed to be engaged in the past, including that of placing skilled and professional personnel. In general, the types of informational services headhunting and employment agencies provide to their (corporate) clients in China include talent (*rencai*) information service, talent assessment, talent training and talent renting.

In addition, some provide personnel agency (*renshi daili*) services to individuals. Under the state economy system, each person must have a personnel file which contains all personal details since high school education. This file is to be kept officially by the school during educational years and then by the employer during employment, or by the local authority in the case of unemployment. Although many firms are now more relaxed about the personnel file when they recruit new staff, the system has not yet been entirely abolished. For those who are changing jobs frequently or are in covert employment, they need a place to keep their personnel file, and employment agencies seize this business opportunity to provide such services.

In terms of ownership structure, there are two types of headhunting and employment agencies operating in the market: domestic agencies and foreign-owned (mostly MNCs) branches. The former have been more protected by the state in their scope of business operations. They are, in general, in their early stage of development as an industry and are facing growing com-petition, in light of the loosening regulatory restrictions, from their foreign competitors which are far more established and well resourced (Liu, D. W. 2000). It is believed that competition is lifting the service standards of employment agencies, and the recent removal of legal constraints by the state means they have more freedom to operate in a much wider range of services.

Caution must be taken, however, to differentiate headhunting and employ-ment agencies. Currently, there is a lack of understanding of the differences between executive search firms and recruitment agencies, in part because many recruitment agencies call themselves executive search when in reality they are not. In addition, employment agencies and job centres are mainly set up by the local labour authorities to help laid-off workers and other unemployed people to (re)gain employment. Private agencies are rarely allowed to set foot in this territory because their profit motive is seen as incompatible with the purpose of existence of these organizations (Lee and Warner 2002).

The use of e-HR

Existing survey studies suggest that the overall picture of e-HR in China is less than promising. For example, Watson Wyatt's Greater China e-HR survey of 268 firms in the region found that the use of HRM software was not as widespread in Greater China as it was in Europe, with 34 per cent of firms employing less than 500 staff not using any software at all for their HR function. Reasons given for this low level of investment in IT for the HR function include: difficulties in proving the anticipated return of investment of the use of IT in the HR system, problems of systems integration, and lack of funding. The survey report concludes that companies in the Greater China region 'have only just started their journey towards enhancing the use of technology in achieving the desired results of improvement in HR processes, efficiency, productivity and cost reduction' (*China Staff*, November 2002: 34).

This conclusion is supported by the findings of other studies in mainland China. For example, Zhao and Wu's (2003) study revealed that most enterprises surveyed only used their IT HR systems for basic HR record keeping rather than for the more sophisticated HR functions, and 25 per cent of the enterprises used the internet for recruitment. Similarly, Zheng's (2003) survey on 1,775 enterprises in China (78 per cent domestic firms and 22 per cent foreign enterprises) found that 70 per cent of the enterprises had not introduced an HR information system. In spite of the fact that the vast majority of the enterprises believed that it was highly necessary to use information technology to transform the HR system, only 30 per cent had ever implemented an IT system, yet most of them were larger firms employing over 500 people. Some 60 per cent of those enterprises that had not introduced any IT system for their HR function planned to introduce one in the next two years. For those that had implemented an IT HR system, over half had introduced them in the two years prior to the survey and 18 per cent planned to renew their system in the next two years. HR professionals faced serious challenges, with more than half having only average IT skills and needing to develop their competence and knowledge on IT HR systems. For those who worked in enterprises that have not introduced any IT HR system, 68 per cent felt that their IT skills were basic.

For the enterprises that had adopted an IT HR system, most only used it for basic HR functions such as keeping their personnel records of wages, attendance, recruitment and welfare. Few used them for strategic planning, performance management, training and career development planning, or self-service purposes. Major challenges reported in the introduction of IT HR systems include the lack of well-developed products and of professional consultancy and training services to facilitate organizations to make informed choices and implement the system smoothly, and the lack of successful cases as examples to follow. In addition, organizations face skills shortages in the management and security protection of the system. Based on the survey findings, Zheng (2003) believes that there is a gap of five to ten years between the state of affair of China's e-HR system and that adopted in the Western countries. Zheng also predicts that e-learning, e-recruitment and employee self-service will be the 'hot' areas of development in e-HR.

However, this seemingly bleak outlook must not be allowed to conceal the oases in the e-HR desert in China. Among them are the governmental and public sector organizations. These state-sponsored organizations are undoubtedly taking the lead in the adoption of e-HR, most notably in recruitment, especially in graduate recruitment and civil servant recruitment. For example, in the 2002–3 recruitment of civil servants for the government in Guangdong Province, all job applications for the 5,400 posts were to be submitted online (*Yangcheng Evening News*, 2 November 2002). All recruitment information related to the posts and organizations was available on the websites. This has significantly increased the transparency and efficiency of the recruitment procedures and processes. There are strong signs which suggest that these practices will be extended to the lower level governments and become more widespread in the less developed provinces.

The West penetrating the East? The role of MNCs and JVs in disseminating HRM in China

Multinational corporations are often regarded as a potential source of convergence in international HRM in that they are expected to use their international perspective to promote the diffusion of 'best practice' HR techniques (Rubery and Grimshaw 2003). This appears to be the case in China, but not until recently.

A review of the studies conducted by (Western) academics in the past fifteen years or so on HR practices of MNCs and JVs in China points to an interesting path of growth in which MNCs and JVs are beginning to enjoy more autonomy and to become a more confident and positive source of influence for all concerned. While earlier research on Western foreign investment enterprises established in China showed that MNCs had to adapt their HRM policies and practices to the Chinese environment (e.g. Child 1991, 1994; Goodall and Warner 1997, 1998), more recent studies (e.g. Lasserre and Ching 1997; Bjorkman and Lu 2001) suggested that there seemed to have been a trend towards introducing more 'Western' HRM policies during the 1990s. For example, Bjorkman and Lu's study (2001) on sixty-three manufacturing Chinese–Western joint ventures found that HRM practices were considerably more similar to those of the MNCs than to those of local manufacturing companies. This result is arguably due to a lack of local pressure for the firms to adopt Chinese-oriented personnel/HRM practices and to Western executives' perception of the need to adopt Western HRM practices to make the joint venture competitive (Bjorkman and Lu 2001). One of the most important consequences of foreign involvement in Chinese joint ventures has been the introduction of a more systematic management approach in that the systems were defined in writing, standardized and operated on a regular basis (Child 1994). Braun and Warner (2002) found that a majority of MNCs in their sample have placed a high strategic importance on the HRM function and have attempted to introduce internally consistent high-performance HRM practices. This finding, according to the authors, was a new development which did not exist in earlier works. Bjorkman and Fan (2002) further observed that the MNCs in their sample had HR practices that tended to be more closely in line with the 'high-performance HRM system' as defined by Western HRM scholars than with the personnel practices found in local Chinese companies. This is in spite of the fact that these HR 'best practices' were mainly Western practices transferred and adapted to suit the Chinese environment.

It must, however, be pointed out here that this is not to suggest that all MNCs and JVs are good employers and that their HR policies are embraced by their employees with enthusiasm. For example, an earlier study by Child (1994) found that, in the thirty JVs studied, there had been various attempts to introduce Western personnel tools with varying, but never significant, degrees of success. A common complaint among Western managers was that Chinese staff were reluctant to accept personal responsibility (Child 1994). Another earlier study (Ilari and Grange 1999) on a Sino–Italian joint venture motor company in southern China also revealed that the Italian partner found it difficult to transfer its firm-specific advantages to China because of the cultural differences in the two employment systems. More specifically, implementation of work concepts such as delegation, broader job responsibilities, and extensive co-operation at both individual and departmental levels were difficult, as was the implementation of a simplified wage structure among technical staff. Legewie's study (2002) on issues related to the control and co-ordination of Japanese subsidiaries in China further highlights the problems of an expatriate-based management system in transferring a typical Japanese firm's strength, namely socialization and networking, abroad and in building up an efficient transnational network of global operations. None the less, there is evidence to suggest that efforts were made by MNC managers to reconcile the twin pressures for control and adaptation rather than satisfying one at the expense of the other (Child and Heavens 1999). A discernible trend is that Western HR policies are gradually being accepted and internalized by the younger generation of the Chinese workforce who can no longer seek job security in the state sector. This is reflected in the fact that MNCs and JVs are the 'first choice' companies for most job candidates. According to an HR survey reported in *Beijing Youth Newspaper*

(15 November 2002), two-thirds of the 'most popular employers' voted by HR managers themselves were MNCs and JVs in China.

An important factor that contributes to the growing influence of MNCs and JVs in China as employers is their changing relationship with local government, supported by the Chinese government's proactive economic policy in attracting foreign investment in the past two decades. While local government officials had strong administrative power to influence the conditions in which MNCs and JVs operated from the early 1980s until the mid-1990s, the bargaining power has been steadily swinging towards MNCs and JVs since the late 1990s. The local government's interfering role has gradually been replaced by a more supportive one. Most local governments now have an important task of attracting foreign investment as one of their key performance indicators. Government officials are keen to help FDIs in any ways they can, from favourable financial policies, positive media coverage and high-profile propaganda to, for some, tolerance of the violation of labour rights. Many MNCs and JVs are treated by their local governments as 'model' companies in the region, with some being national role models. Blue chip MNCs and JVs are generally considered to have a more sophisticated HR system than the Chinese domestic firms. They tend to have a high-profile role in their local areas not only in the economy but also in cultural life and management ideology. They may carry out a range of high-profile activities and sponsorship events. They are considered to be modern and advanced and are often visited by provincial and municipal government officials as model enterprises. Many local organizations visit these 'role-model' firms to adopt their management techniques and organizational procedures, or even the physical layout of the establishment (see e.g. Cooke 2004c). This high publicity serves in turn as an incentive or implicit pressure for these firms to implement progressive HR practices in order to defend and enhance that prestige.

In short, it seems that the role of MNCs and JVs in disseminating Western HR practices in China is set to expand, with an increasing number of high-profile MNCs relocating their Asian-Pacific headquarters, operations or regional offices to China since its accession to the WTO.

Conclusion

There is now a growing body of evidence which suggests that HRM in larger organizations in China is becoming more systematic and, to some extent, more strategic. These organizations are beginning to adopt Western practices of HRM, notably in job analysis and description, recruitment and selection, training and development, and performance management and reward. There is also increasing use of e-HR and external services for the HR function, although the level of uptake is relatively low and lagging behind that in the Western countries. Evidence presented in this chapter and that in previous chapters indicates that HRM is beginning to take root in China, if HRM is to be broadly defined as 'a distinctive approach to employment management which seeks to achieve competitive advantage through the strategic deployment of a highly committed and capable workforce using an array of cultural, structural and personnel techniques' (Storey 1995: 5). There is a growing trend of convergence to Western practices in many aspects, although a strong resemblance in substantive contents should not be expected. Signs of convergence include: more flexibility in strategies of labour utilization, more sophisticated recruitment and selection methods, increasing emphasis on and level of skills training, more diverse methods of financial reward linking with individual and organizational performance, and a renewed interest in enterprise culture, albeit with strong Chinese characteristics. As Ding and Akhtar (2001: 962) observe:

> an increasing number of enterprises will make a clean break from past personnel practices and move towards convergence with HRM practices aimed at developing human capital. The magnitude of convergence will, however, significantly depend upon organizational characteristics (age, size, and particularly ownership), the intervening role of the HR function and the choice of the competitive strategy.

There are several ways in which HRM in China is being influenced by Western practices. One source of influence comes from MNCs and JVs operating in China. While MNCs and JVs may find it necessary to adapt their Western HR practices to fit local cultural values and norms, many domestic firms are beginning to model these Western management practices as 'best practices'. Another source of influence is through firms, mostly international HR consultancy firms, that provide HR services, such as recruitment and training agencies. A third source of influence comes from the individual level. Returned overseas graduates and migrant workers from Hong Kong and Taiwan bring yet more Western management techniques into the Chinese HR system. They may further act as a catalyst in the adoption of the so-called new HR practices in their workplace if local employees feel the need to compete with these employees who are pro or more receptive to these practices. A final force comes from the new generation of Chinese managers who tend to be more open-minded and innovative, and are keen to be seen as modern. They may champion the diffusion of 'advanced' Western management practices in their workplace or at least use 'Western' as a disguise to promote techniques that they favour to bring about changes.

What needs to be pointed out here is that while the adoption of HR techniques in China is on the increase, many managers (interviewed by myself) admit that certain Western HR techniques sound good in theory but prove difficult to implement in practice. Worse still, while many elements of HRM are becoming popular topics as part of the wider embrace of HRM as an 'advanced' management philosophy, if not yet as a reality, these rosy signs necessarily chart the early stage of development of HRM in China. This is because HRM 'best practices' are often being prescribed uncritically without contextual issues and their effectiveness being considered properly. While a more widespread adoption of HR techniques will undoubtedly raise the professional standard of HRM, it poses a serious challenge to HR professionals and academics alike. This issue will be discussed further in the concluding chapter.

10 The future prospects of HRM, work and employment in China

Introduction

This book has provided an overview of HRM, work and employment in China, covering major aspects of HRM and their characteristics in different types of organizations such as SOEs, public sector organizations, foreign firms, JVs, TVEs and domestic private firms. It has highlighted some of the unique features of HRM practices in China. These include: gender inequality in employment; the weak presence of the trade unions and the absence of the workers' voice; the unofficial role of grassroot workers in maintaining the egalitarian distribution system; problems of skills shortages and the associated problems in recruitment, retention and training; and the adoption of Western HR practices, performance management, and enterprise culture management. The discussion of these issues was located in the broader institutional and social context of work organization and employment environment within which HR policies and practices are embedded. These include the labour market segmentation and the ineffectiveness of the minimum wage regulations, for example. It has drawn our attention to the pressures and sources of influence which have helped to shape the new patterns of employment relations in China that have become more diverse and dynamic, marked by shorter employment contracts and tenures and rising levels of labour–management disputes.

This concluding chapter turns to the future prospects of HRM, work and employment in China by contemplating the roles and key challenges facing its main actors, namely the state, the trade unions, the HR function and the research community. The chapter begins by looking at the role and strategic plan of the state in employment creation and skills training. It then discusses the challenges faced by the trade unions and points out their strategic tasks. This is followed by a summary of major challenges to HRM in China and the implications of all these challenges for the HR function in the future. The chapter finally explores a number of research implications for both Chinese and Western academics. It also provides a comparative outline of similarities found between HR features in China and those found in other countries. Although comparative analysis is not the focus of this book, it draws attention to the need for a new approach to comparative study for future works in the field.

The role of the state

It is clear that major economic and social reform initiatives have been implemented by the Chinese government in the past two decades and much has been achieved. As Child and Tse (2001: 19) noted, 'The Chinese leaders are endeavouring to change the country's institutional legacy through a policy of disequilibrium and non-linear progression intended to accommodate basic strains within the system, especially between the goals of reform and social stability.' While the role of the state as an employer is rapidly decreasing, its role as a regulator is increasing and that as an economic manager is becoming more competent. Many of the labour regulations in China were introduced in the past two decades as part of a broader attempt to develop a legislative framework appropriate to the new environment. Despite criticisms of the fairness and effectiveness of these regulations, attempts are being made to improve existing regulations and to introduce new ones to provide a level of protection, at least in principle, to those vulnerable in the labour market. The key issue is, however, how to enforce these regulations effectively.

Moreover, the state is facing the twin pressures of the need to create more employment opportunities and the need for upskilling its labour force, since the skills level of the country is generally low and is severely lagging behind rapid technological change. This is despite the fact that the education and skill levels of the labour force have been rising steadily. So far, job creation initiatives have mainly focused on quantity rather than quality (measured by job security, wage levels and welfare provision), assuming that having a job is better than not having one. In particular, non-standard (informal) employment as a flexible labour strategy has been promoted by the state as a new way to absorb unemployed workers. Favourable policies have been issued by local governments to encourage the creation and uptake of these types of employment. Existing evidence suggests that certain social groups, such as female laid-off workers, older workers and rural migrant workers, are over-represented among temporary, part-time and other forms of non-standard employment which make up more than 20 per cent of the total workforce in the country (Cooke 2004e). These types of work, such as cleaning, security, and other community and domestic services, are often low-skilled, poorly paid and with unsocial working hours and low intrinsic reward. They are created to accommodate workers who have been made redundant by their state employer. They are also designed to target young workers and rural migrant workers who are prepared to accept poor terms and conditions. None the less, these employment opportunities are very important in providing jobs for people who would otherwise be unemployed, thus relieving the burden on the state. They also contribute to the development of the private and informal sector economy since it is within these sectors that most of the non-standard jobs are found. However, what tend to be neglected are the quality of these types of employment and what regulations should/can be implemented to safeguard the employment rights of workers engaged in these types of work so that the quantity of employment is not developed at the expense of its quality.

To some extent, China's focus on job creation rather than quality of employment reflects the social policy stance of other countries. As Rubery and Grimshaw (2003: 95) observe:

> There has been declining confidence in the ability of all countries to generate sufficient high quality jobs for all their potential workforce; and the American model of a high share of junk jobs has found favour amongst some policy makers as a more productive way in which a society can utilize its human resources than parking their labour in long unemployment queues or in inactivity.

Social stability, it is recognized by the Chinese government, is vital in a large country such as China in which consumer purchasing power is limited whereas the underdeveloped labour market is saturated with semi-skilled and unskilled labour. In the absence of the strong back-up of a well-developed social welfare system, the society is unlikely to be able to absorb the vast number of workers who have been laid off or forced into early retirement by their state sector employers. Many are forced to take up contingent employment again to top up their moderate pension to support their family. A growing pressure for the Chinese government is thus to create employment. This pressure is fully recognized by the new premier of China Wen Jiabao who pointed out in his Government Report speech to the 10th National People's Congress (held in Beijing in March 2004) that the task of increasing employment and improving social security was arduous (*Yangcheng Evening News*, 5 March 2004). According to the news announcement issued by the Ministry of Labour and Social Security (www.molss.gov.cn/news/2004), the employment target for the year 2004 was to create nine million jobs for new workers in addition to five million re-employment opportunities for laid-off or unemployed workers in the urban areas. This was to be achieved by promoting labour-intensive industries, small and medium-sized enterprises and the private economy, as well as by encouraging flexible employment and self-employment.

The government is also fully aware of the importance of wider access to knowledge and skills (human resource development) in economic growth, and that displacement, (re)training and re-employment may be a common situation in the (future) labour market. As the reality of 'lifelong employment' comes to an end, the notion of 'lifelong learning' has been given high-profile publication and broadcast by the state, the media and the academics alike. The fact that the state is currently footing the heavy (re)training bill (a costly exercise which may not yield adequate benefits immediately) indicates its willingness to counter the skills problems. According to the news announcement issued by the Ministry of Labour and Social Security (www.molss.gov. cn/news/2004) mentioned above, a dual strategy of promoting skills training and employment was to be adopted in which re-employment training, entrepreneurship training, high-tech skills training and rural worker training were to be fully promoted. More specifically, 100,000 senior technicians were to be trained in 2004, four million people were to receive re-employment training, and 300,000 were to receive entrepreneurship training aimed to help them set up their own businesses. On a longer time span under China's 10th Five-Year Plan (2001–5), 20 per cent of Chinese workers are to be trained as advanced technical workers who are expected to meet international standards. The problems are, however, how to widen access to training and how to improve training relevance and effectiveness which are, again, common problems found in many countries.

Perhaps the most significant new strategic focus of the government is that on the rural workers. According to national statistics, there are ninety-four million rural migrant workers in the urban area. Rural migrant workers now make up 58 per cent of the total workforce in the secondary industrial sector, taking up 68 per cent of manufacturing jobs, nearly 80 per cent of construction, and over 52 per cent of wholesale, retail and catering jobs (*Yangcheng Evening News*, 22 February 2004). This suggests that rural migrant workers have become the main constituent part of the industrial workforce. Recognizing the important role of rural migrant workers in the urban economy, the government has now embarked upon solving the 'rural workers' problems' (*long min gong wen ti*). This is carried out through the shift from a control-oriented policy that poses constraints to a support-oriented policy that aims to create a more friendly working and living environment for rural migrant workers in urban areas. Greater legal protection is to be given to rural migrant workers by ensuring that the minimum wage regulations are strictly adhered to and that wage payment delays should be sorted out as soon as possible. Legal punishment will be enforced on employers who violate the wage regulations. Meanwhile, skills training is to be provided to workers still living and working in rural areas. Major initiatives include, for example, the plan of 'One University Graduate for Each Village' announced by the Ministry of Education on 20 February 2004. This was followed by the announcement of the 'Rural Labour Transition Training Sun Shine Project' in March 2004 which aims to provide skills training to 2.5 million rural workers (*Yangcheng Evening News*, 22 February 2004). The government's new policy initiatives have been well received by the majority of the population, but their impact remains to be seen as the effects of implementation unfold.

The role of the trade unions in the future

Chapter 2 provided a brief overview of the role of the trade unions in China in the past few decades, highlighting the absence of their strength in protecting and advancing workers' interests, especially for those in the new private sector where effective representation of workers is most needed yet unavailable. While the privatization of smaller SOEs has to some extent led to the decline of trade union presence and power in the newly privatized firms, trade unions have not made significant inroads into the rapidly expanding private sector, although progress has been made in union representation in foreign-invested enterprises. More generally, the trade unions are facing fresh challenges under the new form of employment relations in China in which a worker constituency becomes more diverse and the conflict of interest between labour and management/proprietor more evident, with a rising imbalance of bargaining power to the disadvantage of the former. As White (1996: 439) observed,

> On the one hand the trade unions are confronted by more powerful professional managers and a private bourgeoisie, on the other hand, the social character of Chinese workers has also been changing. . . . They are also being pushed in radically different directions: as an organizational component of an embattled sector – urban public enterprises – they are impelled to play a conservative role; as the potential defender of an emergent proletariat in the non-public sector, they are under pressure to support the reforms that created these sectors and to reach out beyond their traditional constituency to deal with new problems in an unfamiliar environment.

It is under this context that the state made a recommendation in the mid-1990s that collective negotiation should be used as a mechanism to reach contractual agreements and resolve industrial relations disputes. Enterprises and their workers are encouraged to establish a collective negotiation system and implement a collective contract system. The collective employment contract system was first implemented in the 1950s, but was abolished in the 1960s. Since the implementation of the Labour Law of China (1995), the collective employment contract system has made a return and gradually been implemented by employing organizations, although most of them are SOEs. This is a function in which the trade unions are expected to play an active role. The Labour Law of China (1995) specifies that workers are one of the two sides (the other being the enterprise) in the collective negotiation. Where a trade union is established, trade union officials participate in the negotiation with workers' representatives and sign the contract on behalf of the workers. Where a trade union is not recognized, workers' representatives participate in the negotiation and sign the contract for the workers they represent. In reality, however, trade union officials are not always familiar with this new role and sometimes mistakenly believe that they are legally one of the two sides in negotiation and bypass the workers' representatives.

Collective negotiation, mainly in wage negotiation, is seen as the main method for trade union organizations to protect and advance workers' interest in the developing market economy in China. However, the negotiation of implementing a collective contract in private firms often proves difficult due to the lack of employer co-operation. Many employers are reluctant to sign a collective contract with their employees because it not only imposes legal constraints on the employers but also reduces employers' flexibility in managing their workers. Many domestic private firms are small organizations with a workforce of diverse nature, making it very difficult to introduce a collective contract to cover the diversity.

The ability to gain employers' recognition and establish a collective negotiation system is also the key to attracting rural migrant workers to join the trade unions, who are the largest and most needy group requiring labour protection in the urban area but the least unionized. For years, the trade unions have not taken seriously the need to represent this expanding group of workers in part because they have the 'farmer' status instead of the 'worker' status and in part because they are highly mobile and transient workers, making it very difficult to capture and organize them. However, this situation is now changing. In early August 2003, one month prior to its 14th National Conference in Beijing, the All-China Federation of Trade Unions made the announcement that rural migrant workers would be considered as part of the workforce and that the ACFTU would attract as many of them as possible to join the unions and represent them. It was reported that in less than two months, over thirty-four million rural migrant workers had joined the trade unions (*Yangcheng Evening News*, 24 September 2003). Action has also been taken to establish a networked union mechanism so that rural migrant workers can travel with their membership and be represented wherever they work. Other plans are also being formulated at local level with the aim of maximizing the union membership level among the rural migrant workers and providing an increasing range of services to the union members.

Efforts are being made by regional trade union headquarters to establish an understanding of the experience of work of the rural migrant workers and what their expectations may be. For example, a questionnaire survey was conducted by the Guangzhou General Trade Union at the end of 2003 on migrant workers in Guangzhou (*Yangcheng Evening News*, 23 February 2004). The survey revealed that over 70 per cent of the migrant workers surveyed came to Guangzhou to work in order to learn skills. Relatedly, over 80 per cent of the migrant workers felt that their biggest reward has been the skills they had learned. In addition, over 40 per cent of them could use the internet to search for information and/or for entertainment. Nearly half of them revealed that their biggest wish was to have a stable job and another quarter expressed that their biggest wish was to receive technical skills training. The vast majority also hoped they would receive more understanding from urban citizens. The survey had 713 returned questionnaires and was the first large survey of its kind in Guangzhou. This indicates that issues related to the employment situation and well-being of migrant workers are becoming a focus of the trade unions and local government. The survey also points to the possibility that the ability to organize and provide skills training to (rural) migrant workers may be an effective way of gaining their membership.

In general, trade union organizations face several challenges in developing their strength in the private sector and they need to formulate an effective strategy to overcome these barriers. First, they have the task of promoting collective negotiation proactively by mobilizing all sorts of media channels internally and externally to increase the awareness of all parties concerned, because collective negotiation is a relatively new phenomenon and many employers and workers are still not familiar with the concept. Second, trade unions should mobilize the support and monitoring role of local authorities to organize collective negotiation at industrial and/or district level (known as 'vertical' and 'horizontal' unionization), instead of negotiating with individual employers, in order to maximize its impact on workers. This strategy is now being adopted by union organizations at municipal district level in large cities, such as Shanghai, where trade union organizations are well established and have a high level of support from local government. Third, at the negotiation table, shop stewards/workers' representatives are in an apparently disadvantaged position largely because they lack the specialized knowledge of wage-setting and negotiation skills. An urgent task for the trade unions is to develop these skills for the shop stewards/workers' representatives in order to raise their negotiation ability. To do this, they need to mobilize resources and provide training. Fourth, although in theory both sides in the negotiation are equal, in reality this equality is difficult, if not impossible, to achieve. This is in part because workers are under the control of managers at work and are expected to show respect and obedience to their superiors, a mindset influenced by the Chinese culture that is difficult to change during negotiation. The threat of job loss also adds to the representatives' fear which affects their performance in negotiations. The state is aware of the possibility of intimidation against shop stewards/workers' representatives and specifies in the Trade Union Law (2001) that it is unlawful for employers to intimidate, threaten, dismiss shop stewards/workers' representatives or move them to other posts because of their union activities. Finally, trade unions should act as a 'think-tank' to provide professional advice to workers' representatives on wage negotiation and other employment-related issues.

In short, trade union organizations in China need to adopt a strategy and role that are more commonly adopted by their Western counterparts to articulate labour interests. They need to be more strategic and operate within a network that reaches well beyond the workplace level. They need to play the monitoring role, the negotiating role, the training role and the advisory role. These are the tasks that prove to be increasingly challenging even for their Western counterparts as a result of reduced state intervention, rising management opposition and intensifying global competition. A net consequence of this has been the global trend of the declining power of trade union organizations in various substantive forms between countries.

Major challenges in HRM in China

The management of human resources in China faces several challenges. While some problems are commonly experienced by employing organizations in both the public and private sectors, others are more specific to the public or private sector. First, it has been argued that the Chinese enterprises in general do not adopt a systematic approach to human resource management. Domestic private firms (many of which are relatively new) in China share a considerable level of similarities in the development of their HR functions. They source their human resources primarily from the labour markets, especially at the start-up of their businesses. They lack a comprehensive HR strategy that provides skills training and career structure. They have not developed an organizational culture to elicit their employees' commitment and loyalty. By comparison, the state sector organizations have a more established HR system due to the fact that they have a much longer history and have been subject to much state influence. However, many elements in their HR system have become outmoded and incompatible with recent developments in the economic environment and the labour markets. The rigidity of the HR system is also a major source of disadvantage to SOEs and public sector organizations. They are faced with two major problems in their HRM: how to retain and attract talent, and how to motivate existing employees.

Second, despite the oversupply of labour, many employers are experiencing recruitment and retention problems of high-performing employees with professional or managerial skills. While foreign firms and JVs operating at the top end of the product markets are able to recruit good-quality university and polytechnic graduates as professionals and skilled workers, many domestic companies are facing recruitment problems. Graduates are unwilling to join or stay with enterprises that offer relatively low pay and have uncertain prospects. While the increasing fluidity of the labour market may be beneficial for individuals who are in advantageous positions, organizations may find it difficult to establish a long-term employment relationship with key workers conducive to the organization's competitiveness. Competition for talent also tends to drive wages upward disproportionally (thus widening the wage gap and social inequality) and to encourage opportunistic behaviour.

Retention of key technical staff has been a tough perennial problem encountered by many SOEs and public sector organizations in recent years. SOE workers are now much more likely to seek high wages in non-state firms

(Ding *et al.* 2001). It is believed that foreign firms and JVs have been poaching key technical personnel from SOEs. For example, a recent investigation by the Beijing City Economy Commission of 150 large and medium-sized enterprises in Beijing on their human resource composition revealed that SOEs had lost 64 per cent of their university graduates since 1982 while high-tech private firms had lost 18.5 per cent (Chu 2002). It has also been reported that the four major state-owned banks had lost many of their talented people to foreign banks in China in the last few years since China relaxed its policy of foreign banks operating in China (Chu 2002). Wang and Fang (2001) in their study of multinational companies in China found that the vast majority of employees in these MNCs were no more than 30 years of age, and over 95 per cent of them possessed at least advanced diploma educational qualifications. Over 64 per cent of the Chinese employees surveyed said that the most important reason for them to join MNCs was that they felt that they could use their talent and realize their own value. High income was the second most important reason (62.5 per cent).

In the past, many SOEs and public sector organizations tried to retain their (key) staff by imposing a penalty clause in their employment contract. Those who wished to leave their employer before the prescribed number of years were fulfilled were often faced with a heavy financial penalty and their personnel file would not be released by their defiant employer. An increasingly popular method now used to retain staff is that of the 'negotiated wage' on an individual basis. This involves abandoning the conventional wage structure that does not differentiate between performance in a real sense to a more tailored package for each individual worker based on his or her competence and market value. This often results in a general wage increase for the individuals concerned (Chen 2002). It needs to be pointed out here that in recent years there has been a reverse trend of talent 'returning' to the well-managed SOEs which offer attractive salaries and individualized reward packages. The relatively high turnover rate of academic staff in the higher education sector has also started to decline over the past few years with substantial wage increases being the main reason in reversing the trend.

A third and related challenge facing HRM in China at the national level is that of the skills shortage and insufficiency of training provision, an intertwined problem that has been discussed in various chapters in this book. The growth of human capital is seriously lagging behind that of the national economy and enterprise profit, and is believed to be the bottleneck in the growth of the high-tech sector. One characteristic of the training system in China is the considerable variation of training provision between different forms of enterprise ownership, in different regions, and among different groups of workers, with little opportunity for those in the secondary labour market to develop their human capital in order to enhance their employment prospects. The effectiveness of the training programmes provided by firms is also called into question. Foreign and domestic private firms face the dilemma of whether to train their employees up for the key skills required at the risk of having them poached or to recruit from the market with attractive employment packages. Firms that provide training may have to readjust their training plan in order to reduce the cost associated with staff turnover, especially for MNCs that send their Chinese employees overseas for training. More importantly, there is little focus on career planning and human resource development, with state sector organizations still following a rigid promotion system largely based on seniority with added emphasis on performance.

A fourth major challenge in HRM in China is the need to change the ideology of reward, distribution and performance. There is a lack of a comprehensive and effective system that links long-term employee motivation and performance to reward. Pay has not been an effective mechanism to reflect workers' performance or to motivate workers, and poor performance has always been a problem haunting SOEs (Korzec 1992; Chiu 2002), if less so for the private firms. Chinese workers have often been criticized by managers of JVs, foreign and domestic private firms for their lack of motivation and pride in their work, with little interest in advancing themselves. Therefore, a challenging task for HRM is to design and implement HR policies that can change the behavioural patterns of workers, to make them more motivated, and to prompt them to take greater ownership and responsibility for their own work and to take greater pride in their organization. If China is to move towards international competition that is based on quality and value-added products, then it should move towards a softer approach to human resource management with a stronger flow of communication and information, which is still primarily top-down and suppressed. There is also a need for a higher level of employee involvement and workers' participation in decision making instead of the master–subordinate relationship that prevails in many workplaces.

It is now evident that HRM in China is becoming more strategic and sophisticated, with an increasing focus on organizational demand rather than labour supply, especially in the state sector. It is also evident that firms in China adopt a mixture of both soft and hard HR practices that may not always be coherent (Cooke 2004d). However, given the fact that the majority of jobs in China are relatively low skilled and poorly paid with limited intrinsic value, it would be unrealistic to expect a macro convergence towards the high-commitment model of HRM. Therefore, one may expect that both hard and soft approaches to HRM will co-exist in China, at least for the foreseeable future, but perhaps with more and more companies adopting more strategic and softer HR practices, while many will still operate in a hire-and-fire mode with sweatshop conditions.

Challenges to the HR function

The above major challenges facing HRM in China have profound implications for the HR function at individual, organizational and national level. At the individual level, there is an urgent need to professionalize the HR function. As has already been pointed out, HRM is a relatively new concept embraced by China. Until the turn of the century, HR management was not considered to be a 'profession' in China. Human resource management as a discipline in higher education did not make its appearance until the mid-1990s, although it has been expanding rapidly since. In 1999, there were only thirty higher educational institutions that provided undergraduate degree courses in HRM. By July 2001, there were over ninety universities that recruited HRM undergraduates (Liao and Chen 2002). In April 2003, the first group of HR officers were awarded their HRM qualification certificates in Beijing on completion of the HRM training. The certificates were issued by the China Research Institute of Human Resource Development. It was reported that the number of people engaged in the profession has been increasing each year, with about three million people currently working in the field (*Yangcheng Evening News*, 14 April 2003). The combination of increased availability of training and a deeper understanding of the importance of the role of HRM is creating a rapidly growing demand for local HR talent. As this pool of local talent begins to emerge, most multinationals have already begun to localize their HR positions. Unfortunately, the new growth of local HR talent remains a small drop in the ocean compared to the needs of the country. The vast majority of HR officers in enterprises have never received any formal training in human resource management, and many come from a non-personnel background. Moreover, the nature of the personnel function is experiencing significant change from the reactive administrative role of the planned economy era to a more proactive and strategic role of the market economy. This is accompanied by an increasing level of labour mobility, more overt labour–management disputes, more complex reward systems, and the introduction of more labour regulations. HR officers therefore need to equip themselves with the understanding of HR theories and labour regulations and their practical implications. They also need to understand the strategic role of HRM in relation to other functions of the organization.

At the organizational level it is likely that in the next few years, the HR function in many Chinese (state-owned) organizations will continue to share its administrative and welfare role with the trade unions. While the rapid expansion of the private sector and the recent amendment of the Trade Union Law (2001) are unlikely to change the power base (or the lack of it) of the unions dramatically, the HR function has yet to be developed to become a strategic part of the business. The majority of entrepreneurs and senior managers in China have insufficient understanding of the strategic importance of HRM to organizational competitiveness and tend to underestimate the technicality of HRM. According to Xu (2001), their ideology of employment relationship is still largely of a transactional nature. The DDI survey (*China Staff*, May 2003) discussed in Chapter 9 also reveals that HR professionals are not as involved in the performance management system as they should be. Therefore, HR professionals have a challenging task to modernize the HR function and to convince their organizational leaders of the added value of human resources and the importance of winning employees' commitment to the success of the organization. What HR professionals should do is to implement an up-to-date IT system for both the administrative and strategic aspects of the HR function. The level of e-HR alone does not represent the level of modernization and professionalism of the HR function itself, but it does play an important role in the delivery of the function.

At the industry and national level, there is a need to establish industrial and national networks to share information on HR, to co-ordinate the HR functions such as skills training and recruitment, and to monitor the labour market trends and the conformity of labour regulations. Equally as important, national professional bodies for HR professionals should be set up, such as the Chartered Institute of Personnel Development (CIPD) founded in the UK, to link HR professionals together and to facilitate the sharing of 'best practices' in HRM. There is evidence that HR enthusiasts have set up human resource management clubs or similar forums in their geographical area to share information and exchange good practices and experience. These pioneer activities have yet to become more widespread and organized in a more systematic manner. It must be pointed out here that there are encouraging signs that a level of 'best practice' sharing is taking place between organizations, albeit often in a spontaneous manner. This is in addition to the rapid growth of HR textbooks and academic and practitioners' journals that have been playing a brokering role in introducing Western HR theories and practices to Chinese readers.

Perhaps the most fundamental challenge to the HR community in China is the need to develop HR theories and practices that are suitable for China. There is currently an absence of debate among academics and practitioners in China as to what human resource management means in the Chinese context and in what ways, if any, it is different from the traditional personnel management approach. Instead, there is a dangerous passion, or rather fashion, in which HRM as a Western imported concept is embraced uncritically as a progressive given. Considerable variations exist in the understanding, interpretation and configuration of HR concepts, a situation which one may justify as HRM with Chinese characteristics. The analysis of the characteristics of enterprise culture management in China in Chapter 9 is a case in point. Most publications in China on human resource management are primarily introductory texts of Western HRM theories and practices with an unquestioned underlying assumption that they are advanced models to be learned by the Chinese organizations if they are to improve their performance. In addition to some of the conventional aspects of the HRM such as recruitment, training, performance and reward, interests are turned increasingly to the softer dimensions such as motivational theories, cultural management, teamworking, emotional investment and organizational commitment that are more 'human' oriented. New trends of HR practices are also covered, including the concept of learning organization, e-learning, and online training. While practitioners' journals on HRM tend to be simplistic and prescriptive, academics have yet to come up with more rigorous analyses, informed by empirical studies, on the appropriateness of these theories in guiding practices in organizations.

Future research agenda

What, then, are the broader research implications on the basis of what has been discussed in this volume? Two main aspects will be covered in this section in terms of the future research agenda of HRM, work and employment in China. One relates to the substantive issues to be researched, and the other relates to the research approach.

Issues to be researched

Although there is now a growing body of literature on human resource management in China, most of it derives from quantitative empirical studies and focuses relatively heavily on MNCs, JVs and SOEs. Data are often obtained through interviewing and/or surveying managers but less so through workers themselves. While this volume has filled some of the gaps in the literature through the discussion of a number of topics that have been insufficiently explored, important topics have also been left out that require further attention. One is the employees'/workers' perspective on the HRM practices in the workplace and in what ways they have internalized the changes that have taken place in recent years. For example, to what extent may those who have survived the SOE lay-offs have changed their psychological contract with their state employers? What are the major post-downsizing management innovations that have taken place? How may these innovations affect workers in terms of the ways they are now expected to work and consequently their experience of work? Are they experiencing a higher level of skills training, wage earning and job satisfaction? If so, are these achieved through job intensification, reduced employees' voice and modified workplace behaviour? How do they identify themselves in their 'new' workplace? To what extent does the relative 'silence' of workers' views on the changes mask any undercurrent that may be simmering? Are these feelings of discontent superseded by the threat of job losses? Or is the workplace harmony an outcome of the displacement of the older generations of workers with the new generation of workers who feel lucky to have a job? In other words, has the legacy of the socialist mentality in SOEs been replaced by a more individualistic mindset of wage and effort bargaining more commonly found in Western societies? Do workers feel that the so-called Western HRM practices introduced into workplaces are really 'Western' practices different from indigenous personnel management or do they see them as just different management techniques? How effective have these HRM practices been in motivating employees? While workers' attitudes towards the existing trade union organizations as the mechanism of workers' representation have been less than enthusiastic, is there a strong demand for an alternative mechanism to voice grassroot concerns? Or is such a demand simply suppressed by (proprietor) management and by job insecurity? Similarly, what is the workforce's attitude towards skills training and career development? What types of skills training do they want and how would they like to be trained? To what extent do they desire jobs with greater intrinsic value and opportunities of career progression? In short, we need more empirical evidence from the workers' perspective on what is happening in the workplace, how this affects them and, importantly, what they want from their employers. The investigation of these issues is crucial if organizations' HR policies are to elicit the maximum amount of effort from the workforce for their competitive advantage.

Another important topic for future research is that of management in China. There is a dearth of Chinese management theory (Ralston *et al.* 1999), and 'research on Chinese managerial learning is limited despite the obvious importance of the topic' (Tsang 2001: 32). Moreover, earlier studies on management in China (e.g. Warner 1992; Ralston *et al.* 1993, 1997; Child 1994; Smith and Wang 1997) have focused on the older breed of managers under the planned economy system. There is very limited research on the new generation of managers in terms of their competence and their managerial philosophy and behaviour, for example. These managers are generally much more highly educated than the previous generations. Many may have been trained in the Western countries (*hai gui pai*) and are playing an important role in disseminating knowledge and good practices, and in bridging the link between China and the rest of the world. As Ralston *et al.* (1999: 425) observe, 'the new generation of Chinese managers appear to be more similar to Western managers than were the previous generations, especially in terms of individualistic behaviour. They are technically more competent and less characterized with traditional Chinese values.'

There appears to be a new breed of Chinese managers who are ambitious and innovative. Most work in MNCs, JVs and (high-tech) domestic private firms. While foreign managers in China are uncertain about what practices may be effective and often look to their headquarters or other MNCs in China for models to be implemented in their Chinese operations (Bjorkman and Lu 2001), many firms are now deploying fewer expatriates and more local Chinese to fill their managerial posts. However, this creates problems of harmonization. As more and more Chinese managers and professionals have acquired management know-how and technical competencies that were once held by expatriate managers and professionals when foreign firms first entered China, this closing gap of knowledge increases the bargaining power of local managers and professionals who are beginning to feel a sense of distributional injustice arising from the differentials between expatriates and local Chinese (Leung *et al.* 2001), and to demand terms and conditions similar to those enjoyed by expatriates. For example, Tsang's (2001) study revealed that one-third of the Chinese managers studied considered that the pay gap between the Chinese managers and the expatriate managers was unfair since their skills and efforts were similar. Expatriate managers also saw the pay gap as the barrier to their integration with their Chinese colleagues who resent pay differentials.

It would therefore be useful to carry out longitudinal studies on the Chinese managers as an occupational group, as an organizational function and as a social class. For instance, what are the most important motivators for their performance? How do they bargain for and determine their own terms and conditions? What are their patterns of learning and management development? What types of organizational governance structure do they prefer? What types of management techniques do they favour? What HRM practices do they perceive to be effective in the Chinese context and how may these perceptions change over time? What are the characteristics of their entrepreneurship and how may they differ from those of their counterparts in other countries? To what extent does the widening earning gap between managers and ordinary employees serve as a barrier to organizational congruence and employee commitment to the organization?

In short, there is much to be researched on HRM, work and employment in China. As Child (1996: xix) remarks, 'China . . . offers one of the most important contexts for business and management in the world today. Understanding it presents a daunting practical and intellectual challenge, but one that cannot be put aside.' This work can only be achieved through collective and cumulative effort by the research community on China, a community that is inspiringly expanding with a growing amount of knowledge. More importantly, issues concerning employment relations in China should be studied in comparison with those of other countries. This is in part because many patterns emerging in China share considerable similarities with those of other countries although key differences remain. It is also in part because China is an integral component of the global political economy in which constituent nations are becoming increasingly interdependent.

Employment relations in China: towards an internationally comparative framework of analysis

It has been noted that employment practices 'do indeed differ significantly between countries and that these differences are likely to persist' (Rubery and Grimshaw 2003: 4). However, from what has been discussed in this volume and from the findings of other studies, we can see that there is also a certain level of convergence of HR and employment strategies across different countries. For example, more and more firms are adopting employment flexibility (e.g. fixed-term, temporary and agency employment) with the aim of reducing costs by transferring (part of) the risk to the workers. Pay systems have become more variable with greater emphasis on performance-related pay. Firms are deploying more sophisticated recruitment methods and using external providers to deliver part of the HR functions, notably in recruitment and training. There is a growing trend for firms to adopt soft HR initiatives, with various degrees of success, that are aimed to elicit employee commitment and thus performance. These initiatives include organizational culture, teambuilding and quality initiatives (e.g. total quality management and ISO 9000 series). While China is a late starter in adopting some of these practices, similarities began to emerge at least a decade ago. For example, Easterby-Smith *et al.*'s (1995) study found that while there were considerable variations in the form of HRM, there were also some surprising similarities between China and the UK, notably in human resource planning systems. There appear to be more similarities 'between companies in China and some of companies in the UK than there were between all the UK companies. This suggests that these elements are not greatly affected by national and cultural differences' (Easterby-Smith *et al.* 1995: 31).

Equally, many tensions and challenges displayed in the employment system in China are also experienced to various degrees in other countries, developed and developing alike. For example, skills shortages and training problems appear to have much in common among nations. In fact, many states are aware of the issues and are taking actions to combat the problems. In European Union countries, the need to combat skills shortages and increasing employability of disadvantaged groups, such as women, older workers and ethnic minorities, are high up on the European Union's social policy agenda. Member states are charged to formulate a skills strategy that aims to improve the quality, relevance and flexibility of skills training, to promote employee development by updating and upgrading vocational skills, and to promote effective training investment by employers. The initiative of lifelong learning is championed by many states as a new way of upskilling their labour force, although the same enthusiasm from the latter has yet to be found. How to improve the performance of the state sector while containing costs, especially those of the public services, poses another challenge to many states. Still another common problem is that the strengthening of employment legislation takes place in parallel with the shrinking of the state sector, the weakening of the trade union's role in protecting workers' interests and the rising level of industrial relations disputes. There is now clear evidence that intensifying global competition has led to the informalization of work and employment which has, to a large extent, led to worsening employment conditions for many working in developed and developing economies alike. Intensifying pressures for productivity and quality in the increasingly integrated global economy and the consequent intensifying pace of restructuring are considered to be the major causes of these problems (Verma *et al.* 1995). State intervention (e.g. in the form of more stringent legislative enforcement) is therefore necessary in order to protect the well-being of this internationally expanding workforce so that the development of the national and global economy is not based on widening inequality and worsening work and employment experience of the workers.

It has been argued that it is 'in the nature of comparative research that opposites tend to attract; that is, countries are selected for study around a particular employment practice precisely because they are known to, or are strongly expected to, display major differences' (Rubery and Grimshaw 2003: 6). There are also tendencies for researchers to avoid comparative study of very different economies (e.g. developed vs. developing) across continents (e.g. Europe vs. Asia), since a taken-for-granted view is that their historical experience, cultural traditions and institutional arrangements are so varied that the outcome is bound to be different. While existing international comparative studies have shed light on HRM and employment-related issues of different nations in the world, these studies have been based mainly on the same type of economy (e.g. advanced economy or developing economy) and/or geographical locations (e.g. Bamber *et al.* 2004; Rowley *et al.* 2004). International and cross-economy comparative studies remain insufficient. The fact is often ignored that issues and tensions which both the developed and developing countries have been facing in recent years may be more similar, as is evidenced by the above examples, than has been allowed for. In light of the increasingly globalized economy and increasing mobility of labour at both domestic (e.g. rural migrant workers) and international (e.g. expatriates, overseas returnees and international migrants) level, how to pay and how much to pay, or who trains, where to train and who is to be trained are no longer decisions to be made in isolation but require more cross-border consideration and co-ordination. This calls for a more integrated analytical framework that should transcend the division of geographic location or level of economic development under which to analyse HRM and wider issues related to the employment policy and practice of individual countries. That way, we will get a much clearer global picture of our stock of human resources.

Bibliography

References in English

Amba-Rao, S. and Pendse, D. (1985) 'Human resources compensation and maintenance practices', *American Journal of Small Business*, 10, Autumn: 19–29.

Bamber, G., Lansbury, R. and Wailes, N. (2004) *International and Comparative Employment Relations: Globalisation and the Developed Market Economies* (4th edn), London: Sage Publications.

Barrett, R. and Rainnie, A. (2002) 'What's so special about small firms? Developing an integrated approach to analysing small firm industrial relations', *Work, Employment and Society*, 16, 3: 415–31.

Becker, G. (1964) *Human Capital: A Theoretical and Empirical Analysis, with Special Reference to Education*, Chicago, IL: University of Chicago Press.

Becon, N., Ackers, P., Storey, J. and Coates, D. (1996) 'It's a small world: managing human resources in small businesses', *International Journal of Human Resource Management*, 7, 1: 83–100.

Benewick, R. and Donald, S. (1999) *The State of China Atlas*, London: Penguin.

Benson, J. and Zu, Y. (2000) 'A case study analysis of human resource management in China's manufacturing industry', *China Industrial Economy*, 4: 62–5.

Benson, J., Debroux, P., Yuasa, M. and Zhu, Y. (2000) 'Flexibility and labour management: Chinese manufacturing enterprises in the 1990s', *International Journal of Human Resource Management*, 11, 2: 183–96.

Bian, Y. (1994) *Work and Inequality in Urban China*, Albany, NY: State University of New York Press.

Bjorkman, I. and Fan, X. C. (2002) 'Human resource management and the performance of Western firms in China', *International Journal of Human Resource Management*, 13, 6: 853–64.

Bjorkman, I. and Lu, Y. (1999a) 'A corporate perspective on the management of human resources in China', *Journal of World Business*, 34, 1: 16–25.

Bjorkman, I. and Lu, Y. (1999b) 'The management of human resources in Chinese–Western joint ventures', *Journal of World Business*, 34, 3: 306–24.

Bjorkman, I. and Lu, Y. (2001) 'Institutionalisation and bargaining power explanations of human resource management in international joint ventures: the case of Chinese–Western joint ventures', *Organization Studies*, 22: 491–512.

Borgonjon, J. and Vanhonacker, W. (1994) 'Management training and education in the People's Republic of China', *International Journal of Human Resource Management*, 5, 2: 327–56.

Bowman, J. S. (1994) 'At last, an alternative to performance appraisal: total quality management', *Public Administration Review*, 54, 2: 129–36.

Boxall, P. and Purcell, J. (2003) *Strategy and Human Resource Management*, Basingstoke: Palgrave Macmillan.

Branine, M. (1996) 'Observations on training and management development in the People's Republic of China', *Personnel Review*, 25, 1: 25–39.

Braun, W. and Warner, M. (2002) 'Strategic human resource management in Western multinationals in China: the differentiation of practices across different ownership forms', *Personnel Review*, 31, 5: 553–79.

Brunner, J., Koh, A. and Lou, X. G. (1992) 'Chinese perceptions of issues and obstacles confronting joint ventures', *Journal of Global Marketing*, 6, 1/2: 97–127.

Bu, N. (1994) 'Red cadres and specialists as modern managers: an empirical assessment of managerial competencies in China', *International Journal of Human Resource Management*, 5, 2: 357–83.

Budhwar, P. and Debrah, Y. (2001) 'Introduction', in P. Budhwar and Y. Debrah (eds), *Human Resource Management in Developing Countries*, London: Routledge, pp. 1–15.

Burke, R. (1984) 'Mentors in organisations', *Group and Organisation Studies*, 9: 353–72.

Burns, P. (2001) *Entrepreneurship and Small Business*, Basingstoke: Palgrave.

Butterfield, F. (1983) *China: Alive in Bitter Sea*, New York: Coronet Books.

Cabestan, J. (1992) 'Civil service reform in China: the draft "provisional order concerning civil servants"', *International Review of Administrative Sciences*, 58, 3: 421–36.

Chan, A. (1995) 'Chinese enterprise reforms: convergence with the Japanese model?', *Industrial and Corporate Change*, 4, 2: 449–70.

Chan, A. (1998) 'Labour relations in foreign-funded ventures', in G. O'Leary (ed.), *Adjusting to Capitalism: Chinese Workers and their State*, Armonk, NY: M. E. Sharpe, pp. 122–49.

Chan, A. (2000) 'Globalisation, China's free (read bonded) labour market, and the Chinese trade unions', in C. Rowley and J. Benson (eds), *Globalisation and Labour in the Asia Pacific Region*, London: Frank Cass, pp. 260–81.

Chan, A. (2001) *China's Workers under Assault: The Exploitation of Labour in a Globalising Economy*, New York: M. E. Sharpe.

Chang, C. and Wang, Y. J. (1994) 'The nature of the township-village enterprise', *Journal of Comparative Economics*, 19: 434–52.

Chen, M. (1997) 'Guanxi dynamics and network building', in M. Warner (ed.), *Comparative Management: Critical Perspectives on Business and Management*, Vol. 3, *Asian-Pacific Management*, London: Routledge, pp. 886–99.

Chew, D. (1990a) 'Civil service pay in China, 1955–1989: overview and assessment', *International Review of Administrative Sciences*, 56: 345–64.

Chew, D. (1990b) 'Recent developments in civil service pay in China', *International Labour Review*, 129, 6: 773–82.

Child, J. (1991) 'A foreign perspective on the management of people in China', *International Journal of Human Resource Management*, 2, 2: 93–107.

Child, J. (1994) *Management in China during the Age of Reform* (hbk edn), Cambridge: Cambridge University Press.

Child, J. (1995) 'Changes in the structure and prediction of earnings in Chinese state enterprises during the economic reform', *The International Journal of Human Resource Management*, 6, 1: 1–30.

Child, J. (1996) *Management in China during the Age of Reform* (pbk edn), Cambridge: Cambridge University Press.

Child, J. and Heavens, S. (1999) 'Managing corporate networks from America to China', in M. Warner (ed.), *China's Managerial Revolution*, London: Frank Cass, pp. 147–80.

Child, J. and Tse, D. (2001) 'China's transition and its implications for international business', *Journal of International Business Studies*, 32, 1: 5–21.

Child, J., Yan, Y. and Lu, Y. (1997) 'Ownership and control in Sino–foreign joint ventures', in P. Meamish and P. Killing (eds), *Global Perspectives on Cooperative Strategies: Asian Perspectives*, San Francisco, CA: The New Lexington Press, pp. 181–225.

China Staff, February 2001, 7, 3: 2.

China Staff, July to August 2001, 7, 8: 2.

China Staff, May 2002, 8, 5: 15–19, 26.

China Staff, June 2002, 8, 7: 18.

China Staff, September 2002, 8, 9: 43.

China Staff, October 2002, 8, 10: 21.

China Staff, November 2002, 8, 11: 34.

China Staff, March 2003, 9, 3: 42.

China Staff, April 2003, 9, 5: 1–5.

China Staff, May 2003, 9, 6: 24–8, 39.

Chiu, W. C. K. (2002) 'Do types of economic ownership matter in getting employees to commit? An exploratory study in the People's Republic of China', *International Journal of Human Resource Management*, 13, 6: 865–82.

Chow, I. and Fu, P. P. (2000) 'Change and development in pluralistic settings: an exploration of HR practices in Chinese township and village enterprises', *International Journal of Human Resource Management*, 11, 4: 822–36.

Chow, K. W. (1991) 'Reform of the Chinese cadre system: pitfalls, issues and implications of the proposed civil service system', *International Review of Administration*, 57: 25–44.

Chow, K. W. (1994) 'An opinion survey of performance appraisal practices in Hong Kong and the People's Republic of China', *Asia Pacific Journal of Human Resources*, 32: 62–79.

Coates, G. (1994) 'Performance appraisal as icon: Oscar-winning performance or dressing to impress?', *International Journal of Human Resource Management*, 5, 1: 165–91.

Cooke, F. L. (2000) 'Manpower restructuring in the state-owned railway industry of China: the role of the state in human resource strategy', *International Journal of Human Resource Management*, 11, 5: 904–24.

Cooke, F. L. (2001) 'Equal opportunities? The role of legislation and public policies in women's employment in China', *Women in Management Review*, 16, 7: 334–48.

Cooke, F. L. (2002) 'Ownership change and the reshaping of employment relations in China: a study of two manufacturing companies', *Journal of Industrial Relations*, 44, 1: 19–39.

Cooke, F. L. (2003a) 'Equal opportunity? Women's managerial careers in governmental organisations in China', *International Journal of Human Resource Management*, 14, 2: 317–33.

Cooke, F. L. (2003b) 'Seven reforms in five decades: civil service reform and its human resource implications in China', *Journal of Asia Pacific Economy*, 18, 3: 381–405.

Cooke, F. L. (2003c) 'New forms of employment in an era of change: non-standard employment in contemporary China and its role in the economy', End-of-project report submitted to the British Council, Beijing, under the scheme of China Studies Small Grants.

Cooke, F. L. (2004a) 'Public sector pay in China: 1949–2001', *International Journal of Human Resource Management*, 15, 4/5: 895–916.

Cooke, F. L. (2004b) 'Vocational and enterprise training in China: policy, practice and prospect', *Journal of Asia Pacific Economy*.

Cooke, F. L. (2004c) 'Foreign firms in China: modelling HRM in a toy manufacturing corporation', *Human Resource Management Journal*, 14, 3: 31–52.

Cooke, F. L. (2004d) 'Women's managerial careers in China in a period of reform', *Asia Pacific Business Review*.

Cooke, F. L. (2004e) 'Informal (sector) employment in China: empirical evidence from the community services sector', paper presented at the *Employment Research Unit Annual Conference*, Cardiff Business School, UK, September.

Cooke, F. L. (forthcoming, 2005) 'Employment relations in small commercial businesses in China', *Industrial Relations Journal*, 36, 1, January.

Cooke, F. L. and Rubery, J. (2002) 'Minimum wage and social equality in China', project report on *Minimum Wage and Employment Equality in Developed and Developing Countries*, Geneva: the International Labour Organisation (ILO).

Cooke, F. L., Shen, J., McBride, A. and Zafar, R. (2004) 'Outsourcing HR: implications for the role of the HR function and the workforce in the NHS', review report conducted under the Policy Research Programme project, *New Ways of Working – A Research Facility to Support HR Policy Making in the NHS*, Department of Health, UK.

Croll, E. (1999) 'Social welfare reform: trends and tensions', *China Quarterly*, 159: 684–99.

Curran, J., Kitchen, J., Abbott, B. and Mills, V. (1993) *Employment and Employment Relations in the Small Service Sector Enterprise – A Report*, ESRC Centre for Research on Small Service Sector Enterprises, London: Kingston University.

Curran, M. (1988) 'Gender and recruitment: people and places in the labour market', *Work, Employment and Society*, 2, 3: 335–51.

Dahlman, C. and Aubert, J. (2001) *China and the Knowledge Economy: Seizing the 21st Century*, New York: World Bank Institute.

Dana, L. (1998) 'Small but not independent: SMEs in Japan', *Journal of Small Business Management*, 36, 1: 73–6.

De Haan, P. and Van Hees, Y. (eds) (1996) *Civil Service Reform in Sub-Saharan Africa*, The Hague: Ministry of Foreign Affairs.

Deyo, F. (1989) *Beneath the Miracle: Labour Subordination in the New Asian Industrialisation*, Berkeley, CA: University of California Press.

Dicks, A. (1989) 'The Chinese legal system: reforms in the balance', *China Quarterly*, 119: 541–76.

Ding, D. and Akhtar, S. (2001) 'The organisational choice of human resource management practices: a study of Chinese enterprises in three cities in the PRC', *International Journal of Human Resource Management*, 12, 6: 946–64.

Ding, D., Fields, D. and Akhtar, S. (1997) 'An empirical study of human resource management policies and practices in foreign-invested enterprises in China: the case of Shenzhen special economic zone', *International Journal of Human Resource Management*, 8, 5: 595–613.

Ding, D., Ge, G. and Warner, M. (2004) 'Evaluation of organizational governance and human resource management in China's township and village enterprises', *International Journal of Human Resource Management*, 15, 4/5: 836–52.

Ding, D., Goodall, K. and Warner, M. (2002) 'The impact of economic reform on the role of trade unions in Chinese enterprises', *International Journal of Human Resource Management*, 13, 3: 431–49.

Ding, D., Lan, G. and Warner, M. (2001) 'A new form of Chinese human resource management? Personnel and labour–management relations in Chinese township and village enterprises: a case study approach', *Industrial Relations Journal*, 32, 4: 328–43.

Ding, D. and Warner, M. (1998) 'Labour law, industrial relations and human resource management in China: an empirical field study in central and south China', *Working Paper No. 17/98*, Cambridge: Judge Institute of Management Studies.

Ding, D. and Warner, M. (1999) '"Re-inventing" China's industrial relations at enterprise-level: an empirical field-study in four major cities', *Industrial Relations Journal*, 30, 3: 243–60.

Easterby-Smith, M., Malina, D. and Lu, Y. (1995) 'How culture-sensitive is HRM?', *International Journal of Human Resource Management*, 6, 1: 31–59.

Economist, The (1998a) 'Zhu takes on the red-tape army', 14 March: 83.

Economist, The (1998b) 'China pedals harder', 13 June: 73.

Edwards, P., Collinson, D. and Rocca, G. (1995) 'Workplace resistance in Western Europe: a preliminary overview and a research agenda', *European Journal of Industrial Relations*, 1, 3: 283–316.

Eraut, M., Steadman, S., Trill, J. and Parkes, J. (1996) 'The assessment of NVQs', *Research Report No. 4*, Brighton: University of Sussex.

Folger, R. and Cropanzano, R. (1998) *Organisational Justice and Human Resource Management*, London: Sage.

Forrester, P. and Porter, R. (1999) 'The politics of management in People's China: from CMRS to modern enterprise and beyond', in M. Warner (ed.), *China's Managerial Revolution*, London: Frank Cass, pp. 47–72.

Fox, A. (1974) *Beyond Contract: Work, Power and Trust Relations*, London: Faber and Faber.

Frenkel, S. and Peetz, D. (1998) 'Globalisation and industrial relations in East Asia: a three-country comparison', *Industrial Relations*, 37, 3: 282–310.

Freud, E. (1998) 'Downsizing China's state industrial enterprises: the case of Baoshan Steel Works', in G. O'Leary (ed.), *Adjusting to Capitalism: Chinese Workers and the State*, New York: M. E. Sharpe, pp. 101–21.

Garnaut, R. (2001) 'Twenty years of economic reform and structural change in the Chinese economy', in R. Garnaut and Y. P. Huang (eds), *Growth with Miracles: Readings on the Chinese Economy in the Era of Reform*, Oxford: Oxford University Press, pp. 1–18.

Gilman, M., Edwards, P., Ram, M. and Arrowsmith, J. (2002) 'Pay determination in small firms in the UK: the case of the response to the national minimum wage', *Industrial Relations Journal*, 33, 1: 52–67.

Golhar, D. and Deshpande, S. (1997) 'HRM practices of large and small Canadian manufacturing firms', *Journal of Small Business Management*, 35, 3: 30–8.

Goodall, K. and Warner, M. (1997) 'Human resources in Sino–foreign joint ventures: selected case studies in Shanghai and Beijing', *International Journal of Human Resource Management*, 8, 5: 569–94.

Goodall, K. and Warner, M. (1998) 'HRM dilemmas in China: the case of foreign-invested enterprises in Shanghai', *Asia Pacific Business Review*, 4, 4: 1–21.

Granick, D. (1990) *Chinese State Enterprises: A Regional Property Rights Analysis*, Chicago, IL: University of Chicago Press.

Granick, D. (1991) 'Multiple labour markets in the industrial state enterprise sector', *China Quarterly*, 126: 269–89.

Gray, C. (1992) 'Growth orientation and the small firm', in K. Caley, E. Chell, F. Chittenden and C. Mason (eds), *Small Enterprise Development: Policy and Practice in Action*, London: Paul Chapman.

Grint, K. (1993) 'What's wrong with performance appraisal? A critique and a suggestion', *Human Resource Management Journal*, 3, 3: 61–77.

Gu, E. (1997) 'Foreign direct investment and the restructuring of Chinese state-owned enterprises (1992–1995): a new institutionalist perspective', *China Information*, 12, 3: 46–71.

Hakim, C. (1996) *Key Issues in Women's Work: Female Heterogeneity and the Polarisation of Women's Employment*, London: Athlone.

Hare, D. (1999) '"Push" versus "pull" factors in migration outflows and returns: determinants of migration status and spell duration among China's rural population', in S. Cook and M. Maurer-Fazio (eds), *The Workers' State Meets the Market: Labour in China's Transition*, London: Frank Cass, pp. 45–72.

Hassard, J., Sheehan, J. and Morris, J. (1999) 'Enterprise reform in post-Deng China', *International Studies of Management and Organisation*, 29, 3: 54–83.

Hastings, S. (2000) 'Grading systems and estimating value', in G. White and J. Druker (eds), *Reward Management: A Critical Text*, London: Routledge, pp. 84–105.

Henley, J. and Nyaw, K. (1987) 'The development of work incentives in Chinese industrial enterprises – material versus non-material incentives', in M. Warner (ed.), *Management Reforms in China*, London: Frances Pinter.

Hoffman, C. (1981) 'People's Republic of China', in A. Albert (ed.), *International Handbook of Industrial Relations*, Westport, CT: Greenwood Press.

Holliday, R. (1995) *Investigating Small Firms: Nice Work?*, London: Routledge.

Howe, C. (1973) *Wage Patterns and Wage Policies in Modern China 1919–1972*, London: Cambridge University Press.

Hughes, N. C. (1998) 'Smashing the iron rice bowl', *Foreign Affairs*, 77, 4 (July/August).

Ilari, S. and Grange, A. (1999) 'Transferring ownership-specific advantages to a joint venture in China', in M. Warner (ed.), *China's Managerial Revolution*, London: Frank Cass, pp. 119–46.

International Labour Organisation (ILO) (1988) *Assessing the Impact of Statutory Minimum Wages in Developing Countries: Four Country Studies*, Geneva: International Labour Office.

Jackson, S. (1992) *Chinese Enterprise Management Reforms in Economic Perspective*, Berlin: De Gruyter.

Johnson, T. (1990) 'Wages, benefits, and the promotion process for Chinese university faculty', *China Quarterly*, 125: 137–55.

Keasey, K. and Watson, R. (1993) *Small Firm Management: Ownership, Finance and Performance*, Oxford: Blackwell.

Keith, R. (1997) 'Legislating women's and children's "Rights and Interests" in the PRC', *China Quarterly*, 149: 29–55.

Kessler, I. (1995) 'Reward systems', in J. Storey (ed.), *Human Resource Management: A Critical Text*, London: Routledge, pp. 254–79.

Kessler, I. (2000) 'Remuneration systems', in S. Bach and K. Sisson (eds), *Personnel Management*, Oxford: Blackwell, pp. 264–86.

Khan, A. R. and Riskin, C. (1998) 'Income and inequality in China: composition, distribution and growth of household income, 1988 to 1995', *China Quarterly*, 154: 221–53.

Kinnie, N., Purcell, J., Hutchinson, S., Terry, M., Collinson, M. and Scarbrough, H. (1999) 'Employment relations in SMEs: market-driven or customer-shaped?', *Employee Relations*, 21, 3: 218–35.

Klauss, R. (1981) 'Formalised mentor relationships for management and development programmes in federal government', *Public Administration Review*, July–August: 489–96.

Knight, J., Song, L. and Huaibib, J. (1999) 'Chinese rural migrants in urban enterprises: three perspectives', in S. Cook and M. Maurer-Fazio (eds), *The Workers' State Meets the Market: Labour in China's Transition*, London: Frank Cass, pp. 73–104.

Kochan, T. (1996) 'Shaping employment relations for the 21st century: challenges facing business, labor, and government leaders', in J. Lee and A. Verma (eds), *Changing Employment Relations in Asian Pacific Countries*, Taiwan: Chung-Hua Institution for Economic Research.

Kondo, D. (1990) *Crafting Selves: Power, Gender and Discourses of Identity in a Japanese Workplace*, Chicago, IL: University of Chicago Press.

Korabik, K. (1994) 'Managerial women in the People's Republic of China: the long march continues', in N. Adler and D. Izraeli (eds), *Competitive Frontiers: Women in a Global Economy*, Oxford: Blackwell, pp. 114–26.

Korzec, M. (1992) *Labour and the Failure of Reform in China*, London: Macmillan.

Kram, K. (1983) 'Phases of the mentoring relationship', *Academy of Management Journal*, 26: 608–25.

Kram, K. (1985) *Mentoring at Work: Development Relationships in Organisational Life*, Glenview, IL: Scott, Foresman.

Laaksonen, O. (1988) *Management in China During and After Mao*, Berlin and New York: Walter de Gruyter.

Lasserre, P. and Ching, P. S. (1997) 'Human resource management in China and the localisation challenge', *Journal of Asian Business*, 13: 85–99.

Lee, C. K. (1998) 'The labour politics of market socialism: collective inaction and class experiences among state workers in Guangzhou', *Modern China*, 24, 1: 3–34.

Lee, C. K. (1999) 'From organised dependence to disorganised despotism: changing labour regimes in Chinese factories', *China Quarterly*, 157: 44–71.

Lee, E. (1997) 'Globalisation and labour standards: a review of issues', *International Labour Review*, 136, 2: 173–89.

Lee, G. and Warner, M. (2002) 'Labour-market policies in Shanghai and Hong Kong: a study of "One Country, Two Systems" in Greater China', *International Journal of Manpower*, 23, 6: 505–26.

Legewie, J. (2002) 'Control and co-ordination of Japanese subsidiaries in China: problems of an expatriate-based management system', *International Journal of Human Resource Management*, 13, 6: 901–19.

Leung, K., Wang, Z. and Smith, P. (2001) 'Job attitudes and organisational justice in joint venture hotels in China: the role of expatriate managers', *International Journal of Human Resource Management*, 12, 6: 926–45.

Levine, M. (1997) *Worker Rights and Labour Standards in Asia's Four New Tigers: A Comparative Perspective*, New York: Plenum Press.

Liff, S. and Ward, K. (2001) 'Distorted views through the glass ceiling: the construction of women's understandings of promotion and senior management positions', *Gender, Work and Organization*, 8, 1: 19–36.

Lin, J. (1998) 'State intervention, ownership and state enterprise reform in China', in R. I. Wu and Y. P. Chu (eds), *Business, Markets and Government in the Asia Pacific: Competition Policy, Convergence and Pluralism*, London: Routledge, pp. 70–85.

Lindholm, N. (2000) 'Standardised performance management? A study of joint ventures in China', in M. Warner (ed.), *Changing Workplace Relations in the Chinese Economy*, Basingstoke: Palgrave Macmillan, pp. 163–84.

Lockett, M. (1988) 'Culture and the problems of Chinese management', *Organisation Studies*, 9: 475–96.

Lubman, S. (1995) 'Introduction: the future of Chinese law', *China Quarterly*, 141: 1–21.

Lucas, R. (1988) 'On the mechanics of economic development', *Journal of Monetary Economics*, 32: 3–42.

Luo, Y. D., Tan, J. and Shenkar, O. (1998) 'Strategic responses to competitive pressure: the case of township and village enterprises in China', *Asia Pacific Journal of Management*, 15: 33–50.

McCourt, W. (2001) 'Towards a strategic model of employment reform in developing countries: explaining and remedying experience to date', *International Journal of Human Resource Management*, 12, 1: 56–75.

McEvoy, G. (1984) 'Small business personnel practices', *Journal of Small Business Management*, 22, 10: 1–8.

Marchington, M., Carroll, M. and Boxall, P. (2003) 'Labour scarcity and the survival of small firms: a resource-based view of the road haulage industry', *Human Resource Management Journal*, 13, 4: 5–22.

Marshall, A. (1920) *Principles of Economics* (8th edn), Book Six, Chapter 4, p. 3, New York: Macmillan.

Marshall, V. (1994) 'Beware employers: don't lose control of NVQs', *Personnel Management*, March: 30–3.

Matley, H. (1999) 'Employee relations in small firms: a micro-business perspective', *Employee Relations*, 21, 3: 285–95.

Meng, X. (2000) *Labour Market Reform in China*, Cambridge: Cambridge University Press.

Morris, J, Sheehan, J. and Hassard, J. (2001) 'From dependency to defiance? Work–unit relationships in China's state enterprise reforms', *Journal of Management Studies*, 38, 5: 697–717.

Nelson, J. and Reeder, J. (1985) 'Labour relations in China', *California Management Review*, 27, 4: 13–32.

Nelson, R. (1987) 'Promotion of small enterprises', in P. Neck and R. Nelson (eds),

Small Enterprise Development: Policies and Programmes, Geneva: International Labour Office, pp. 1–15.

Ng, S. H. and Warner, M. (1998) *China's Trade Unions and Management*, London: Macmillan.

Nunberg, B. (1997) *Rethinking Civil Service Reform: An Agenda for Smart Government*, Washington, DC: World Bank, Poverty and Social Policy Department.

Nyaw, M. K. (1995) 'Human resource management in the People's Republic of China', in L. Moore and P. Jennings (eds), *Human Resource Management on the Pacific Rim*, Berlin: Walter de Gruyter.

Parris, K. (1999) 'The rise of private business interests', in M. Goldman and R. MacFarquhar (eds), *The Paradox of China's Post-Mao Reforms*, Cambridge, MA: Harvard University Press, pp. 262–82.

Pomfret, R. (1991) *Investing in China: Ten Years of the Open Door Policy*, Ames, IA: Iowa State University Press.

Poole, M. and Jenkins, G. (1998) 'Human resource management and the theory of rewards: evidence from a national survey', *British Journal of Industrial Relations*, 36, 2: 227–47.

Potter, P. (1999) 'The Chinese legal system: continuing commitment to the primacy of state power', *China Quarterly*, 159: 673–83.

Rainnie, A. (1989) *Industrial Relations in Small Firms*, London: Routledge.

Ralston, D., Gustafson, D., Cheung, F. and Terpstra, R. (1993) 'Differences in managerial values: a study of US, Hong Kong and PRC managers', *Journal of International Business Studies*, 24, 2: 249–75.

Ralston, D., Holt, D., Terpstra, R. and Cheng, Y. K. (1997) 'The impact of national culture and economic ideology on managerial work values: a study of the United States, Russia, Japan and China', *Journal of International Business Studies*, 28, 1: 177–207.

Ralston, D., Egri, C., Stewart, S., Terpstra, S. and Yu, K. C. (1999) 'Doing business in the 21st century with the new generation of Chinese managers: a study of general shifts in work values in China', *Journal of International Business Studies*, 30, 2: 415–28.

Ram, M. (1994) *Managing to Survive: Working Lives in Small Firms*, Oxford: Blackwell.

Ram, M., Edwards, P., Gilman, M. and Arrowsmith, J. (2001) 'The dynamics of informality: employment regulations in small firms and the effects of regulatory change', *Work, Employment and Society*, 15, 4: 845–61.

Randell, G. (1994) 'Employee appraisal', in K. Sisson (ed.), *Personnel Management in Britain*, Oxford: Blackwell, pp. 221–52.

Rees, T. (2000) 'Models of equal opportunities: tinkering, tailoring, transforming', paper presented to the *International Seminar on the Legal Protection of Women's Employment Rights*, April, Shanghai, China.

Reskin, B. and Ross, C. (1992) 'Jobs, authority, and earnings among managers: the continuing significance of sex', *Work and Occupations*, 19: 342–65.

Romer, P. (1990) 'Human capital and growth: theory and evidence', *Carnegie-Rochester Conference Series on Public Policy*, 32: 251–86.

Rowley, C., Benson, J. and Warner, M. (2004) 'Towards an Asian model of human resource management? A comparative analysis of China, Japan and South Korea', *International Journal of Human Resource Management*, 15, 4/5: 917–33.

Rubery, J. (1995) 'The low paid and the unorganised', in P. Edwards (ed.), *Industrial Relations in Britain*, Oxford: Blackwell, pp. 543–68.

Rubery, J. (1997) 'Wages and the labour market', *British Journal of Industrial Relations*, 35, 3: 337–66.

Rubery, J. (2003) 'Pay equity, minimum wage and equality at work: theoretical framework and empirical evidence', *Working Paper 19*, Geneva: International Labour Organisation.

Rubery, J. and Grimshaw, D. (2003) *The Organisation of Employment: An International Perspective*, Basingstoke: Palgrave Macmillan.

Saich, T. (2001) *Governance and Politics of China*, Basingstoke: Palgrave.

Scase, R. (1995) 'Employment relations in small firms', in P. Edwards (ed.), *Industrial Relations: Theory and Practice in Britain*, Oxford: Blackwell, pp. 569–95.

Schiavo-Campo, S., de Tommaso, G. and Mukherjee, A. (1997b) 'An international statistical survey of government employment and wages', *Policy Research Working Paper 1806*, The World Bank.

Schultz, T. (1961) 'Investment in human capital', *American Economic Review*, March: 1–17.

Scott, M., Roberts, I., Holroyd, G. and Sawbridge, D. (1989) 'Management and industrial relations in small firms', *Research Paper No. 70*, Department of Employment, Britain.

Sheehan, J. (1999) *Chinese Workers: A New History*, London: Routledge.

Shirk, S. L. (1981) 'Recent Chinese labour policies and the transformation of industrial organisation in China', *China Quarterly*, 88: 575–93.

Smith, P. and Wang, Z. M. (1997) 'Leadership, decision-making and cultural context: event management within Chinese joint ventures', *Leadership Quarterly*, 8, 4: 413–31.

Sparrow, P. (2000) 'International reward management', in G. White and J. Druker (eds), *Reward Management: A Critical Text*, London: Routledge, pp. 196–214.

South China Morning Post, 21 June 1998, Hong Kong.

Stockman, N. (1994) 'Gender inequality and social structure in urban China', *Sociology*, 28, 3: 759–77.

Stockman, N., Bonney, N. and Sheng, X. W. (1995) *Women's Work in East and West: The Dual Burden of Employment and Family Life*, London: UCL Press.

Stokes, D. (1998) *Small Business Management: A Case Study Approach* (3rd edn), London: Letts Educational.

Storey, D. (1994) *Understanding the Small Business Sector*, London: International Thomson Business Press.

Storey, J. (1995) *Human Resource Management: A Critical Text*, London: Routledge.

Straussman, J. and Zhang, M. Z. (2001) 'Chinese administrative reforms in international perspective', *International Journal of Public Sector Management*, 14, 5: 411–22.

Sun, B. (2000) 'Pay and motivation in Chinese enterprises', in M. Warner (ed.), *Changing Workplace Relations in the Chinese Economy*, London: Macmillan, pp. 205–23.

Sunday Telegraph, 24 April 2001.

Sutherland, J. and Rainbird, H. (2000) 'Unions and workplace learning: conflict or co-operation with the employer?', in H. Rainbird (ed.), *Training in the Workplace*, London: Macmillan, pp. 189–209.

Takahara, A. (1992) *The Politics of Wage Policy in Post-revolutionary China*, London: Macmillan.

Tanner, M. (1995) 'How a bill becomes a law in China: stages and processes in lawmaking', *China Quarterly*, 141: 39–65.

Taylor, B. (2002) 'Privatisation, markets and industrial relations in China', *British Journal of Industrial Relations*, 40, 2: 249–72.

Tong, C. H., Straussman, J. and Broadnax, W. (1999) 'Civil service reform in the People's Republic of China: case studies of early implementation', *Public Administration and Development*, 19: 193–206.

Tsang, E. (1994) 'Human resource management problems in Sino–foreign joint ventures', *International Journal of Manpower*, 15, 9/10: 4–21.

Tsang, E. (2001) 'Managerial learning in foreign-invested enterprises of China', *Management International Review*, 41, 1: 29–51.

Tung, R. (1991) 'Motivation in the Chinese industrial enterprise', in R. Steers and L. Porter (eds), *Motivation and Work Behaviour*, New York: McGraw-Hill.

Tziner, A. (1999) 'The relationship between distal and proximal factors and the use of political considerations in performance appraisal', *Journal of Business and Psychology*, 14, 1: 217–31.

United Nations Development Programme (2003) *Human Development Report*, Oxford: Oxford University Press.

Verburg, R. (1996) 'Developing HRM in foreign–Chinese joint ventures', *European Management Journal*, 14, 5: 518–25.

Verma, A. and Yan, Z. M. (1995) 'The changing face of human resource management in China: opportunities, problems and strategies', in A. Verma, T. Kochan and R. Lansbury (eds), *Employment Relations in the Growing Asian Economies*, London: Routledge, pp. 315–35.

Verma, A., Kochan, T. and Lansbury, R. (1995) 'Employment relations in an era of global markets', in A. Verma, T. Kochan and R. Lansbury (eds), *Employment Relations in the Growing Asian Economies*, London: Routledge, pp. 1–26.

Verser, T. (1987) 'Owners' perceptions of personnel problems in small business', *Mid-American Journal of Business*, 2, September: 13–17.

Vinnicombe, S. and Colwill, N. (1995) *The Essence of Women in Management*, London: Prentice Hall.

Wager, T. (1998) 'Determinants of human resource management practices in small firms: some evidence from Atlantic Canada', *Journal of Small Business Management*, 36, 3: 13–23.

Walder, A. (1986) *Communist Neo-Traditionalism: Work and Authority in Chinese Industry*, Berkeley, CA: University of California Press.

Walder, A. (1987) 'Wage reform and the webs of factory interests', *China Quarterly*, 109: 90–102.

Walder, A. (1989) 'Factory and managers in the era of reform', *China Quarterly*, 118: 22–43.

Wang, Y. Y. (2004) 'Observations on the organizational commitment of Chinese employees: comparative studies of state-owned enterprises and foreign-invested enterprises', *International Journal of Human Resource Management*, 15, 4/5: 649–69.

Warner, M. (1988) 'China's management education at the crossroad', *Journal of General Management*, 14, 1: 78–91.

Warner, M. (1990a) 'Developing key human resources in China: an assessment of university management schools', *International Journal of Human Resource Management*, 1, 1: 87–106.

Warner, M. (1990b) 'Chinese trade unions: structure and function in a decade of economic reform, 1979–1989', *Management Studies Research Paper No. 8/90*, Cambridge University.

Warner, M. (1992) *How Chinese Managers Learn: Management and Industrial Training in the PRC*, London: Macmillan.

Warner, M. (1993) 'Human resource management "with Chinese characteristics"', *International Journal of Human Resource Management*, 4, 4: 45–65.

Warner, M. (1995) *The Management of Human Resources in Chinese Industry*, London: Macmillan.

Warner, M. (1996a) 'Human resources in the People's Republic of China: the "Three Systems" reforms', *Human Resource Management Journal*, 6, 2: 32–42.

Warner, M. (1996b) 'Chinese enterprise reform, human resources and the 1994 labour law', *International Journal of Human Resource Management*, 7, 4: 779–96.

Warner, M. (1997a) 'Management–labour relations in the new Chinese economy', *Human Resource Management Journal*, 7, 4: 30–43.

Warner, M. (1997b) 'China's HRM in transition: towards relative convergence?', *Asia Pacific Business Review*, 3, 4: 19–33.

Warner, M. (1998) 'China's HRM in transition: towards relative convergence?', in C. Rowley (ed.), *Human Resource Management in the Asia Pacific Region: Convergence Questioned*, London: Frank Cass, pp. 19–33.

Warner, M. (1999a) 'Human resources and management in China's "hi-tech" revolution: a study of selected computer hardware, software and related firms in the PRC', *International Journal of Human Resource Management*, 10, 1: 1–20.

Warner, M. (ed.) (1999b) *China's Managerial Revolution*, London: Frank Cass.

Warner, M. (2000) 'Society, organisation and work in China', in M. Maurice and A. Sorge (eds), *Embedding Organisations*, Amsterdam and Philadelphia, PA: Benjamin, pp. 257–2.

Warner, M. (2001a) 'The new Chinese worker and the challenge of globalisation: an overview', *International Journal of Human Resource Management*, 12, 1: 134–41.

Warner, M. (2001b) 'Human resource management in the People's Republic of China', in P. Budhwar and Y. Debrah (eds), *Human Resource Management in Developing Countries*, London: Routledge, pp. 19–33.

Warner, M. and Ng, S. H. (1998) 'The ongoing evolution of Chinese industrial relations: the negotiation of "Collective Contracts" in the Shenzhen Special Economic Zone', *China Information*, 12, 4: 1–20.

Warner, M. and Ng, S. H. (1999) 'Collective contracts in Chinese enterprises: a new brand of collective bargaining under "market socialism"?', *British Journal of Industrial Relations*, 37, 2: 295–314.

White, G. (1996) 'Chinese trade unions in the transition from socialism: towards corporatism or civil society?', *British Journal of Industrial Relations*, 34, 3: 433–57.

White, G. (2000) 'Determining pay', in G. White and J. Druker (eds), *Reward Management: A Critical Text*, London: Routledge, pp. 25–53.

Wilkinson, A. (1999) 'Employment relations in SMEs', *Employee Relations*, 22, 3: 206–17.

World Bank, The (1993) *The East Asian Miracle: Economic Growth and Public Policy*, New York: Oxford University Press.

World Bank Report 1995: Workers in the Globalised World (1995) Beijing: China Financial and Economic Publishing House.

You, J. (1998) *China's Enterprise Reform: Changing State/Society Relations after Mao*, London: Routledge.

Yu, K. C. (1998) 'Chinese employees' perceptions of distributive fairness', in A. M. Francesco and B. A. Gold (eds), *International Organisational Behavior*, Englewood Cliffs, NJ: Prentice Hall, pp. 302–13.

Zhao, M. H. and Nichols, T. (1996) 'Management control of labour in state-owned enterprises: cases from the textile industry', *China Journal*, 36: 1–21.

Zhu, C. and Dowling, P. (2002) 'Staffing practices in transition: some empirical evidence from China', *International Journal of Human Resource Management*, 13, 4: 569–97.

Zhu, C. and Nyland, C. (2004) 'Marketization and social protection reform: emerging HRM issues in China', *International Journal of Human Resource Management*, 15, 4/5: 853–77.

Zhu, Y. (1995) 'Major changes under way in China's industrial relations', *International Labour Review*, 134, 1: 37–49.

References in Chinese

All-China Women's Federation (2000) 'The situation of women entrepreneurs in non-public sectors', *Research in Women*, 2: 34–9.

Beijing Youth Newspaper (2002) 'The most popular employers in the eyes of HR managers', 15 November.

Chen, B. (2002) '"Negotiated wage": a method to stop staff turnover in SOEs', *Development and Management of Human Resources*, 4: 11–12.

Chen, C. Y. and Lin, Y. M. (2002) *China Modern Enterprise Management*, Beijing: China Development Publishing House.

Chen, D. J. and Zhang, Y. P. (1999) 'Wage system reform and social insurance', *Liaoning Educational College Journal*, 1: 24–6.

Chen, J. G., Lu. Z. and Wang, Y. Z. (2001) *China Social Security System Development Report*, Beijing: Social Science Document Publishing House.

Chen, L. (2001) 'Minimum wage is not plausible', *21st Century Economic Report*, 2 April.

Chen, Q. T. (2003) 'Promoting the healthy growth of private economy', *Xinhua Wenzhai*, 4: 40–2.

Chen, Y. D. and Wang, C. C. (1994) 'On the minimum wage and its determination', *Journal of Zhongnan University of Finance*, 5: 71–6.

Chen, Z. G., Lu, S. M., Liu, H. H. and Xu, W. (1996) 'Problems and strategies in the implementation of minimum wage policies', *Trade Union Theory and Practice*, 3: 40–2.

Cheng, X. W. (2000) *Public Sector Reform in China: Choice and Direction*, Beijing: Democracy and Construction Publishing House.

Chi, F. L. (2001) *Operations and System Design of Employee Share Ownership in China*, Beijing, China Economy Publishing House.

China Education Statistics Yearbook (2001) Beijing: China Education Publishing House.

China Labour Statistics Yearbook (1997) The Ministry of Statistics, China.
China Labour Statistics Yearbook (2000) The Ministry of Statistics, China.
China Labour Statistics Yearbook (2003) The Ministry of Statistics, China.
China Private Economy Yearbook (2003) Beijing: China Industrial and Commercial Association Publishing House.
China Statistics Yearbook (1996) The Ministry of Statistics, China.
China Statistics Yearbook (1997) The Ministry of Statistics, China.
China Statistics Yearbook (1998) The Ministry of Statistics, China.
China Statistics Yearbook (1999) The Ministry of Statistics, China.
China Statistics Yearbook (2000) The Ministry of Statistics, China.
China Statistics Yearbook (2001) The Ministry of Statistics, China.
China Statistics Yearbook (2002) The Ministry of Statistics, China.
China Statistics Yearbook (2003) The Ministry of Statistics, China.
China Trade Union Statistics Yearbook (1997) The Ministry of Statistics, China.
China Trade Union Statistics Yearbook (2001) The Ministry of Statistics, China.
Chu, L. Q. (2002) 'Can your enterprise retain talent after the WTO?', *Development and Management of Human Resources*, 5: 7–8.
Chu, Y. D. (1998) 'Some thoughts on enterprise employee education and training', *China Vocational and Technical Education*, 6: 14–15.
Deng, Y. (1998) 'The impact of labour rights and interests on women intellectuals', *Shenghuo shibao*, 26 March.
Diao, Y. F. (2000) 'Improving the strategy of the minimum wage system', *China Labour*, 5: 14–16.
Dong. Y. X. (2001) 'Thoughts on the reform of the personnel system in higher education in the new era', *China Metallurgy Education*, 6: 12–14.
Fourth Census of China, The (1993) China Statistics Publishing House.
Fu, K. S. (1995) 'An economic analysis of the implementation of the minimum wage system', *Jianghuai Forum*, 6: 70–4.
Guan, Y. B. and Xu, Y. Q. (1999) *Employee Share Ownership System and Legal System*, Beijing: Economic Science Publishing House.
Guangzhou Daily (2000) 27 August.
Guo, H. M. (2000) 'Gender discrimination in women's employment and the completion of relevant laws and regulations', paper presented to the *International Seminar on the Legal Protection of Women's Employment Rights*, April, Shanghai, China.
Guo, W. Y. (1996) *Theory of Administrative Management in China*, Beijing: The Central Communist Party School Publishing House.
Head Project Team of the 'Positional Training System in China' (1998) 'A study on establishing the positional training system in China', *Educational Studies*, 8: 9–14.
Hong Kong Commercial Daily News (2002) 17 March: A10.
Hu, J. and Liu, J. M. (1994) 'Choices of wage reform in the dual system', *Economy Debate*, 2: 52–6.
Hu, X. Y. and He, P. (eds) (1992) *The Implementation of the Post-plus Skills Wage System*, Beijing: Wage Research Institute of the Ministry of Labour of China.
Hu, Y. H. (2001) 'New characteristics of rural population mobility in China in 2000', *China National Conditions and Power*, 9: 18–20.
Hu, Y. H. (1998) 'Vocational education needs to follow the law: developing a trans-millennium strategy', *Vocational and Technical Education in China*, 12: 14–15.

Huang, L. H., Mong, Q. X., Cheng, X. B. and Cao, Z. W. (2002) 'Urbanisation of farmers', *China National Conditions and Power*, 1: 21–6.

Huang, M. T. (1998) 'A discussion on the implementation of position wage', *Reform and Management*, bimonthly, 5, Guangzhou Railway Corporation: 18–21.

Hunan Team of the Agricultural Research Team of Ministry of Statistics (2001) 'A bright spot of increasing farmers' income: Research Report III on rural hot issues', *China National Conditions and Power*, 11–12: 37–44.

Jiang, Y. P. (2000) 'State intervention in the employment of urban women', paper presented to the *International Seminar on the Legal Protection of Women's Employment Rights*, April, Shanghai, China.

Jin San Jiao (1998) 'Preventing the re-expansion of government organisations', *Jin San Jiao*, 4: 15.

Jin, Y. H. (2002) 'Media's influence on women's participation in politics as seen from the public's cognition of the question', *Collection of Women's Studies*, 2: 15–22.

Kang, S. Y. (1996) *Wage Theory and Wage Management*, Beijing: China Labour Publishing House.

Labour Market Wage Prices in Large and Medium Sized Cities (1999) The Ministry of Labour and Social Insurance, China.

Li, M. F. (1995) 'The determination of a minimum wage and mechanism for adjustment', *Labour Science of China*, 5: 37–40.

Li, X. Y. (2000) 'The implications of China's accession to the WTO for its continuous education', *Zhejiang Social Science*, 5: 83–5.

Li, Y. G. and Bai, R. P. (2000) 'Problems in and strategy for enterprise culture building in China', *Scientific Management Research*, 3: 58–60.

Li, Z. W., Zhao, J. F. and Wang, Z. H. (2000) 'Some thoughts on employee training in SOEs', *Education and Occupation*, 5: 44–5.

Liao, C. W. and Chen, W. S. (2002) 'Human resource management employee training system', *Development and Management of Human Resources*, 7: 22–6.

Lin, Y. F. (2000) 'The calculation of minimum wage needs to be standardised urgently', *Jiangsu Statistics*, May: 30.

Liu, C. S. and Liu, Y. (1999) 'Strategy for new challenges faced by vocational and technical education', *New Vocational Education*, 9: 3–6.

Liu, D. W. (2000) 'Focus: head hunting agencies', *Administrative Personnel Management*, 1: 2–3.

Liu, G. H. (1998) 'The organisation of vocational education and motivation mechanism', *Higher Education Studies and Exploration* (Nanjing), 1–2: 131–5.

Liu, G. X. (1999) 'On the minimum wage social security system', *Journal of Heilongjiang Agricultural College*, 3: 30–1.

Liu, L. X. (2000) 'Employee training in SOEs in China', *Enterprise Operations and Management*, 7: 63–7.

Liu, L. X. (2001) 'Employee training in SOEs: problems and suggestions', *Human Resource Development in China*, 3: 12–15.

Liu, T. (1989) 'Chinese workers and employees participate in democratic management of enterprises', *Chinese Trade Unions*, China, 2: 5–10.

Liu, Y. (2001) 'Chinese women in politics in the new century', *China National Conditions and Strength*, 107, 11–12: 28–9.

Liu, Z. W. and Yang, H. P. (2001) *Legal Protection of Non Public-owned Industries*, Beijing: Xi Yuan Publishing House.

Lu, X. X. (1999) 'Characteristics of the labour–management relations in the period of economic transition in China', *Economic Issues*, 11: 13–15.

Lu, L. J. and Wang, Z. J. (2003) 'A study of private enterprise capital, labour and distribution relations', *Labour Economy and Labour Relations*, 3: 42–7.

Lu, Q. and Zhao, Y. M. (2002) 'Gender segregation in China since the economic reform', *Journal of Southern Yangtze University* (Humanities and Social Sciences), 1, 2: 22–48.

Lu, X. J. (2000) 'An analysis of the reform of the standard of unemployment insurance benefits in China', *Journal of Beijing Economic Management Institute*, 3: 8–10.

Luo, P. (2000) 'Retirement age and protection of women's employment rights', paper presented to the *International Seminar on the Legal Protection of Women's Employment Rights*, April, Shanghai, China.

Ma, H. C. and Liu, H. R. (1999) 'On the new round of reform of the personnel system of higher education', *China Higher Education*, 5: 4–7.

Ma, J. F. (1999) 'Building a sustainable vocational training system', *New Vocational Education*, 4: 8–10.

Market (2001) Internet version, 13 September.

Meng, X. (1998) 'Male–female wage determination and gender wage discrimination in China's rural industrial sector', *Labour Economics*, 5: 67–89.

Ministry of Statistics (1999) 'Annual report of the development of labour and social insurance service, 1998', *China Labour Insurance News*, 6: 17.

Mu, Z. and Bi, S. H. (1994) 'Reflections on the socialist enterprise culture', *Xue Hai (Sea of Learning)*, 3: 39–44.

Niu, Z. (1998) 'On the reform of employment system and the development of vocational education', *Education and Occupation*, 6: 4–7.

Pan, J. T. (2002) 'Gender (dis)advantages in pension social insurance: on the retirement age of men and women', *China Social Science*, 2: 118–31.

Peng, J. F. (2003) 'Talent market focus in China', *Development and Management of Human Resources*, 3: 4–9.

Project Team of the Second National Survey of Women's Social Position in China, The (2001) 'Report of the main findings of the Second National Survey of Women's Social Position in China', *Collection of Women's Studies*, 5: 4–12.

Project Team of Social Situation Analysis and Prediction of China, The (2002) 'General report of social situation analysis and prediction of China: 2001–2002', *Management World*, 1: 17–26.

Project Team of the State Education and Development Research Centre, The (2002) 'A report on the employment choice and situation of university graduates in China', *China Youth Studies*, 1: 5–9.

Project Team of the Study on the Social Stratification of Private Enterprise Owners in China, The (1994) 'Operational situations of private enterprises and group characteristics of private enterprise owners in China', *Social Science in China*, 4: 60–72.

Sai, F. and Yin, Z. W. (1995) 'Problems in the implementation of the minimum wage system in China', *Management World*, 3: 198–203.

Shanghai All-China Women's Federation, The (1997) 'Re-employment of laid-off female workers in Shanghai: Problems and strategy', *Collection of Women's Studies*, 1: 36–9.

Shi, L. J. (1999) 'Strategy on deepening the reform of the personnel system of higher education', *Science and Economy of Inner Mongolia*, 2: 26–8.

Shi, Q. Q. (2002) 'Opportunities and challenges for women entrepreneurs in China', *Macro Economy Studies*, 10: 54–5.

Song, S. M. (1999) 'Local government reform', *Xinhua Wenzai*, 10: 18–20.

Specialist Team, The (1999) 'A review of employee education and training', *Vocational and Technical Education*, 21: 4–9.

Tan, W. S. and Liu, F. (2003) 'The individualisation tendency in HRM in private businesses', *China Human Resource Development*, 2: 12–13.

Tien, Y. (2000) 'Pay reform in China: characteristics and prospects', *Commercial Research*, 1: 93–4.

Wang, B. F. and Du, W. X. (1999) 'Differences in men and women's motivations to success', *Journal of Jinan University*, 9, 3: 35–8.

Wang, C. G. and Fang, W. (2001) 'Cultural adaptation and co-operation: an important aspect that MNCs face in China', *Xinhua Wenzhai*, 12: 19–24.

Wang, C. H. (1999) 'Gender differences in their perceptions and ideologies among political cadres', *Collection of Women's Studies*, 2: 17–20.

Wang, C. H. (2003) 'How much do university teachers earn?', *Xinhua Wenzhai*, 2: 182–5.

Wang, D. (2002) 'Did you train today?', *Development and Management of Human Resources*, 6: 8–10.

Wang, F. C., Shen, Y. W. and Han, B. (2002) 'Reinforcing the achievement of the personnel system reform in higher education through scientific assessment', *China Metallurgy Education*, 2: 12–14.

Wang, H. L. (2002) 'Enterprise labour disputes in China', *Population and Economics*, 10: 180–1.

Wang, J. F. (2000) 'Safeguarding women's working rights and interests', paper presented to the *International Seminar on the Legal Protection of Women's Employment Rights*, April, Shanghai, China.

Wang, J. P. and Niu, Y. J. (1996) 'Minimum wage: prospects and problems', *Workers' Daily*, Beijing, 23 May: 7.

Wang, Q. J. (2003) '"Wage" opportunity', *Development and Management of Human Resources*, 5: 35–41.

Wang, Y. J. (2003) 'Current situation of private investment development and policy direction', *Xinhua Wenzhai*, 4: 43–45.

Wei, X. M. (1999) 'An investigation of the technical education and competency development in Suzhou City', *Journal of Vocational and Competency Training and Education*, 4: 11–12.

Workers' Daily (2002) 29 November.

Wu, F. S. (1998) 'Problems and key issues in the development of vocational education in China under the socialist market economy condition', *Education and Occupation*, 8: 4–7.

Wu, J. (1997) 'Vocational and technical education must deal with the two fundamental changes effectively', *Journal of Sichuan Education College*, 3: 34–9.

Wu, J. (2003) 'Review of talent market in 2002', *Development and Management of Human Resources*, 3: 10–12.

Wu, Y. B. (1999) 'Vocational and technical education in China: a historic overview and analysis of the current situation', *Occupational and Technical Education*, 5: 5–9.

Xiao, B. S. (1999) 'Some thoughts on the agricultural vocational training system', *Education and Vocation*, 1: 40–2.

Xinhua Monthly (1995) 'An outline of Chinese women's development 1995–2000', 10: 48–55.

Xu, L. (2000) 'Enterprise training: some thoughts at the new millennium', *Journal of Changzhou Technical College*, 9: 25–7.

Xu, Y. L. (2001) 'Current situation of HRM in China', *Development and Management of Human Resources*, 2: 8–10.

Xu, Z. (2000) 'On format, style and methods of employee training', *China Smelter Education*, 6: 79–80.

Yang, F. (1996) 'Barriers to and strategies for women's career progression', *Women's Studies*, 2: 20–2.

Yang, F. (1999) 'Increasing five types of awareness for women in politics', *Human Resource Development*, 2: 36–7.

Yang, S. W. and Gao, F. L. (2001) 'Reforms of the civil service pay system in China', *Economy and Management Studies*, 6: 23–9.

Yangcheng Evening News (2002) 26 June.

Yangcheng Evening News (2002) 2 November.

Yangcheng Evening News (2002) 21 November.

Yangcheng Evening News (2003) 23 February.

Yangcheng Evening News (2003) 14 April.

Yangcheng Evening News (2003) 4 July.

Yangcheng Evening News (2003) 9 July.

Yangcheng Evening News (2003) 14 August.

Yangcheng Evening News (2003) 24 September.

Yangcheng Evening News (2004) 22 February.

Yangcheng Evening News (2004) 23 February.

Yangcheng Evening News, (2004) 5 March.

Yu, Q. M. (1994) 'Current situation and characteristics of enterprise culture in China', *Journal of Guizhou Normal University*, 2: 84–7.

Yu, Q. N. (1998) 'An exploration of a reform model for the vocational educational system', *Jilin Educational Science*, 6: 17–20.

Zhang, H. Y. and Ming, L. Z. (1999) *The Development of Private Enterprises in China: Report No. 1*, Beijing: Social Science Documentation Publishing House.

Zhang, H. Y., Ming, L. Z. and Liang, C. Y. (2002) *The Development of Private Enterprises in China: Report No. 3*, Beijing: Social Science Documentation Publishing House.

Zhang, K. H. (2003) 'Issues of labour capital relations in the WTO framework', *Labour Economy and Labour Relations*, 1: 60–3.

Zhang, M. and Zhao, L. L. (1999) 'The situation of labour protection for female workers in Gangdong Province', *China National Conditions and Strength*, 12: 37.

Zhang, Z. B. (2000) '"The Seventh Revolution": developments in the reform of governmental organisations', *Xinhua Wenzai*, 11: 64–7.

Zhang, Z. J. (2000) 'Practices and observations of the "flexible pay" distribution in the public sector', *The Economist* (China), 1: 67–8.

Zhang, Z. W. (2000) *Modern Government and Civil Servant System*, China: Shichuan People's Publishing House.

Zhang, Z. and Huang, M. H. (2000) 'The effect of rural labours', *Economics Information*, 7 April.

Zhao, S. M. and Wu, C. S. (2003) 'A survey study of the current state of HRM in China', *Development and Management of Human Resources*, 7: 27–38.

Zheng, D. Q. (2003) 'A survey on the e-HR situation in China', *Development and Management of Human Resources*, 5: 4–7.

Zheng, X. Y. (2001) 'Census and gender statistics', *Collection of Women's Studies*, 40, 3: 11–15.

Zheng, X. Y., Jiang, L. W. and Zheng, Z. Z. (1995) *Women Population Issues and Development in China*, Beijing: Beijing University.

Zhong, W. Hu, X. D. and Wu, D. M. (1999) 'An overview of the higher educational distance learning and assessment', *Higher Education Studies*, 2: 81–7.

Zhu, F. M., Yao, S. R., Zhou, Y. and Hu, S. F. (1998) *Private Economy in China: Changing Realities, Problems and Prospects*, Beijing: China City Publishing House.

Zhu, H. (2000) 'Civil service reform', *Ban Yuan Tan*, September, 2: 35–40.

Zhu, L. M. (2000) 'Innovating the training system for civil servants', *China Vocational Training and Education*, 2: 41–2.

References from websites

www.molss.gov.cn, News, 'Municipal Minimum Wage Standard "Bottom Line"', 26 October 2001, accessed June 2002.

www.molss.gov.cn, News, 'The Fourth Season of 2003 News Announcement by the Ministry of Labour and Social Security', 16 February 2004, accessed April 2004.

Index